STEPHEN HUTCHINGS

LANDSCAPES FOR THE END OF TIME

Glenbow Museum

Contents

previous: ***Sky*** (detail), 2010, oil and charcoal on canvas

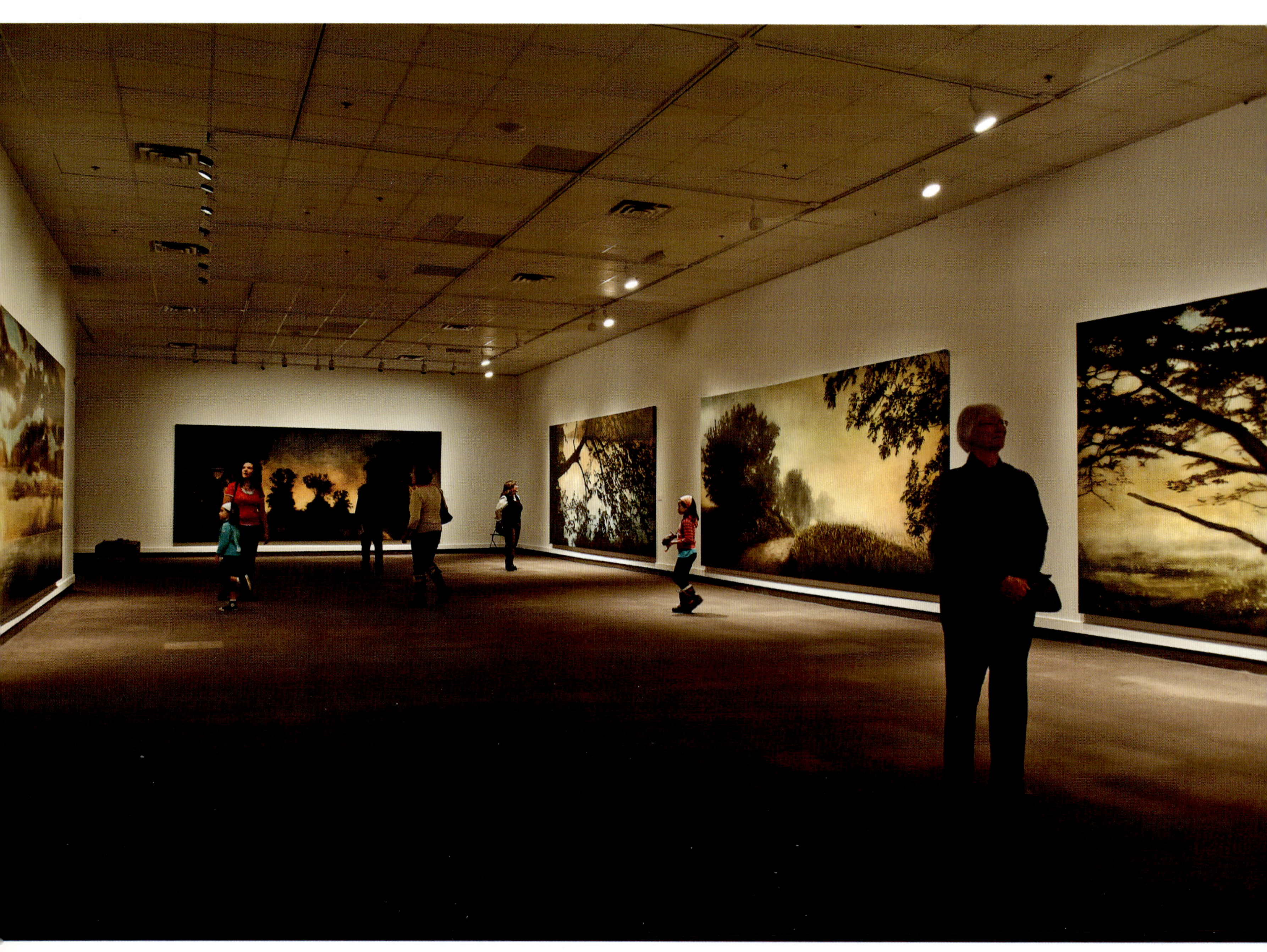

Installation shot of *Landscapes for the End of Time* at the Glenbow Museum, 2011

Preface

Landscapes for the End of Time is a show consisting of
eight paintings and two videos. All the paintings are the same
proportional format and are all made with charcoal and oil paint on
canvas. Six of the paintings are very large, 8' × 18', with the other
two being somewhat smaller at 4' × 9'. The two videos, which are
thematically related to the paintings, are each about eight minutes
long, with soundtracks written specifically for them.

The concept for the show as well as many other topics related to
the work are discussed in the various essays in this book. Suffice
it to say for now, however, that the title of the show, as well as the
primary thesis for the work, finds its genesis in French composer
Olivier Messiaen's famous *Quartet for the End of Time.* Writing it
during World War II while he was a prisoner of war facing probable
death, Messiaen focused on the Biblical reference to the ending
of time in the Revelation of St. John. However, the music and the
performance of it in the prison camp in January 1941 ultimately
led to the release of Messiaen and the other musicians involved,
thereby establishing an optimistic and somewhat ironic context for
the composition.

Landscapes for the End of Time examines ideas of temporality,
permanence, and eternity. Although we experience time as a
continuous presence, to suggest that there is an end to time brings
up questions concerning the nature of our knowledge. Can the life
span of an individual be reconciled with the idea of eternity, or of
an existence beyond the constraints of time? Can a sense of place
that is realised through a specific landscape effectively suggest the
universal?

— Stephen Hutchings, Ottawa, 2011

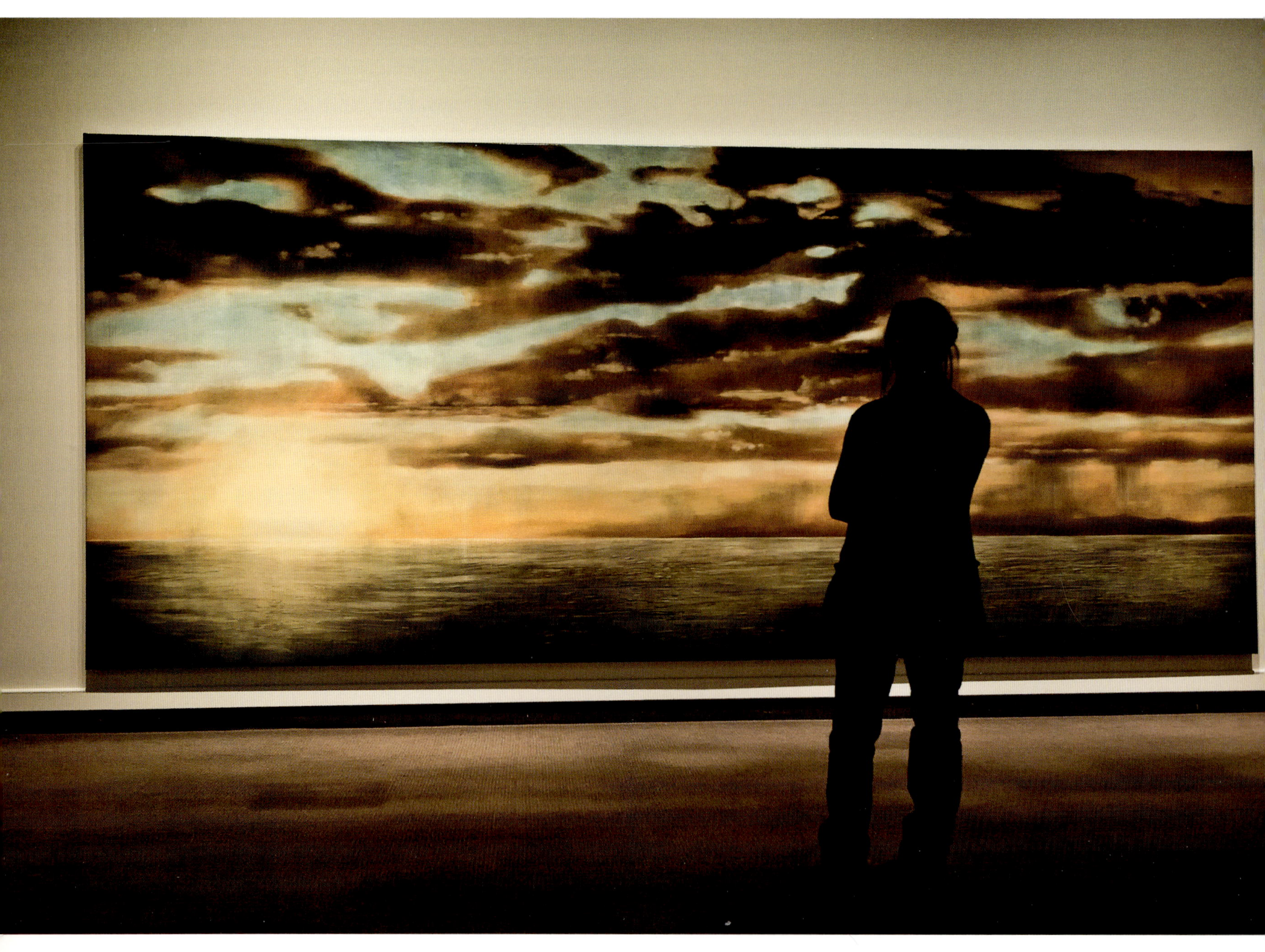

Sky, installation at the Glenbow Museum, 2011

Introduction
Colleen Sharpe

The Glenbow Museum is pleased to be able to present Landscapes for the End of Time, *an exhibition of works by Stephen Hutchings, on exhibit from December 10, 2010 until March 15, 2011.*

In the eighteenth and nineteenth centuries, landscape painting was an act of faith in nature, as fervent as religious faith. The arts in general, including music, attempted to capture and express the divinity found in nature. This was at the core of inspiration for French composer Olivier Messiaen (1908-1992), whose composition *Quatuor pour la fin du temps (Quartet for the End of Time)* informed the concept of this exhibition.

Quartet for the End of Time separates rhythm from meter and, in doing so, literally accomplishes the end of time musically. Both Olivier Messiaen and Stephen Hutchings have found a way to create the end of time through their art.

Also akin to Messiaen, Hutchings creates with his art a heaven on earth, attempting to capture a sense of eternity beyond the grasp of the human construct of time. At the same time, the paintings explore philosophical ideas of dualism: good cannot exist without evil, light cannot exist without darkness, hope exists alongside despair. In their physical form, the landscapes literally encapsulate dualism in the way heavy charcoal is repeatedly applied and rubbed away. Hutchings applies darkness and removes it, erasing and exposing the light of canvas beneath.

These landscape paintings are deliberately ambiguous and full of paradox. Photographs of unnamed places, from unknown times, become realistic paintings of the unreal. In this way, Hutchings posits for our consideration the artificial, artifice, art. There is little clue to the viewer as to what moment in recorded history the landscapes document, if any. Hutchings's creations are imbued with a sense of the divine in nature and yet are confined to presentation in a constructed gallery environment.

Historically, by the early 1900s, the introduction of landscape photography signalled the end of naturalistic painting, yet in the way his process and techniques reference the Pictoralists and eighteenth-century landscape painters, Hutchings reunites these movements.

From its inception, photography has attempted to capture and record moments

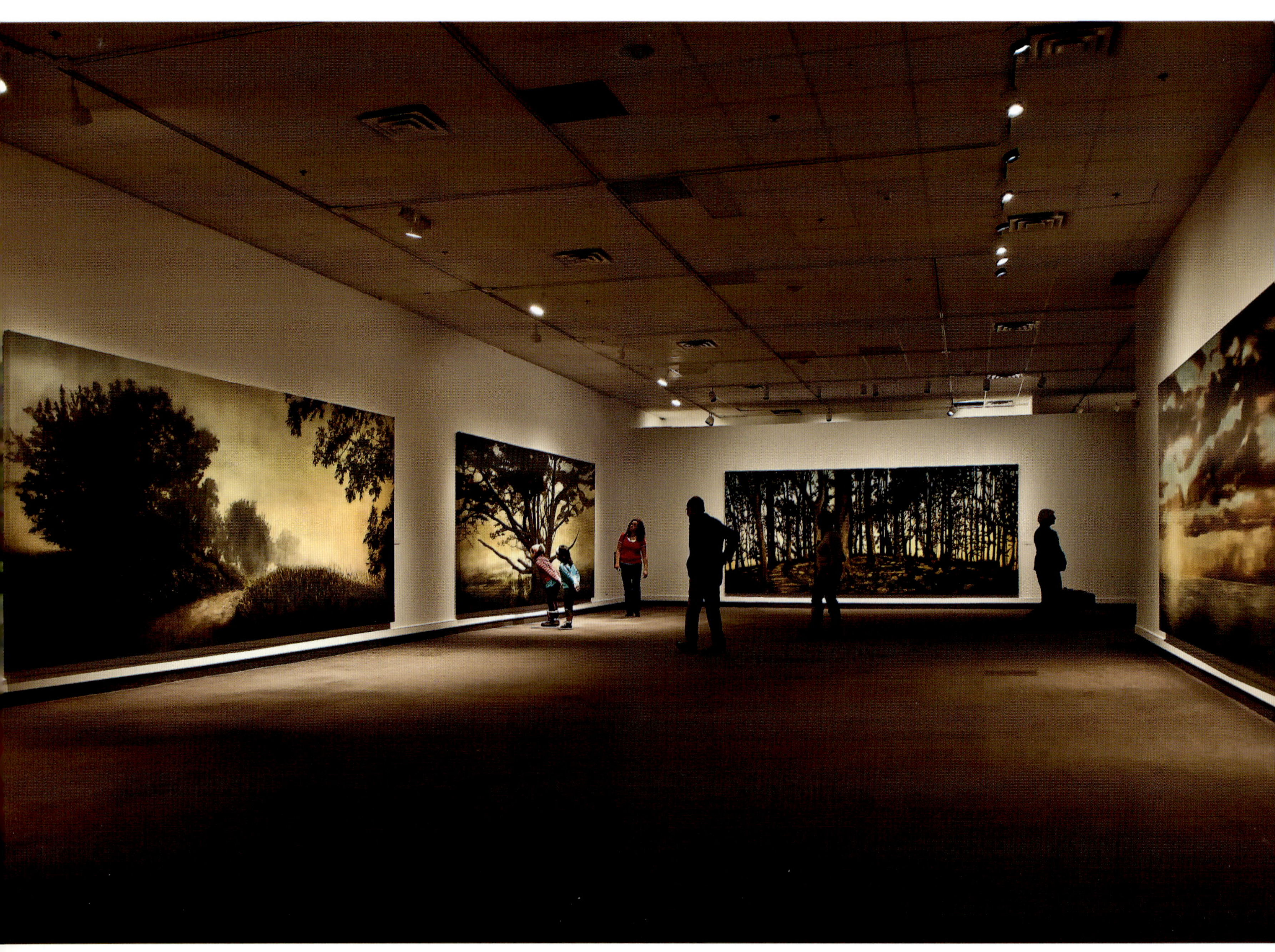

Installation of *Landscapes for the End of Time* at the Glenbow Museum, 2011

perceived by humans. Its innate technical and chemical process forces photography to carefully regard time, and consequently, images captured in photographs are considered "timeless."

The French photographer Gustave Le Gray (1820-1884) astonished the world in 1856 with his picture *Brig on the Water,* in which the luminosity of sea and sky suggested a transcendent experience. Le Gray had managed to depict what people had only been able to previously achieve through memory.

Landscapes for the End of Time are contemporary paintings that allude to such seminal historic landscapes. Because they are so tangibly influenced by history, Hutchings's paintings play with the human perception of time. In a sense he reintroduces naturalistic painting but accomplishes this through technology. For example, he uses digital photography and projection that reference an earlier invention, the camera lucida. This device used a prism, suspended at eye level, to allow the viewer to see both object and drawing paper. Hutchings's process confronts the photographic necessity of visually capturing a moment, as each painting contains an entire past and an entire future layered into one imagined moment, where the artist has frozen it for our consideration.

Interpretations of Hutchings's artworks are multiple and endless. The paintings attempt to capture human memory, emotion, and con-sciousness. Hutchings invites the viewer to see beyond the paintings to also consider the philosophical beginning and end of his process—if there is an end at all. The viewer is the necessary final part of Hutchings's compositions. Those who experience his paintings invoke many possible memories and perspectives. As Susan Sontag has said, photography "fills the gaps in our mind of the present and the past." Hutchings's work melds Sontag's idea with naturalism in landscape painting and, in execution, seeks to capture in two-dimensional form the essence of a moment.

Landscapes for the End of Time encourages dialogue among artistic, religious, environmental and philosophical communities. Just as *Landscapes for the End of Time* invites dialogue about time and art, the Glenbow Museum endeavors to offer new perspectives for today and for the future. I share the Glenbow's ambition that this exhibition and publication will present new perspectives for now and for the end of time.

Colleen Sharpe is Curator of Art at the Glenbow Museum.

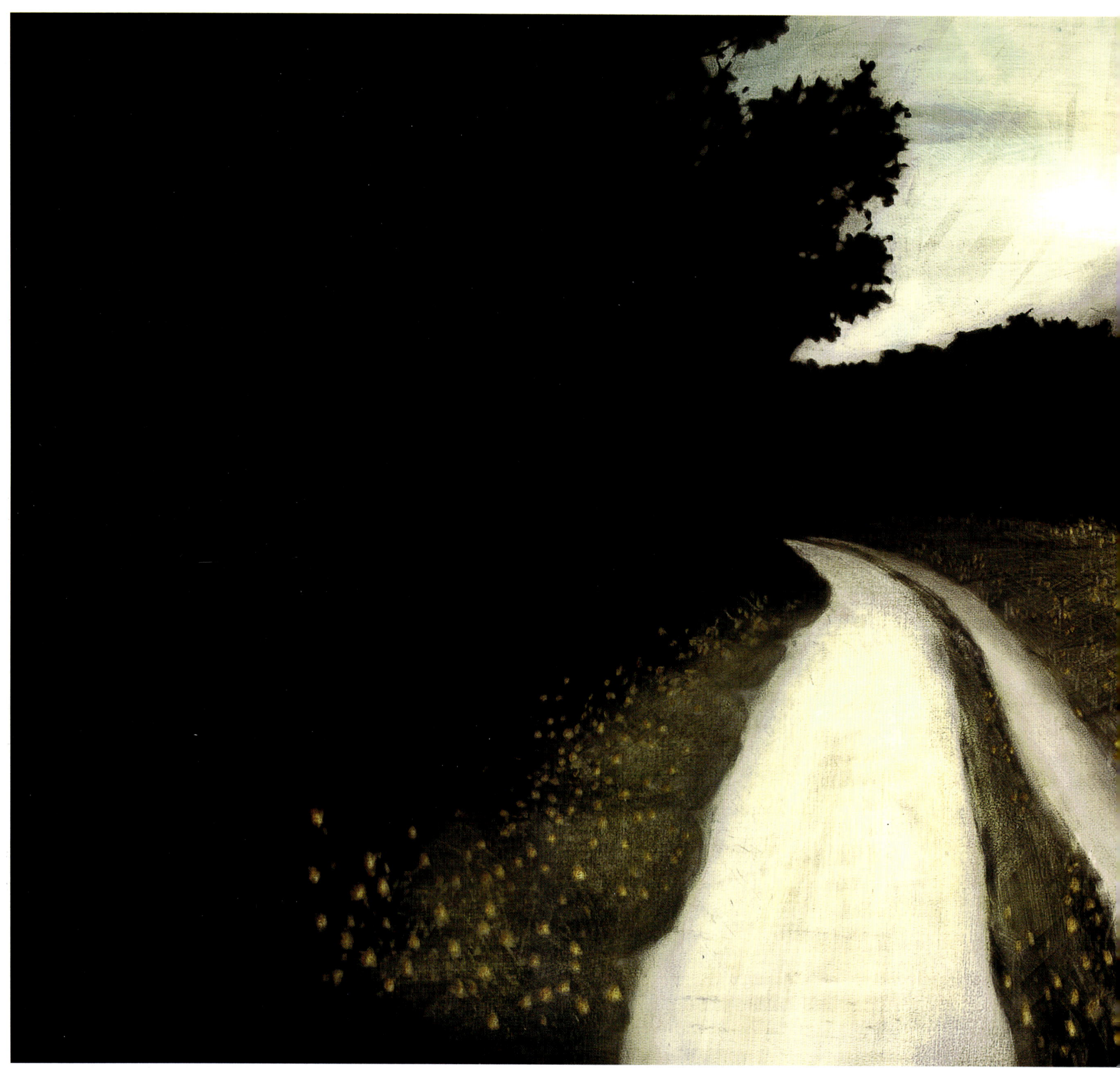

Approach, 2010, oil and charcoal on canvas, 4' x 9'

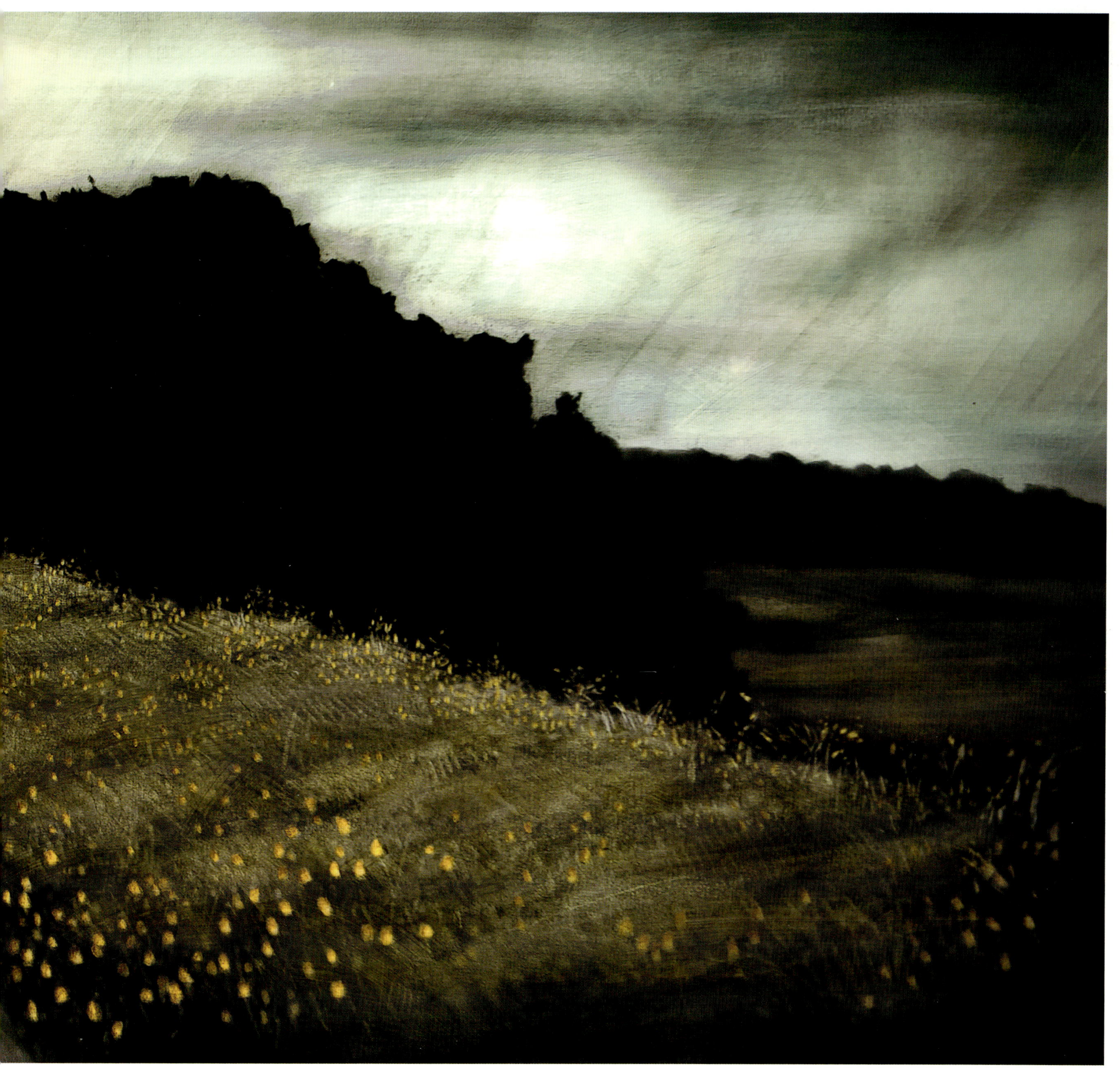

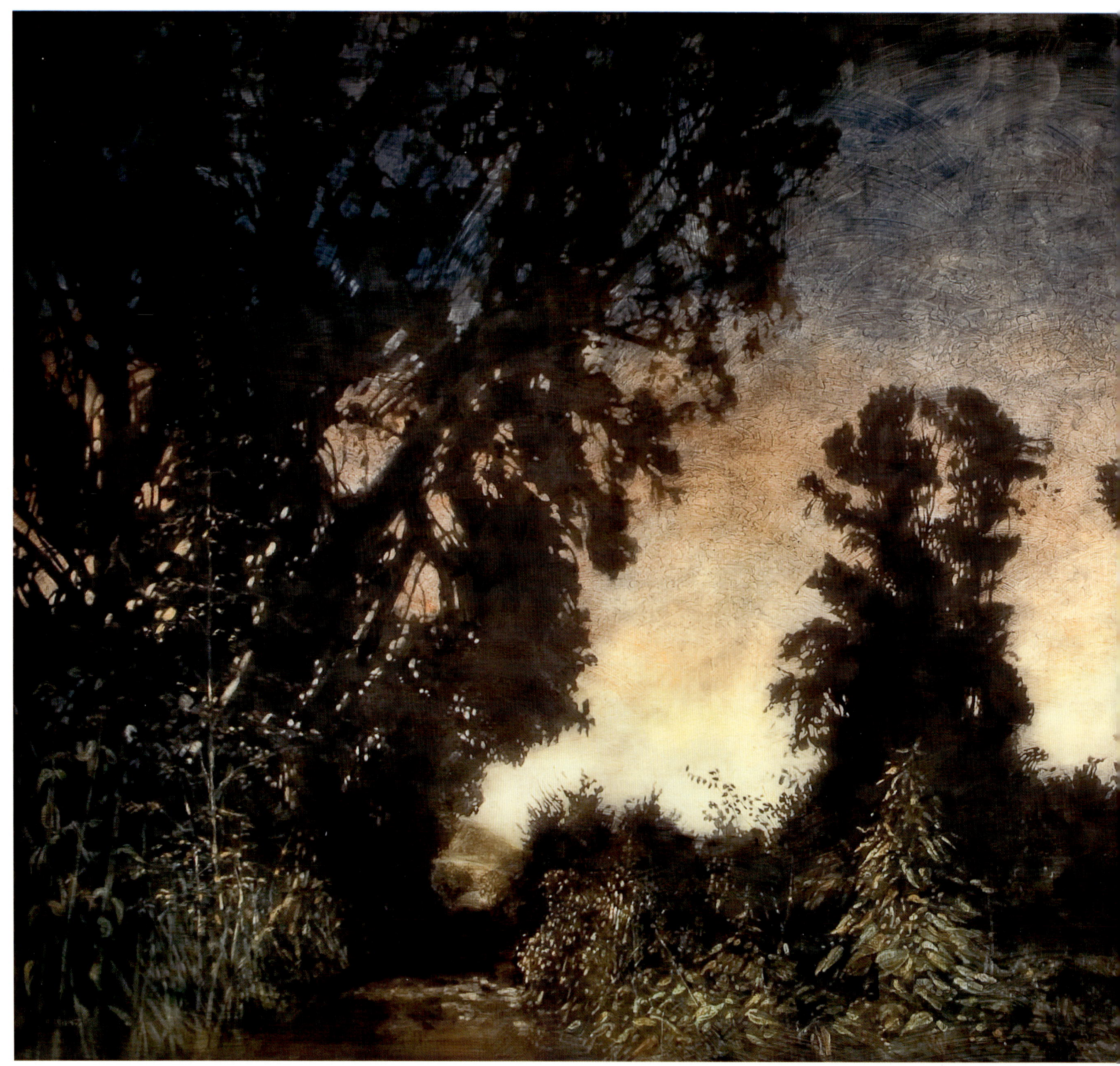

Roads 2010, oil and charcoal on canvas, 8' x 18'

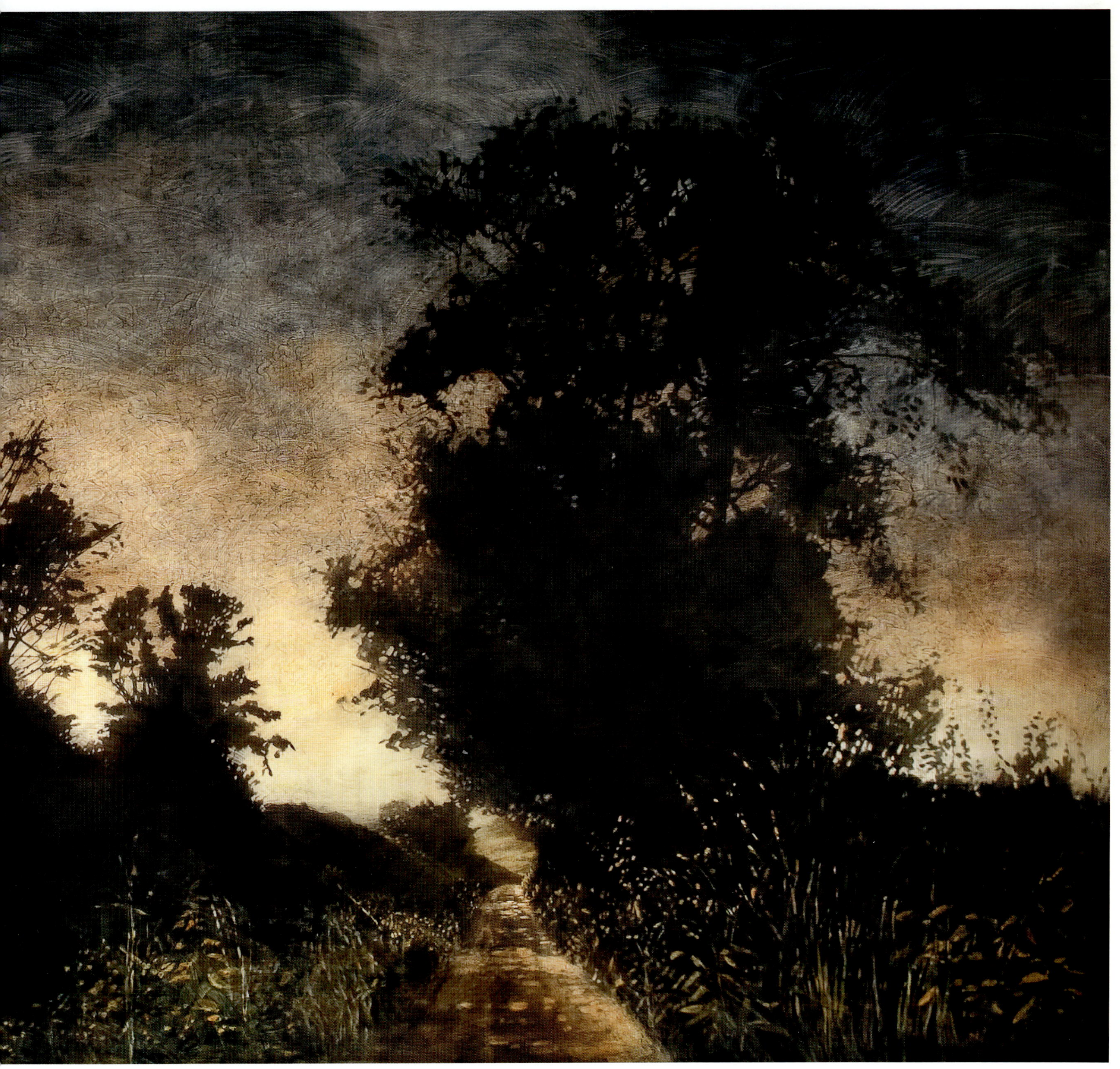

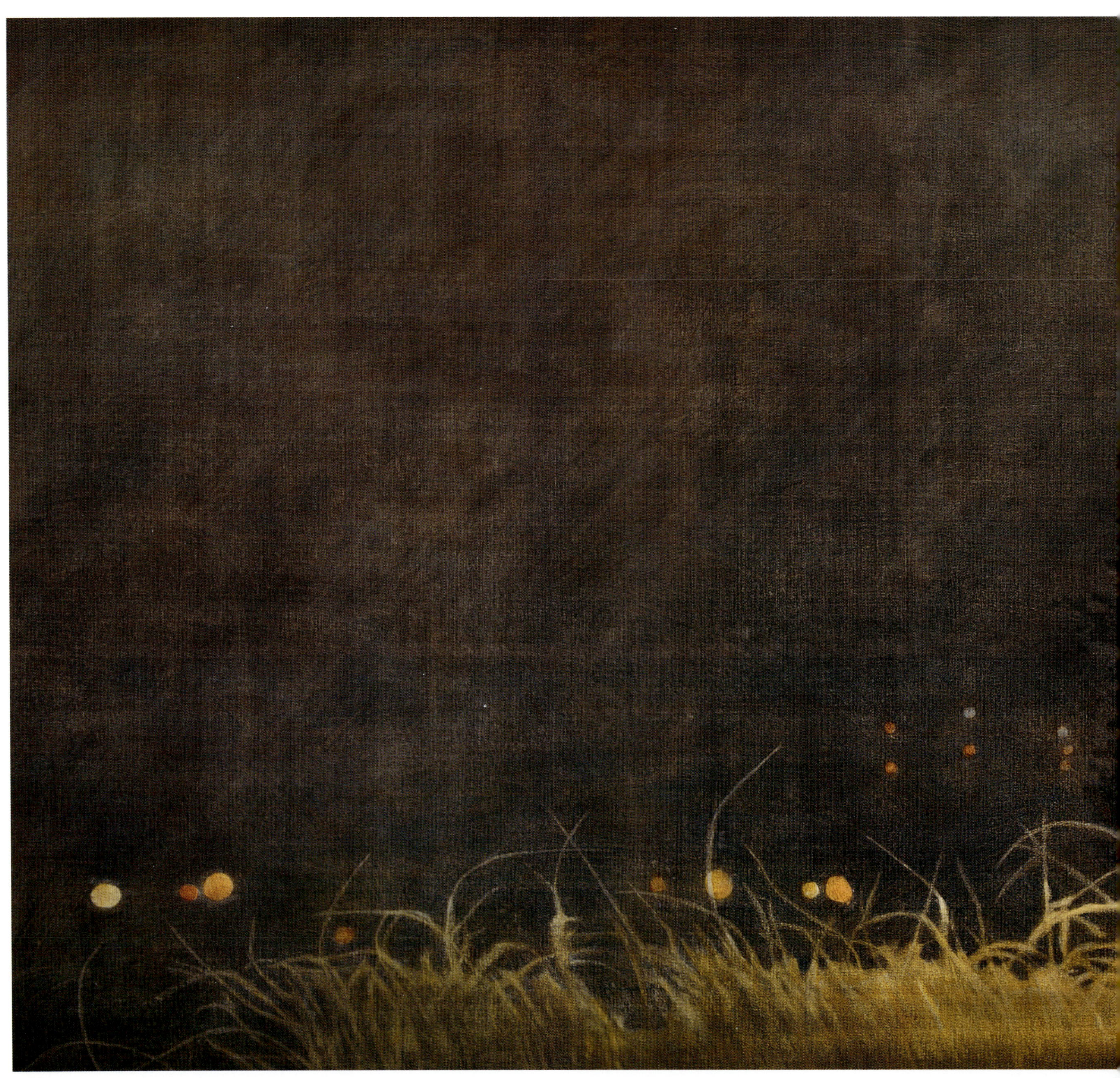

Abyss, 2010, oil and charcoal on canvas, 4' x 9'

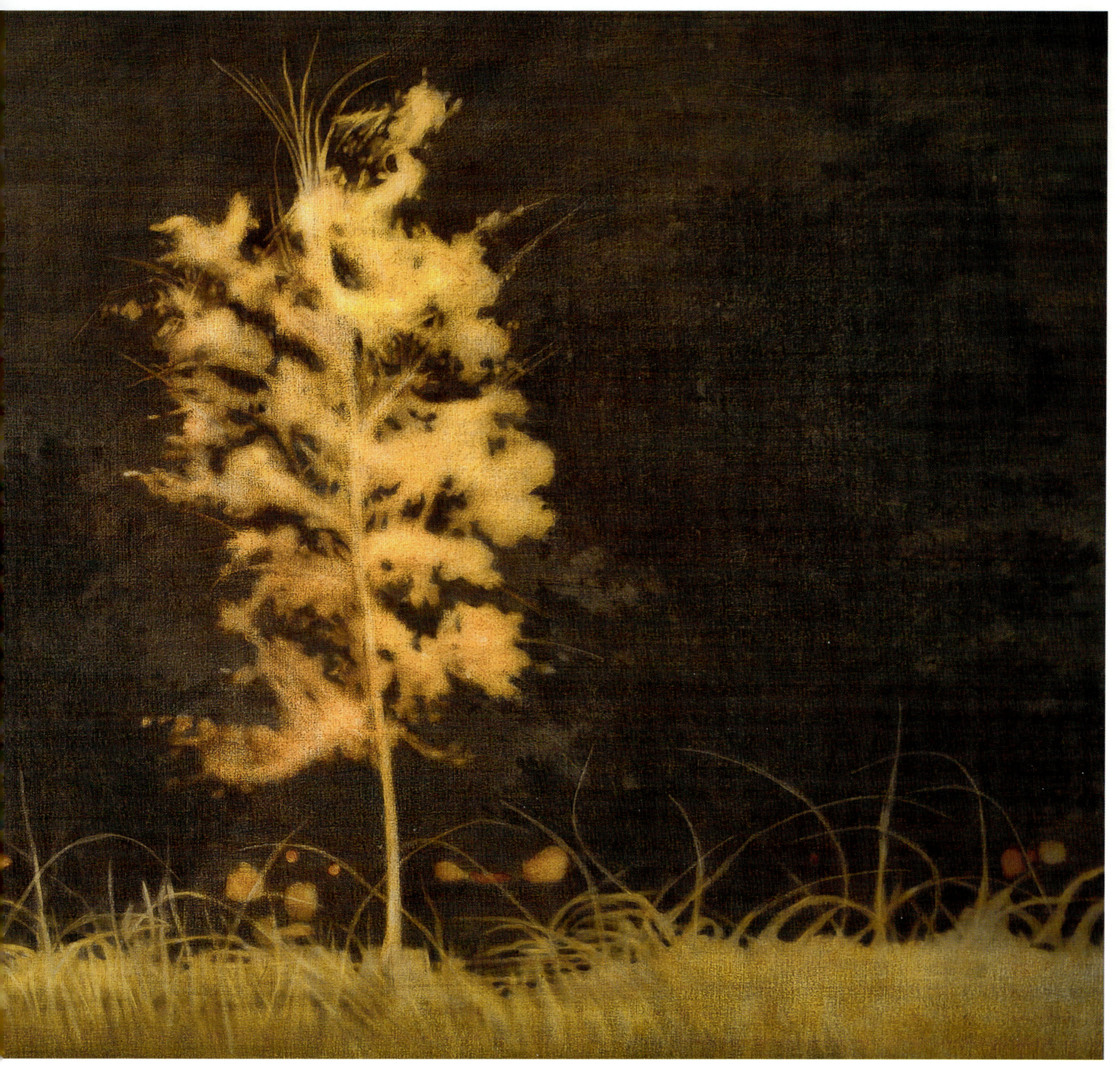

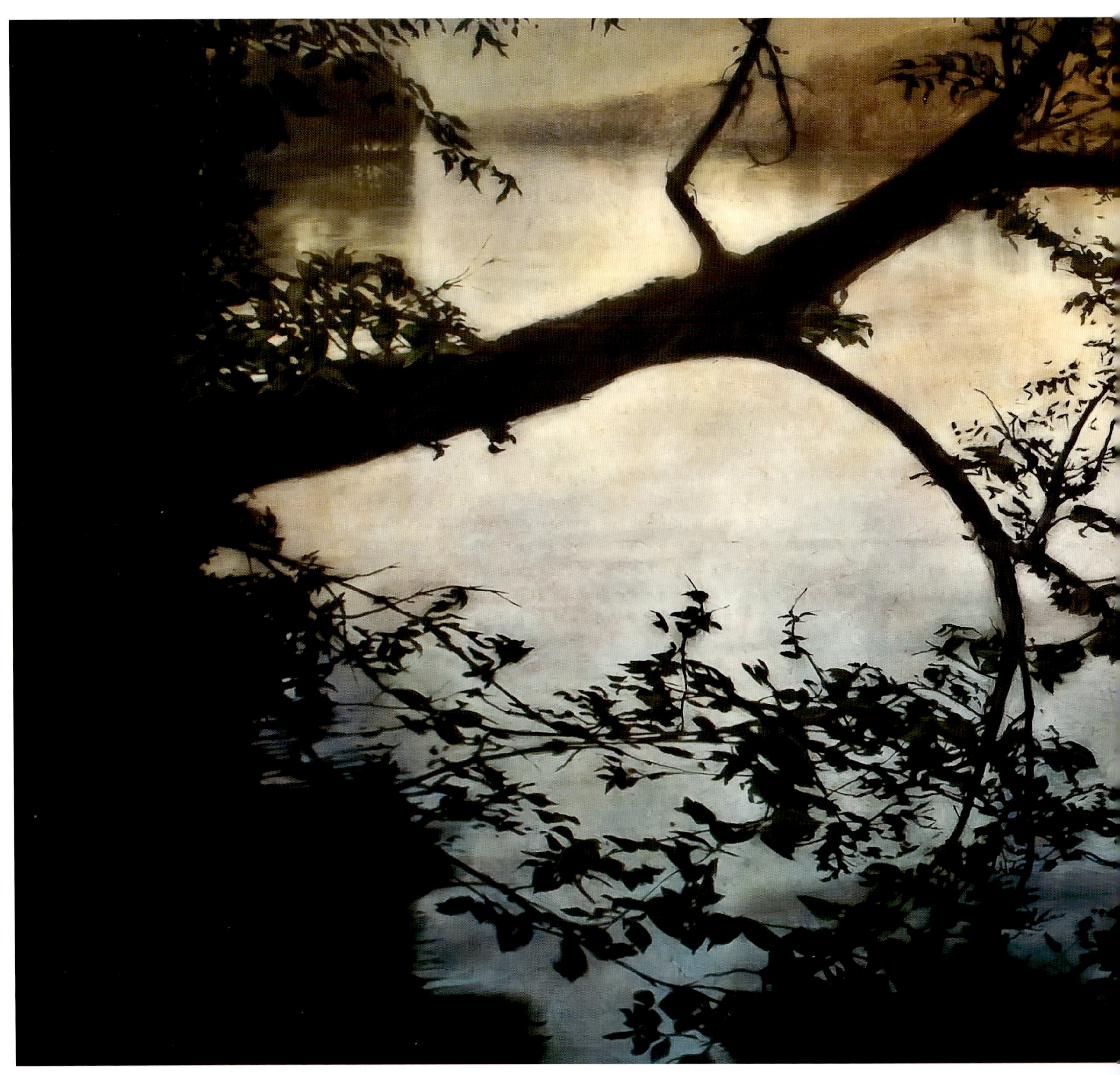

Branch, 2010, oil and charcoal on canvas, 8' x 18'

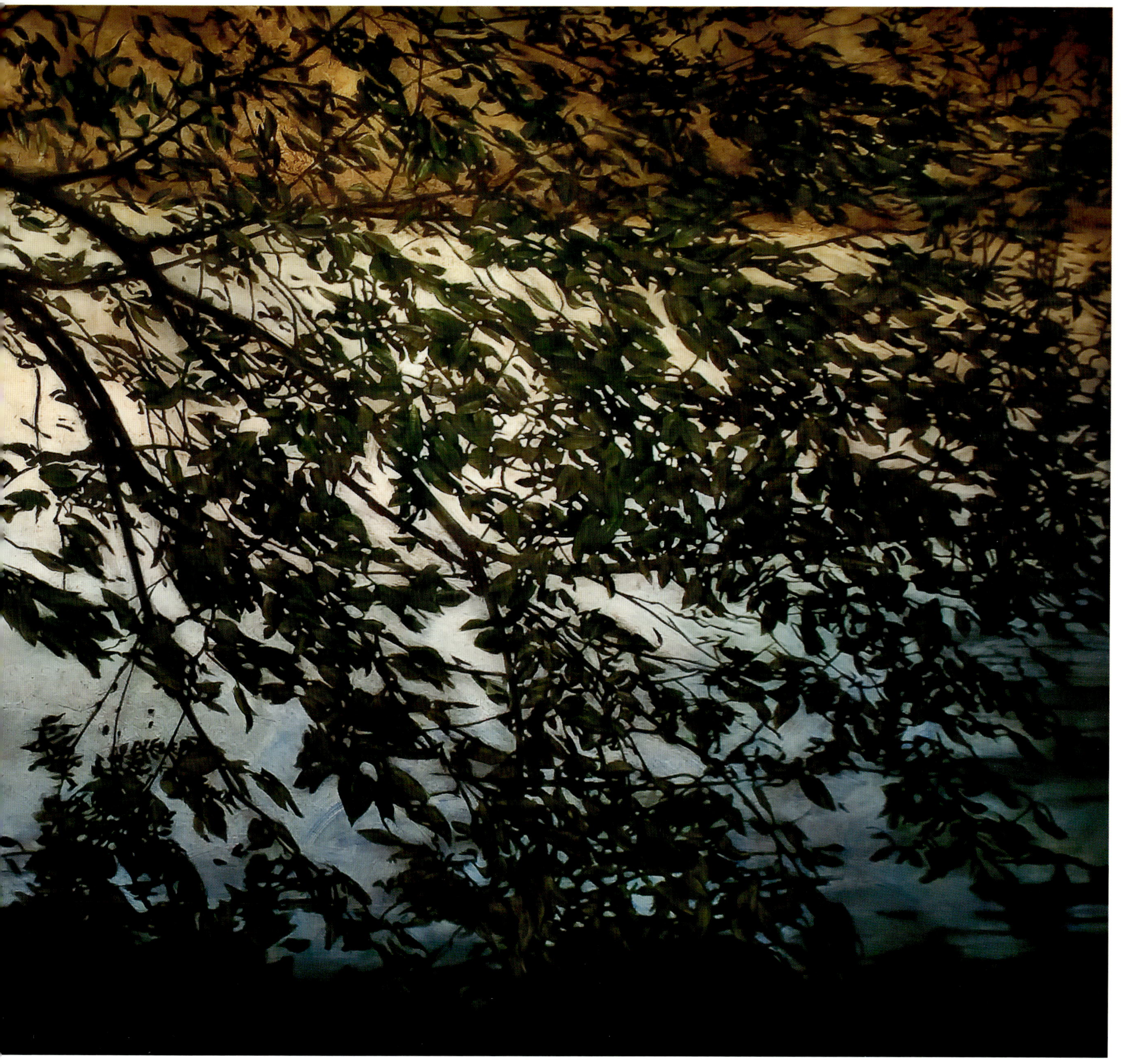

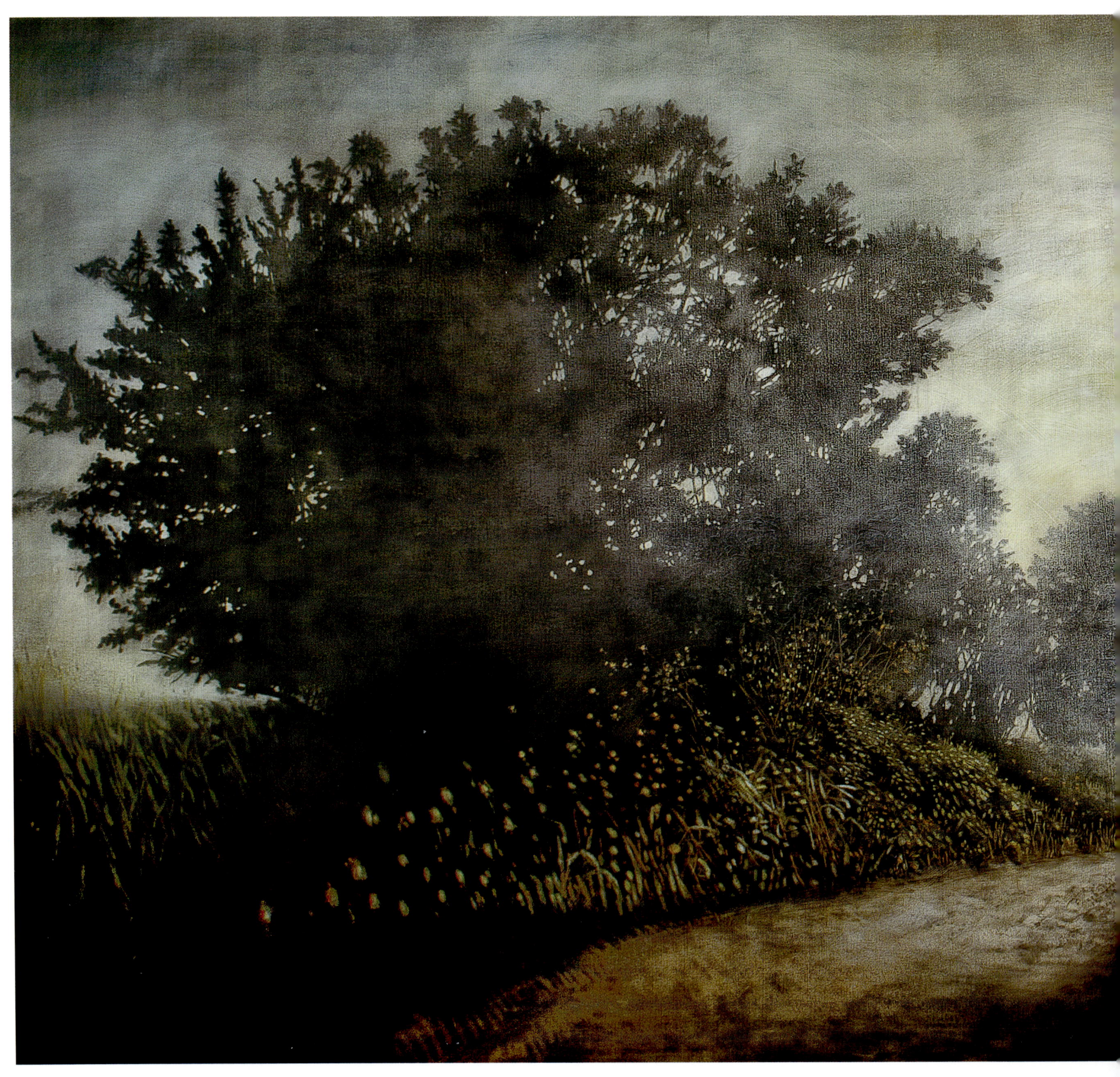

Hill, 2010, oil and charcoal on canvas, 8' x 18'

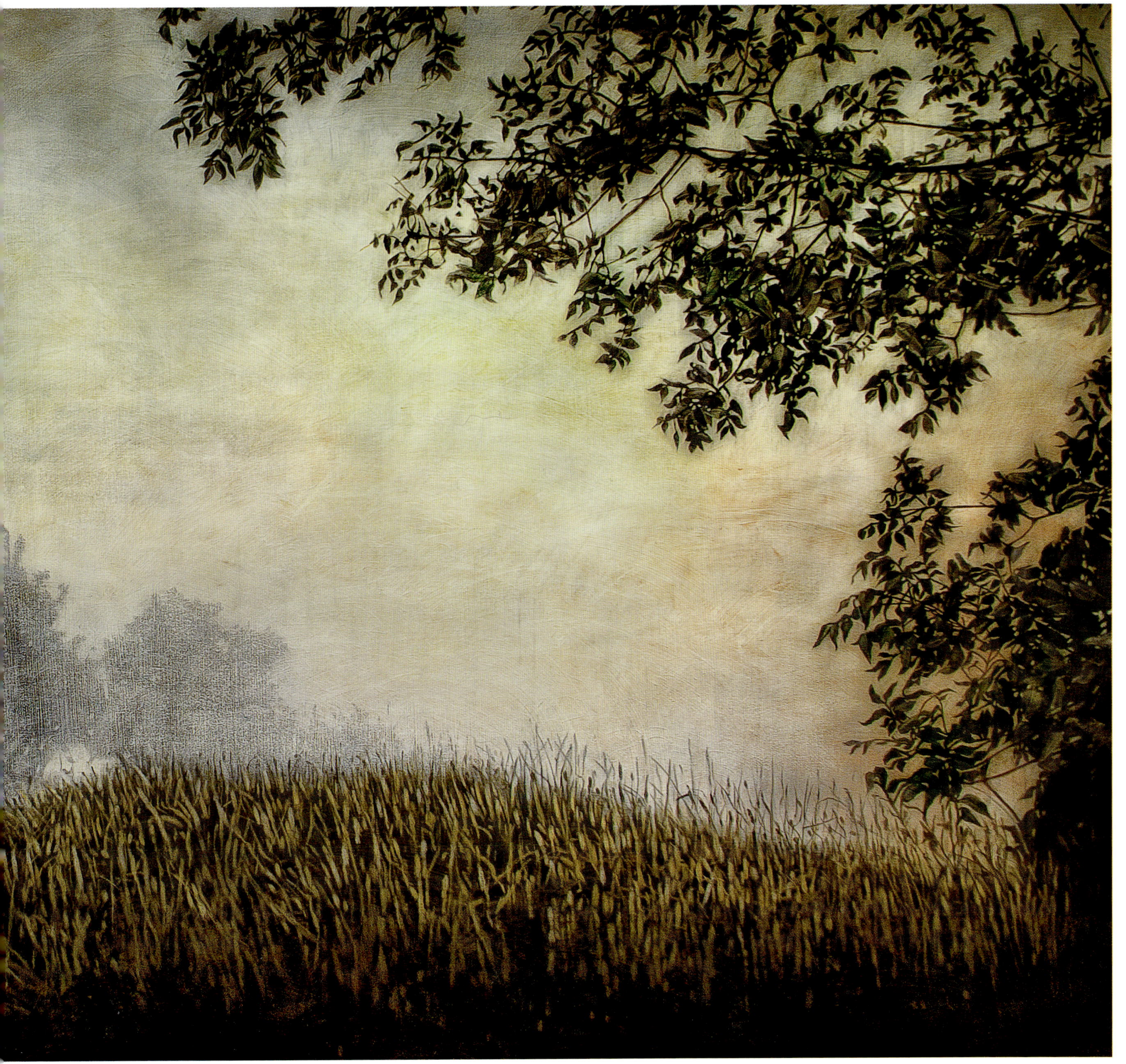

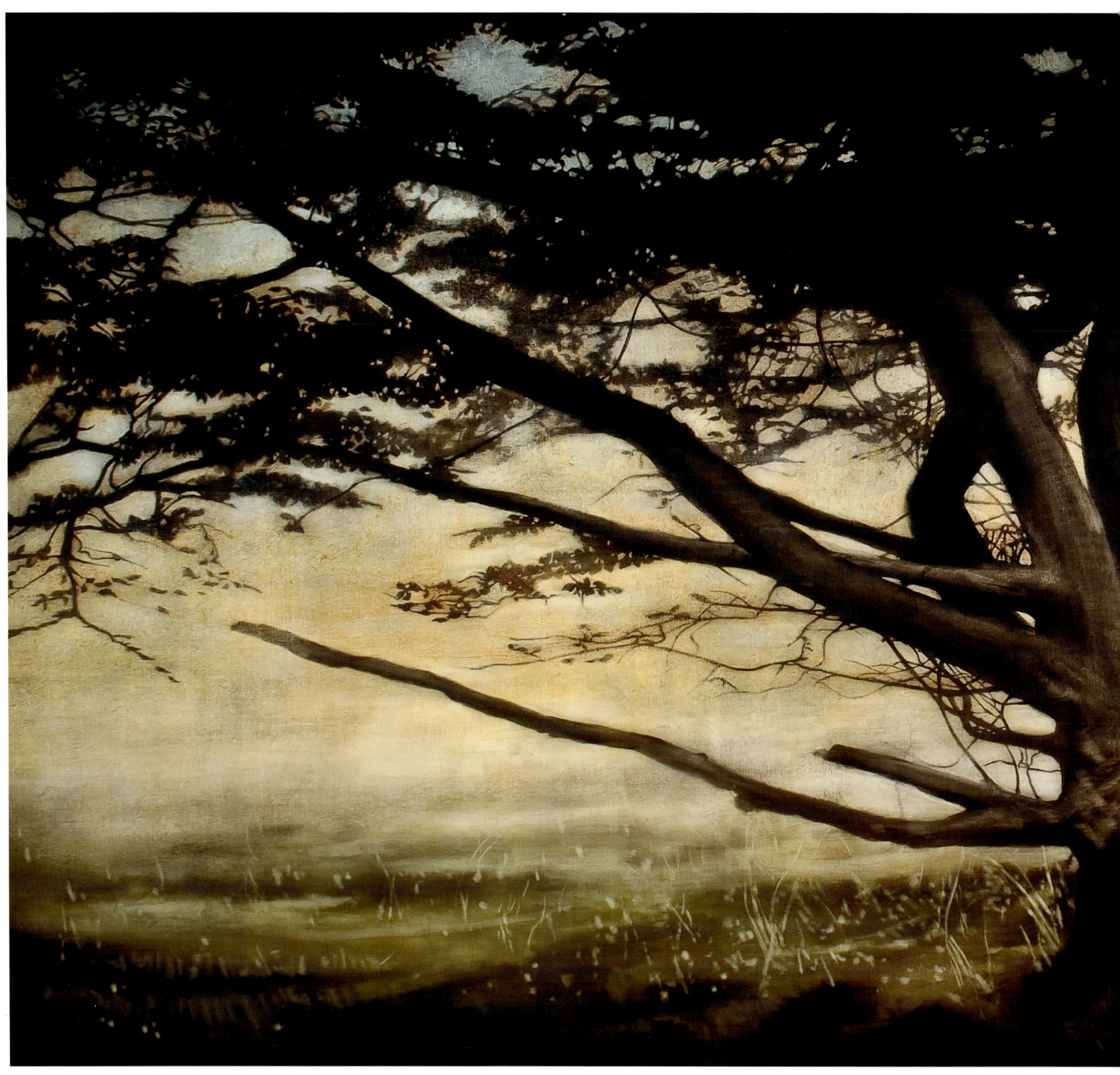

Tree, 2010, oil and charcoal on canvas, 8' x 18'

TREE, FROM THE SERIES *LANDSCAPES FOR THE END OF TIME*

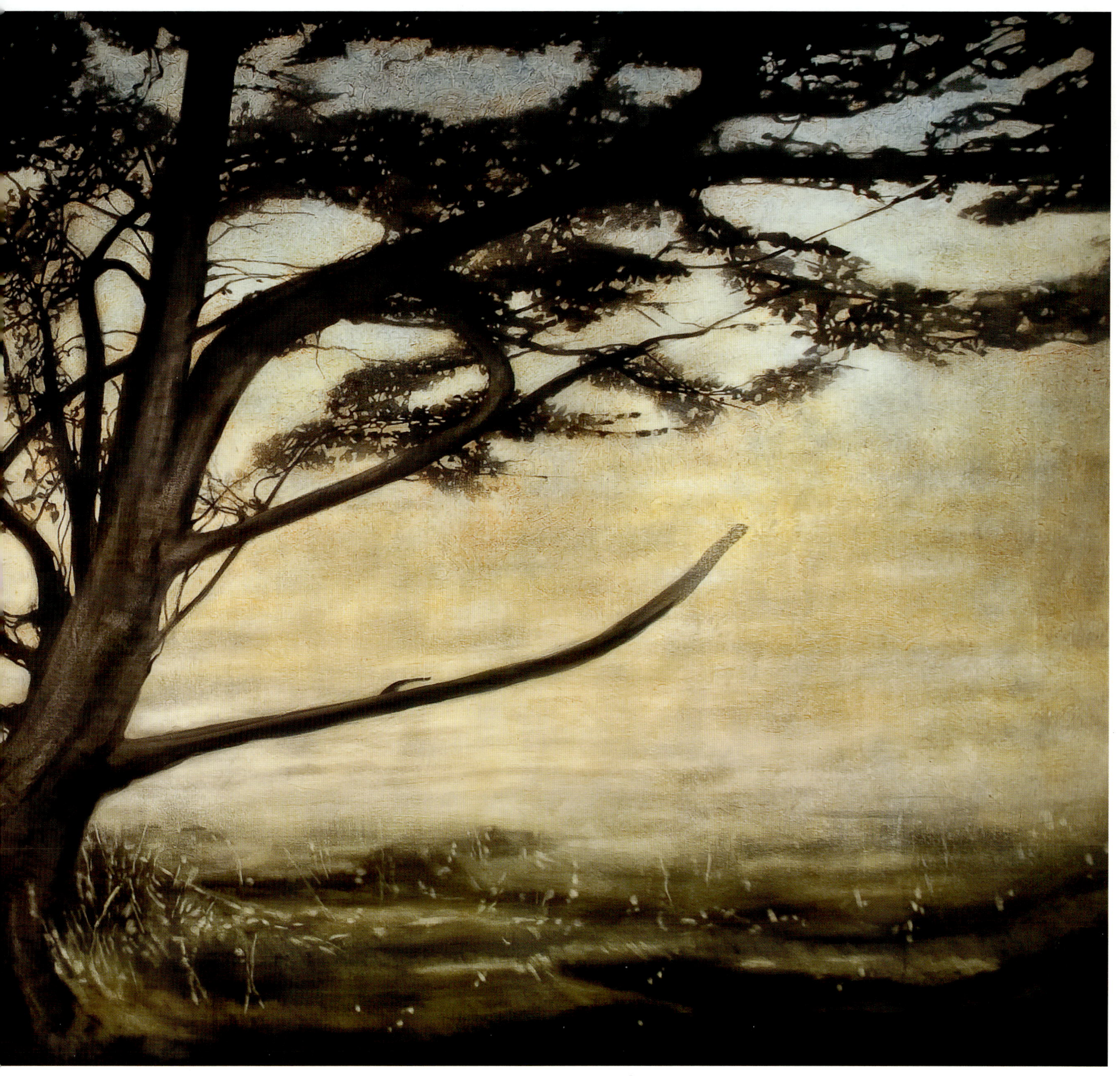

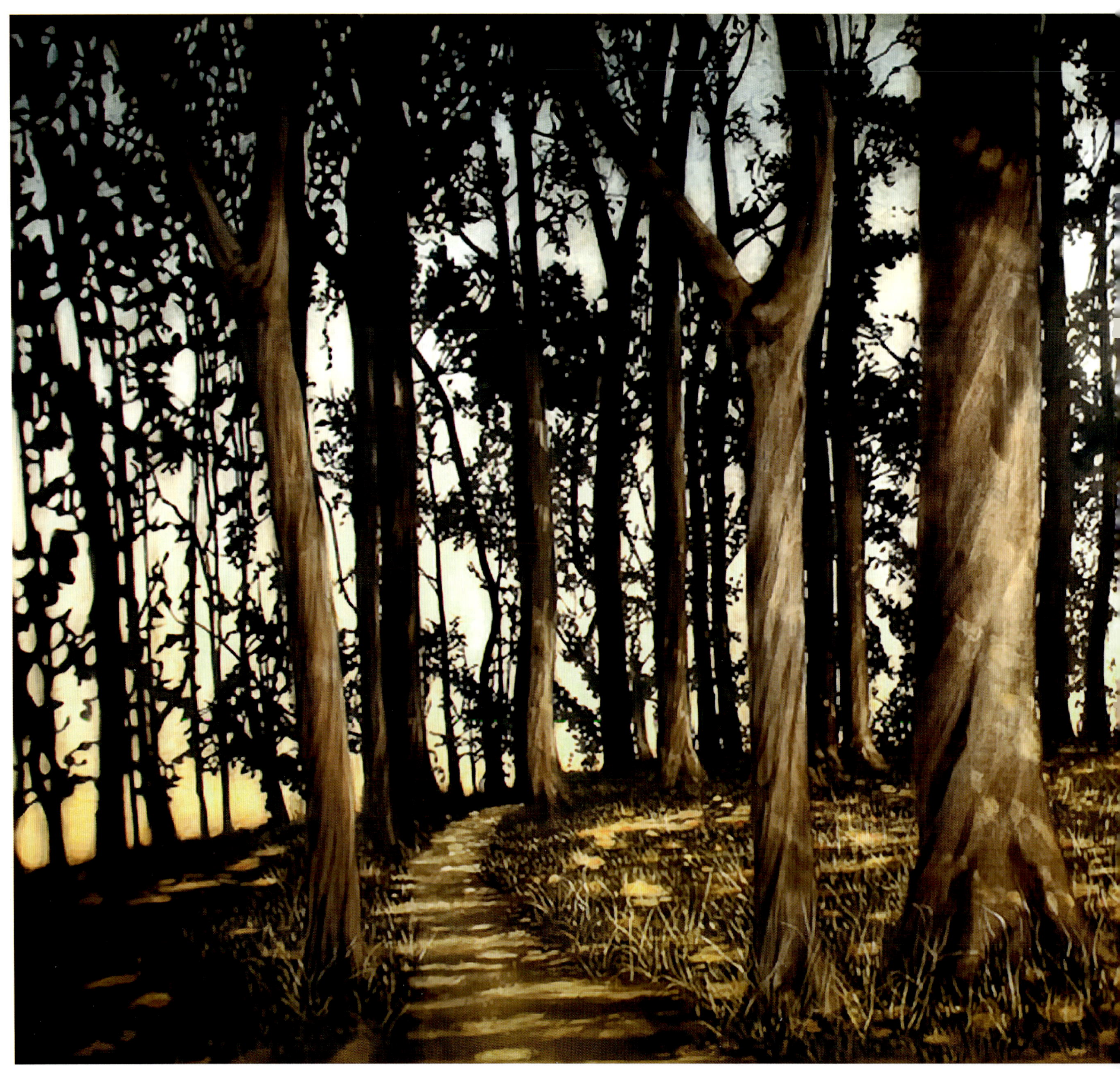

Grove, 2010, oil and charcoal on canvas, 8' x 18'

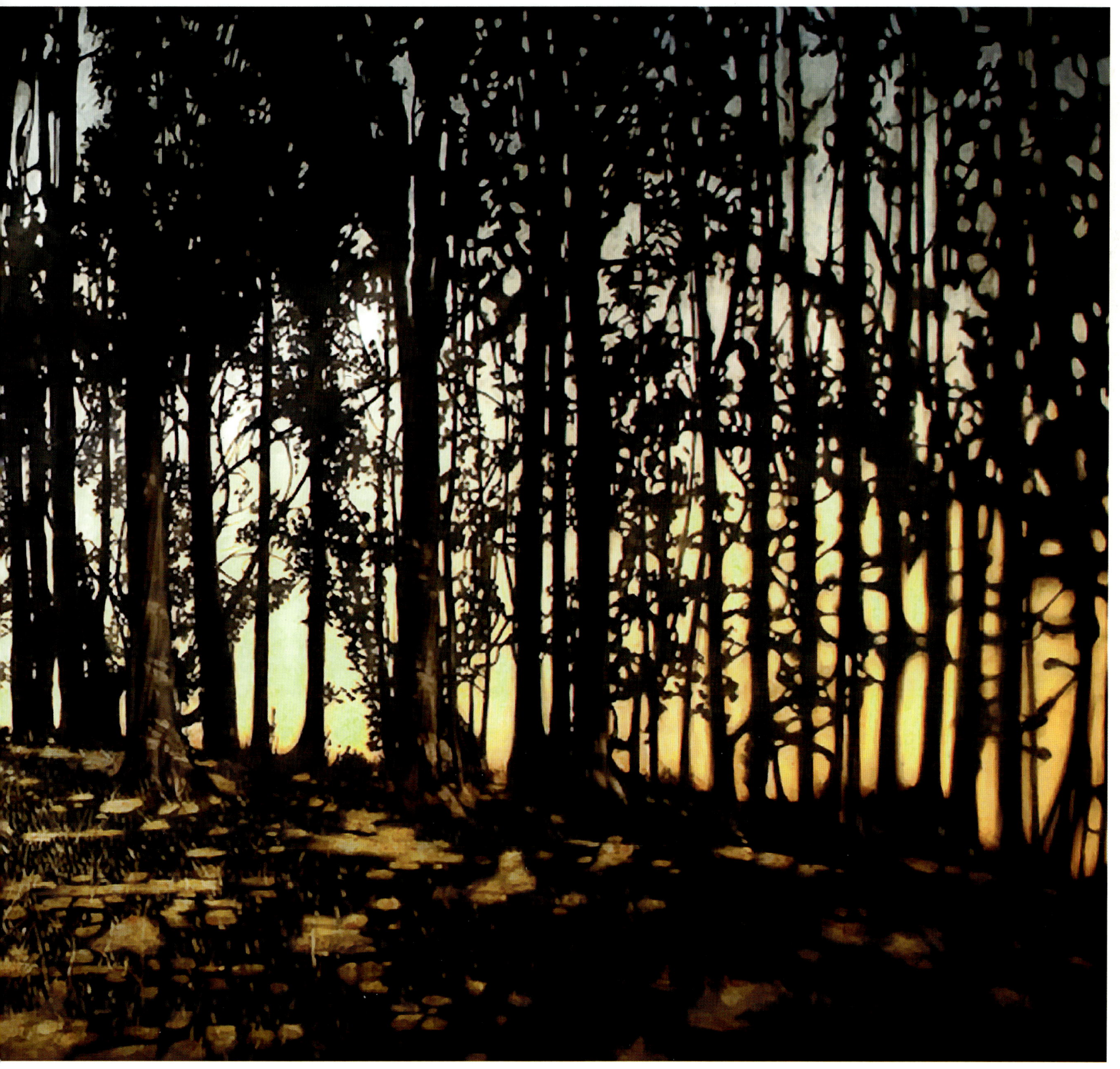

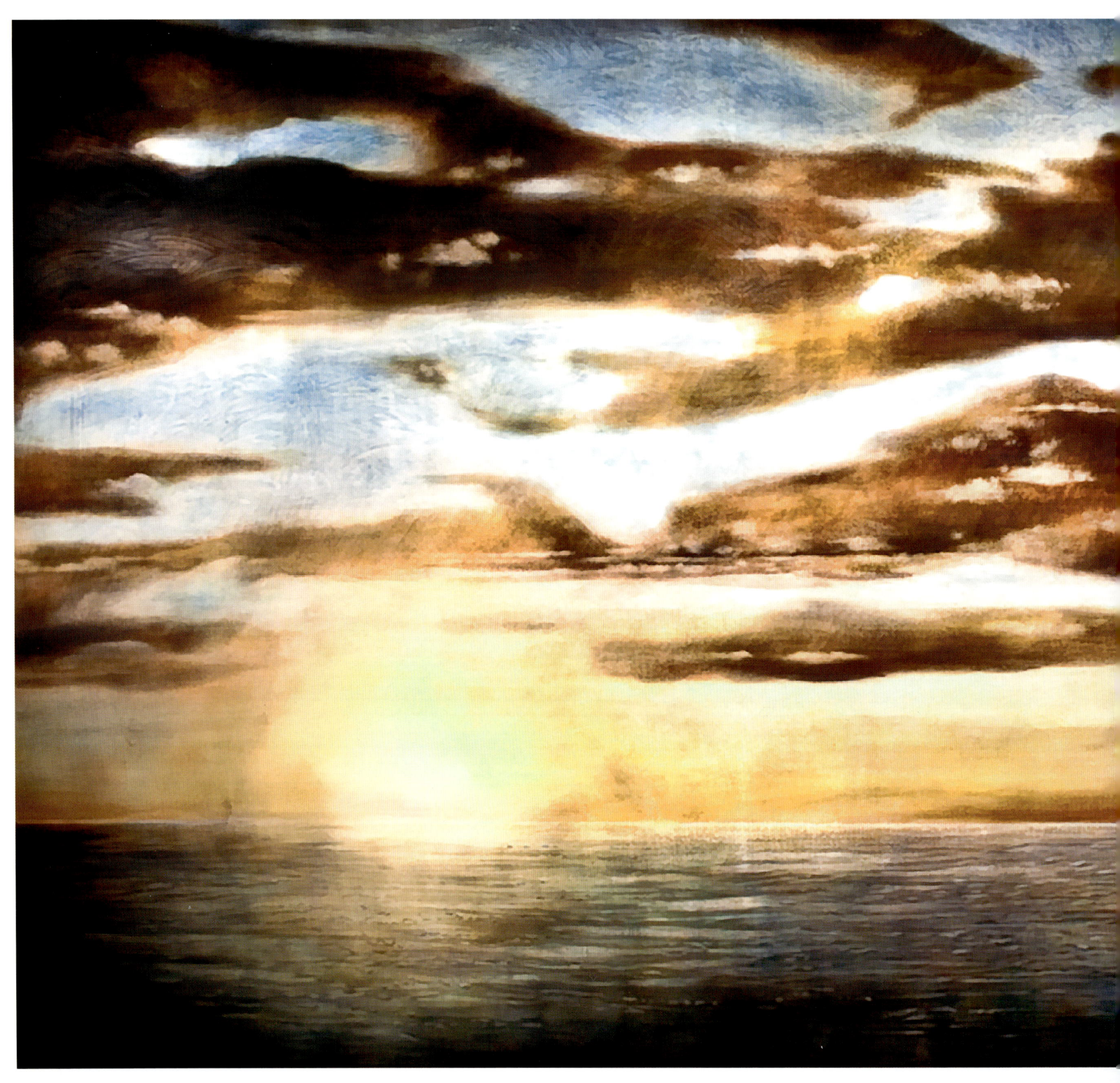

Sky, 2010, oil and charcoal on canvas, 8' x 18'

SKY, FROM THE SERIES *LANDSCAPES FOR THE END OF TIME*

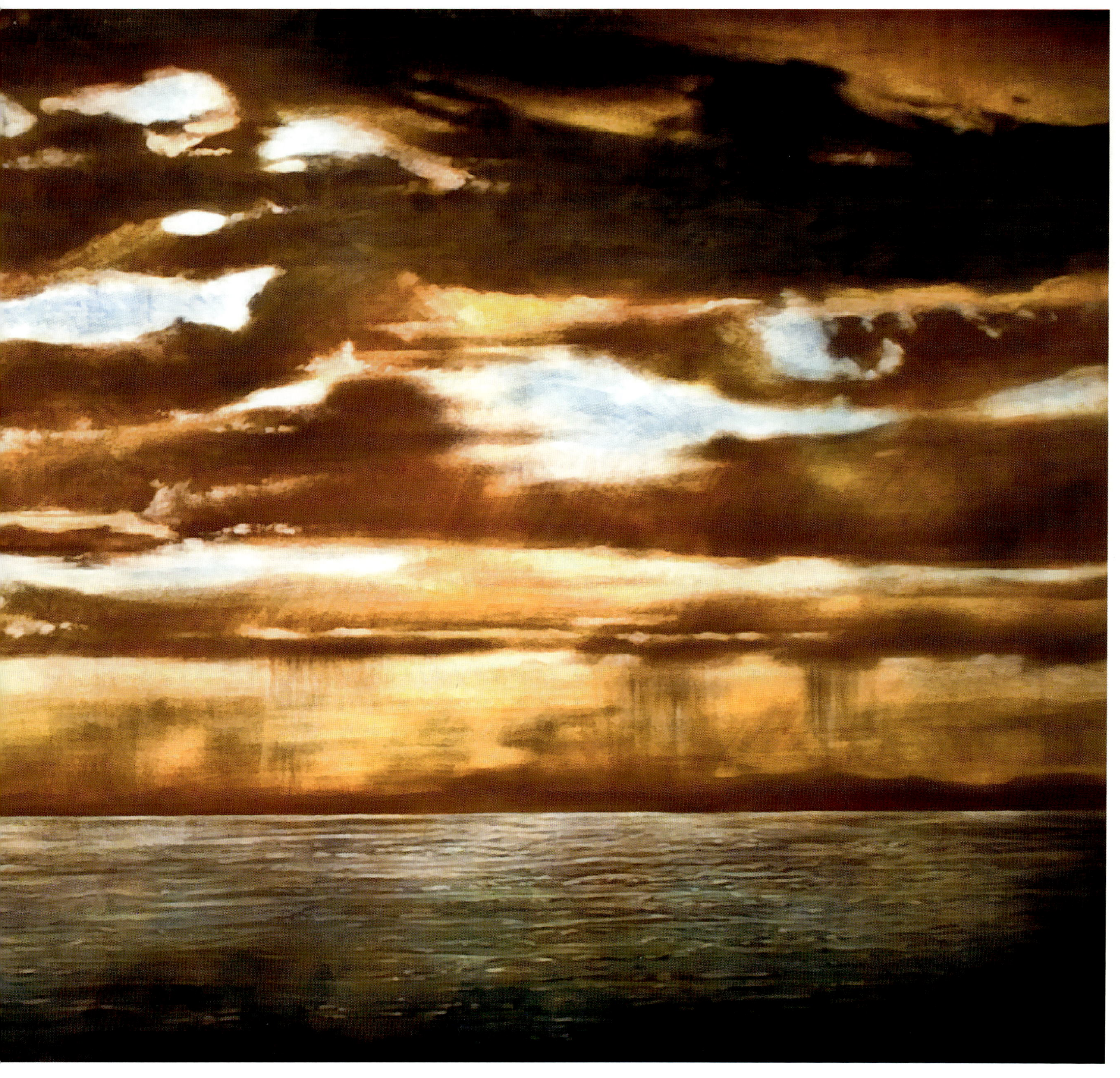

Keeping Ruin and Promise Together: Stephen Hutchings's *Landscapes for the End of Time*

Petra Halkes

This is the edge of the world
Where clouds converge and keep on gathering,
Trees turn their backs and face the wrong direction,
The sound of the sea is an unchanging roar,
Patterns in the sand perspective into a whisper,
The sky is a mist,
The horizon the edge of the mirage.

Here the face of the clock is blank,
Magnets forget their axes,
This is where fingerprints flatten out,
Parallel lines meet, space folds back
Unsettling the seat of gravity.
Solids swirl into shadows,
Press into planes,
Compress into lines,
Define the edge of the world.

Look back at the world losing its definition:
The sky searching its co-ordinates,
Stars as black as burnt-out holes,
Your last footprint
Erased.

— H. Masud Taj

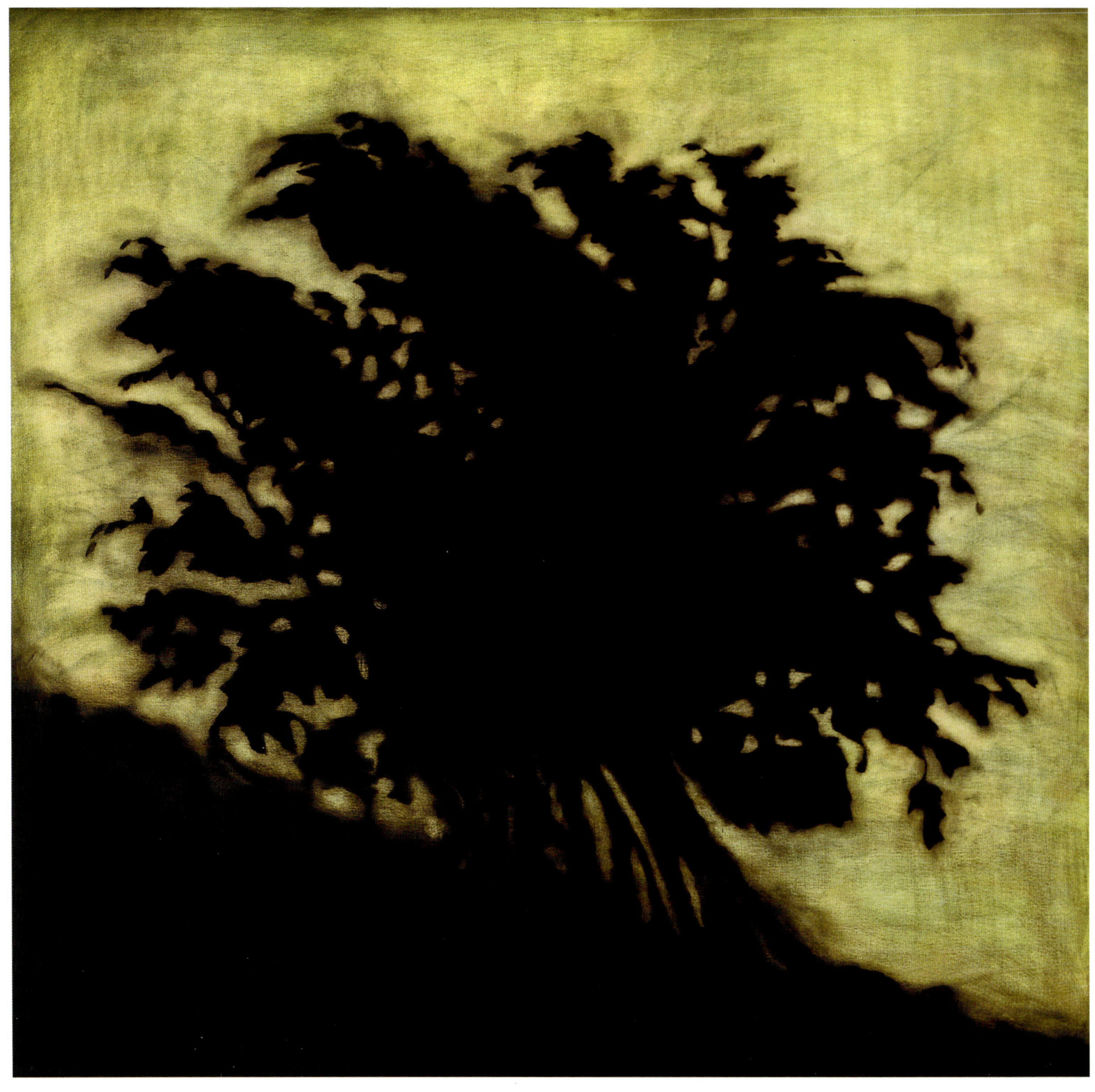

Bush, June 1991, 1991, oil on canvas, 108" x 108"

In Stephen Hutchings's Landscapes for the End of Time, "the face of the clock is blank."[1] Leaving behind nature's historical realities of place and time, the paintings show hauntingly unreal, or, more accurately, hyper-real landscapes that remain uncannily familiar, as if visited in a dream. In Hutchings's paintings, as in H. Masud Taj's poem, the end of time is felt not as an actuality but as a restless yearning blowing through the landscape, disturbing rather than creating unity. Forests thin out to lines of trees, intense luminosity highlights single leaves and blades of grass, while trees, and whole scenes, show their eerie doubles. *Landscapes for the End of Time* show that time is inescapable, even if the clock has been effaced.

Hutchings's paintings come alive with an unresolved tension between the desire for divine infinity and finite human existence. In Hutchings's earlier paintings from the 1990s, scepticism weighted this tension in favour of the existential finite. At that time, his series of *Plants, Bushes, and Hedges* — flat, dark forms on screen-like backgrounds — emphatically denied the possibility of timelessness in nature.[2] At the same time, they formed allegorical emblems of *desire* for a fusion of temporal existence into a timeless absolute.

In his more recent paintings, including *Landscapes for the End of Time,* the desire for the infinite hangs heavier in the balance than the reality of finite life. Space opens up in scenes with distant horizons. Where a bush from 1991 stood out against an empty background (*Bush, June 1991*) (page 28), trees in 2007 are placed near a river that shows both shorelines (*The Far Shore,* 2007). Winding roads and wide, brooding skies make room for a desire to be transported to an illuminated "edge of the world," from which to leave behind "your last footprint."[3]

In other recent works, nature appears to provide a divine immanence, as in the secluded forest of *Grove* (2010) (see image on pages 22 –23), or a sheltering security, as in *Single tree with small bush* (2009) (page 30). Still others show the countryside with picturesque motifs, but the Arcadian dream is disturbed by intense luminosity and slightly skewed compositions that transform idyllic scenes of rural harmony into blazing signs of existential yearning. The paintings speak of a longing to lose our individual selves — always marked by a beginning and end of consciousness — into a larger, timeless order. But Hutchings, as we shall see, remains the allegorist, honouring the *desire* for oneness — the end of time — as much as showing the unstoppable passage of time here on earth.

Allegory: The Romantic Symbol's Underside of Doubt

Hutchings's connection to Romanticism is undeniable, but needs to be specified. The varied and fluid Romantic movement, with its long

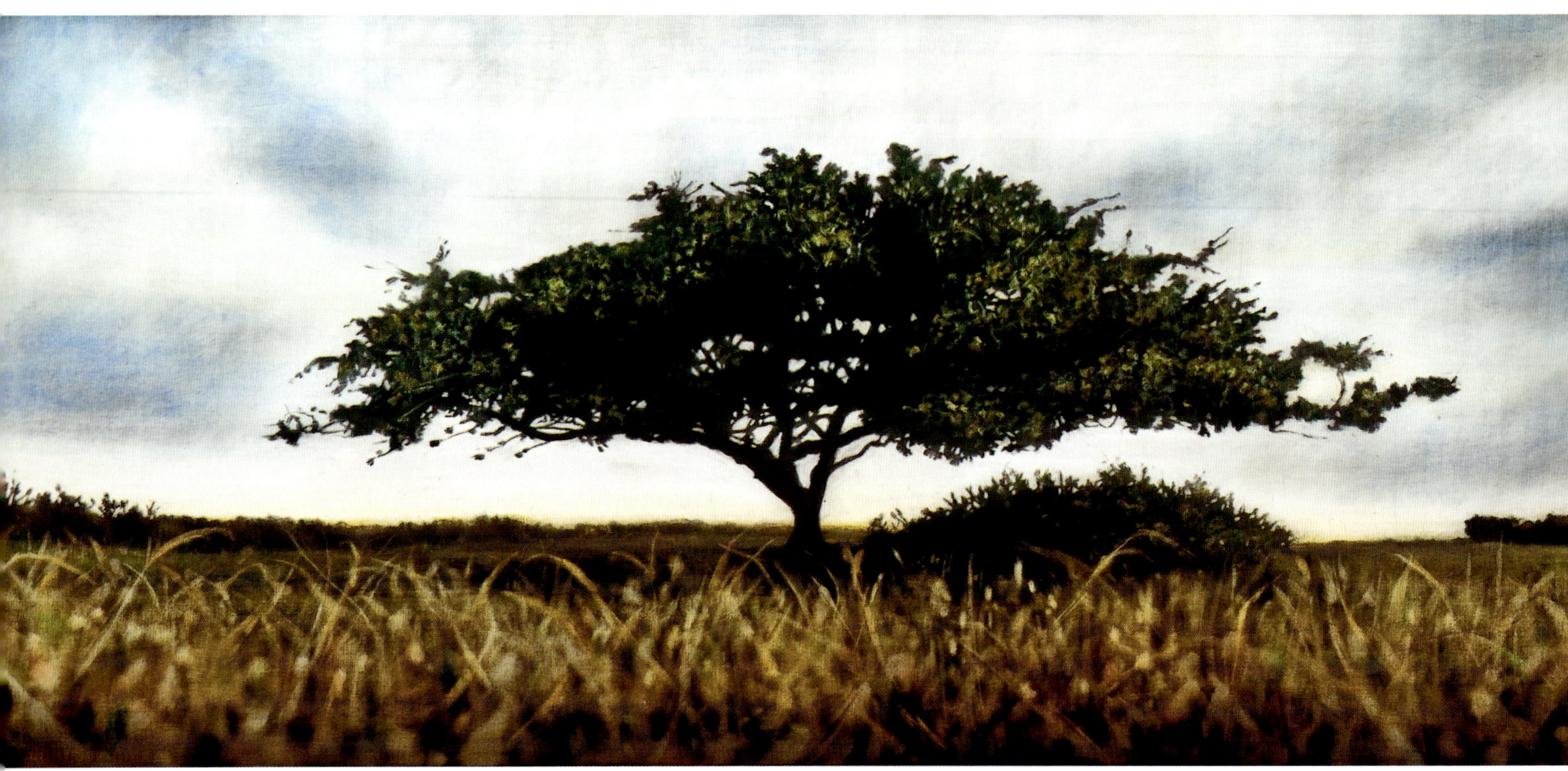

outgrowths and influences that reach into the present, can never be generalized. Romanticism centres on the desire to reconcile oppositions of culture and nature, of mind and spirit, of finite and infinite time. The movement originated at the end of the eighteenth century when prevailing rational Enlightenment ideas and codified religious practices lost their grip in the bewildering chaos of revolution, terror, and the advances of industry and science. The search for an end to conflict, for harmony between self and other, led some Romantics to see nature as a symbol for the pure Other — a pure objectiv-

ity to be brought into communion with what was thought to be the pure subjectivity of the inner mind.

Through a myriad of different artistic styles and literary genres that developed throughout the nineteenth and twentieth centuries, Romantics expressed both belief and doubt in the construct of pure objectivity and subjectivity and their mystical reconciliation. Belief and skepticism are not always easy to distinguish in Romantic art because a desire for oneness animates both. But the trope of modern allegory stands out against Romantic symbolism as

Single tree with small bush, 2009, oil and charcoal on canvas, 40" x 90"

skepticism does against belief.

In Romantic symbolism, a presumed essential, timeless commonality between a sign and what this sign refers to creates an unbroken conduit between landscape representations, nature, and absolute, divine truth. The viewer, following the painter, *enters* the picture and follows its lead to contemplate a disembodied, spiritual oneness with divine infinity. The Romantic symbol expresses a *belief* in a mystical transcendence of the self, while modern allegory forms the Romantic symbol's dark underside of doubt. It dwells on the entangled, time-bound interconnectedness between the individual and the world, which brings forth a deep scepticism that the construct of autonomous object and subject will hold. The allegorist sees that subjectivity is always marked by a beginning and end of consciousness, and that nature itself, as became increasingly clear during the nineteenth century, is subject to ruination. Nature is no more a pure object than the self can be a pure subject.[4]

The end of differences, the end of time, can only be yearned for — *mourned* — in allegory. Images and words can never be more than signs, mere representations of an unrealizable unity. Where the Romantic symbol presupposes a transparency between the object and its symbolic representation, allegory "says one

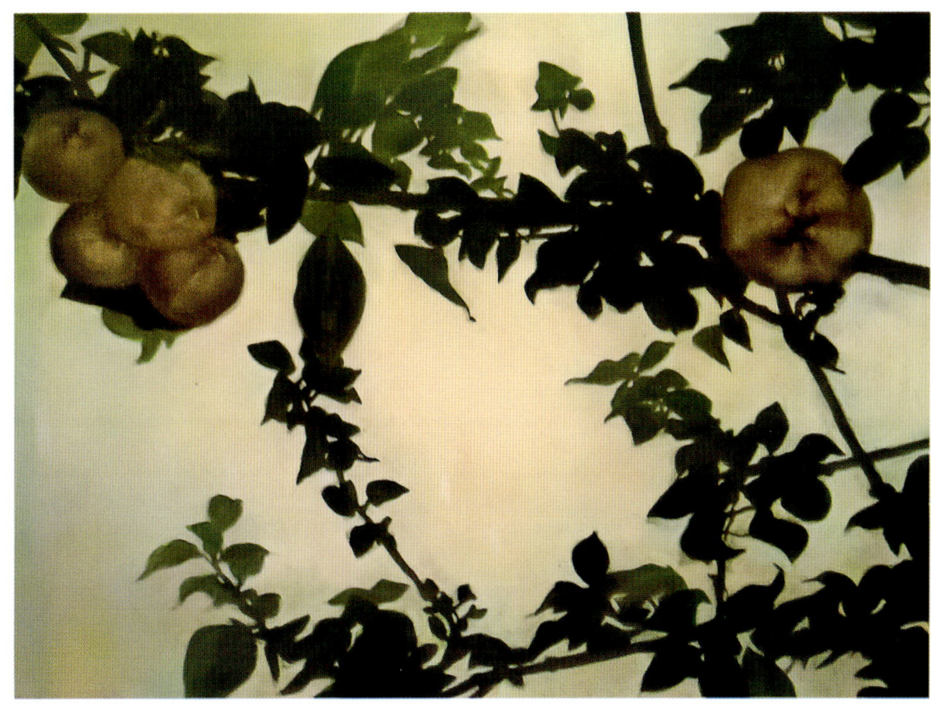

thing and means another."[5] Pried from its premodern fixed hermeneutics, modern allegory retains its quality as artificial sign, not related in any essential way to the object it refers to. The symbol, however, remains in the foreground as an ideal, as a sign for the divine unity it ultimately yearns for.

Toward the End of Time: *Plants, Bushes,* and *Hedges* of the 1990s

Hutchings's works of the 1990s can be read as a series of allegorical signs. In "The Allegorical Impulse in Stephen Hutchings's *Plants, Bushes, and Hedges,*"[6] I suggested that he shares a clear scepticism regarding Nature's pure objectivity and its unmediated representation in art with

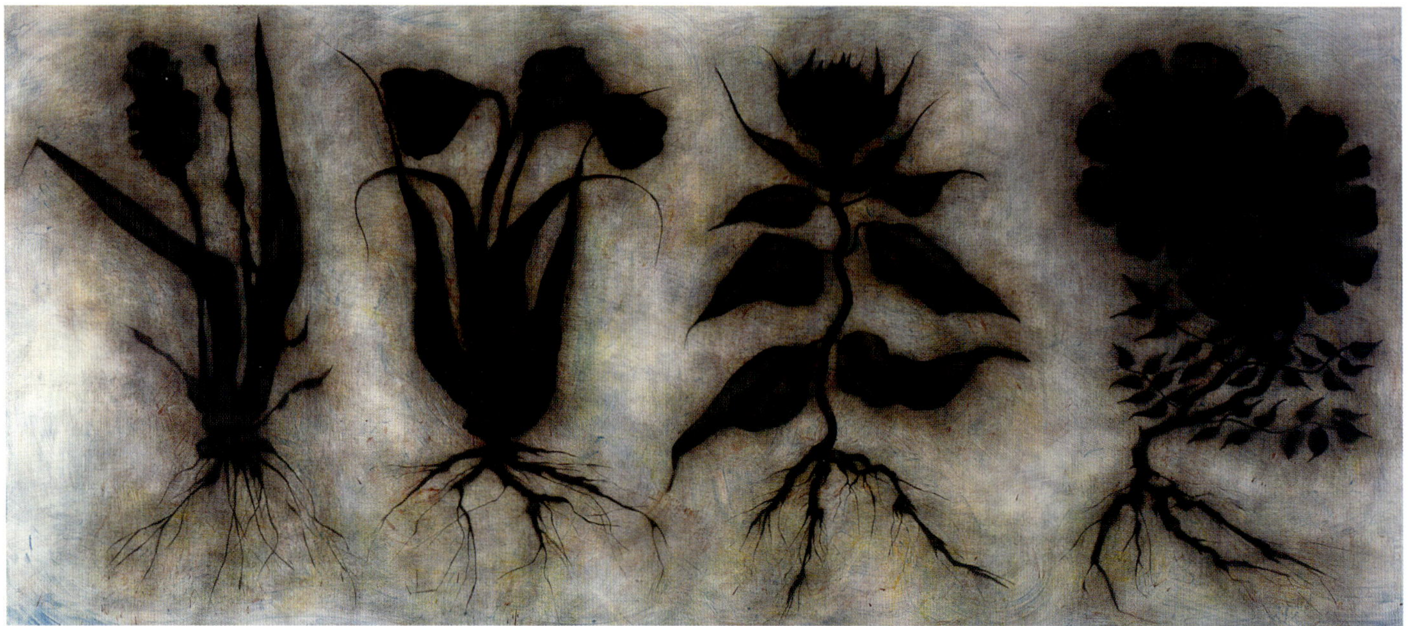

early German Romantics such as Friedrich, Runge and Carus.[7] The modern allegorist, as theorized by Walter Benjamin in *The Origin of German Tragic Drama,* takes an image from the past and divests it from its traditional, cultural meaning. Emptied out, the image is now ready to become something other, to receive a different meaning from the allegorist. The allegorical structure welcomes rather than resists language-based interpretation. Unlike the Romantic symbol, it does not hide the constructed, conventional nature of all representations, and thus questions whether absolute truth can ever be represented. Benjamin's allegorist depletes objects of their conventional meaning in order to let the *desire* for ultimate meaning travel from sign to sign. The allegorical objects become signs of passion pointing to

a final truth that is forever deferred, but remains a point of destination that sustains allegory's dynamism. Allegorical objects become stepping stones toward an impossible place where representation and object would coincide.

The paintings that comprise Hutchings's series, *Plants, Bushes,* and *Hedges,* form ruins of absolute knowledge. *Plants,* in particular, appear to be in a process of disintegration, their edges bleeding into the background. Although *Plant #17* is represented in a realistic manner and has lost nothing in line detail, it has lost, with its life, its volume and colour. Mute, passive, separated by a forceful black wooden frame, this plant poses as a scientific specimen, reminiscent of historical Romantic investigations into the wonders of nature. Yet it has no connection to such scientific natural history.

Four plants, 1996, oil and charcoal on canvas, 48" x 84"

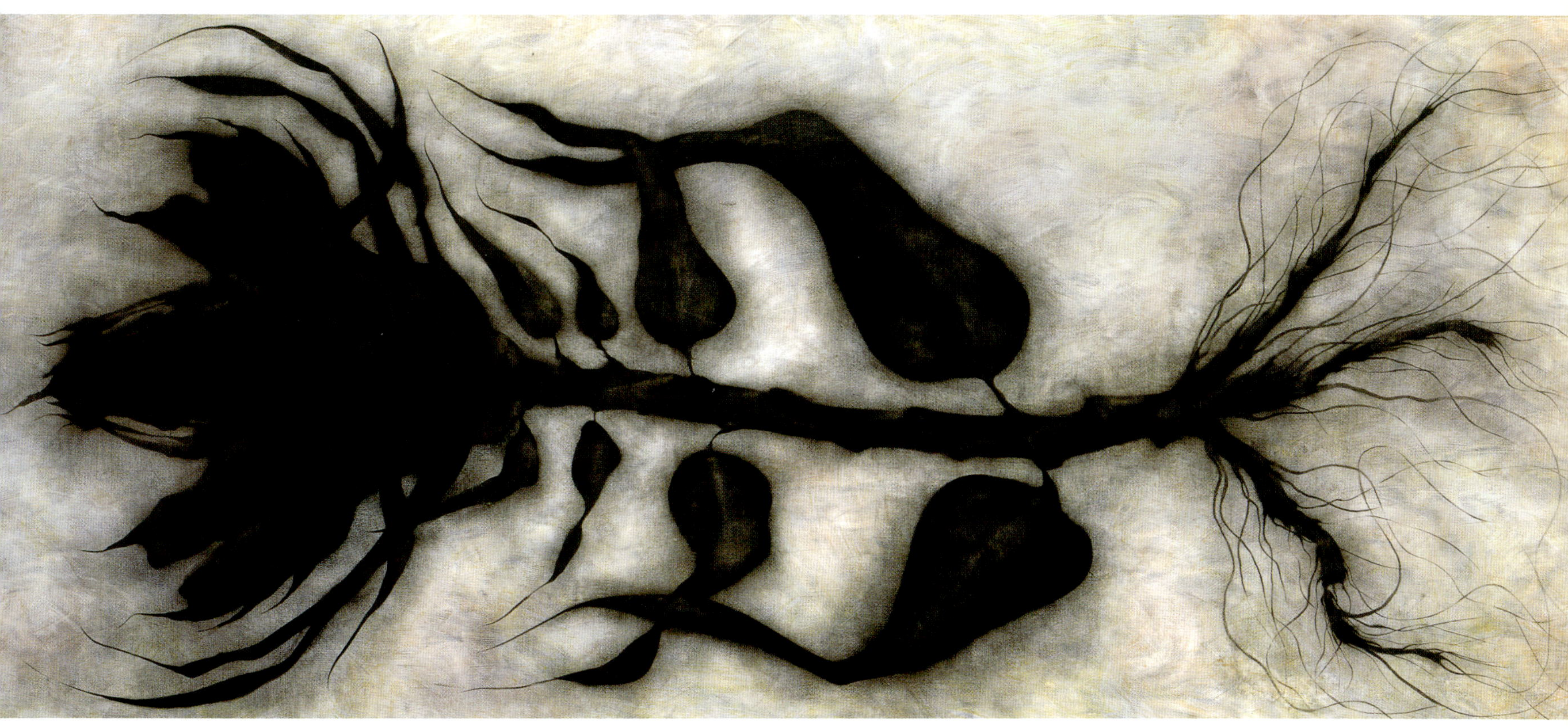

Hutchings invented this plant while he painted, as he did the others in the series. By taking away the specimen's scientific definition, the image is readied for non-scientific interpretations.

The shimmering effect created by layers of white paint with highlights of pink, ochre, and blue does remind the viewer of the luminous Romantic paintings in which light symbolizes the source of life and radiates through the objects represented. But this significance has been subverted here through the concealment of the light's source and direction: it is unclear whether the screens are lit from the front or the back. The light in these paintings shows only the thinness and flatness of the plant. In places, light almost penetrates the blackness; the plants' bleeding edges signal the threat that the image could dissolve into the screen. Romantic radiance is transformed into the mundane light of the slide projector.

The fate of *Plant #17*, its leaves stretched out like arms towards its flowering head, becomes my fate as a human. The personified *Plants* reflect the pernicious result of science's need for objective examination — a strict division between mere objective "matter" and conscious human subjectivity. The words of environmentalist Neil Evernden could apply to this

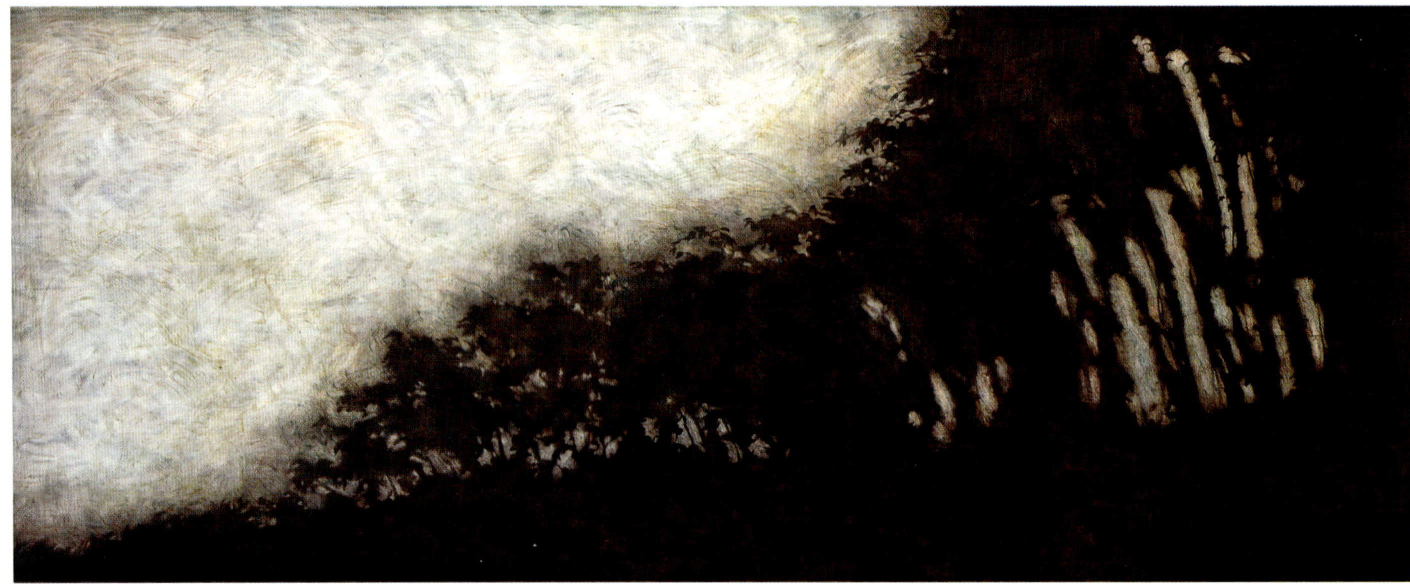

picture: "At first, nature was ours, our domesticated category of regulated otherness. Now we are nature's, one kind of object among all the others awaiting final explanation."[8]

The dark blooms in some of Hutchings's paintings from the *Plants* series speak to a longing to dim the Romantic fusing light in order to make space for a deeper, even more Romantic desire: for the absolute end of difference, in the absorption of death, or in the prelapsarian wholeness before birth. The blurry blooms of *Plant #3* and *Plant #6* cling tenuously to the edges of the canvas. The silhouettes seem to be emptying out the centre, pushing all tremulous energy to those edges. The heads of these plants, so large compared to their leaves and roots, are reminiscent of images of a fetus in the womb. While Hutchings, as an allegorist, reminds us that the fusing light, or total darkness, may be the desired end of time in which painful divisions between self and other are finally eradicated, he returns us to the reality of human existence and shows us that our own finality is part of nature's. *Plant #3* and *Plant #6* show not an absorbing blackness, but rather flat, two-dimensional silhouettes that barely cover the lighted background. The Romantic ideal of undifferentiated unity collapses into the disintegrating form of the plant, and into the reality of the heavy wooden black frame.

Landscapes for the End of Time: Borrowing Pictorialist Desires

In *Landscapes for the End of Time,* art-historical references to late Romanticism become more obvious and intentional. The intensely luminous skies, the sepia tones and play of shadows

Hedge (2), 1995, oil and charcoal on canvas, 60" x144"

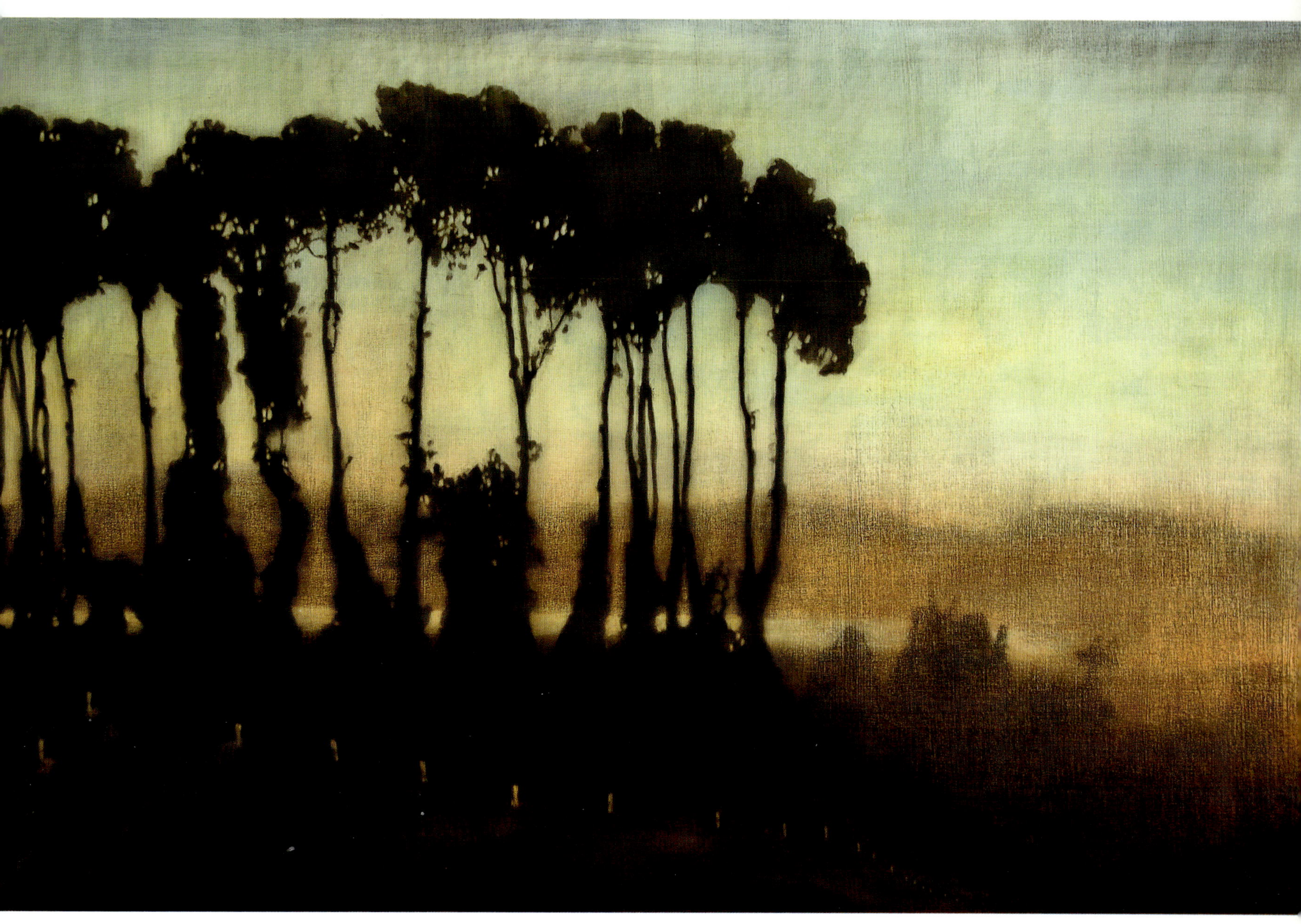

and light create a contemplative atmosphere of loss that points to the Pictorialism of photographers Demachy, Coburn, and Steichen, to name a few. Some Pictorialist works are quoted and even appropriated outright in several paintings.[9] Hutchings is clearly borrowing from this specific movement in photography, a movement that can be considered an outgrowth of Romanticism.

Pictorialism had its heyday at the end of

Demachy's pines #1, 2007, oil and charcoal on canvas, 42" x 84"

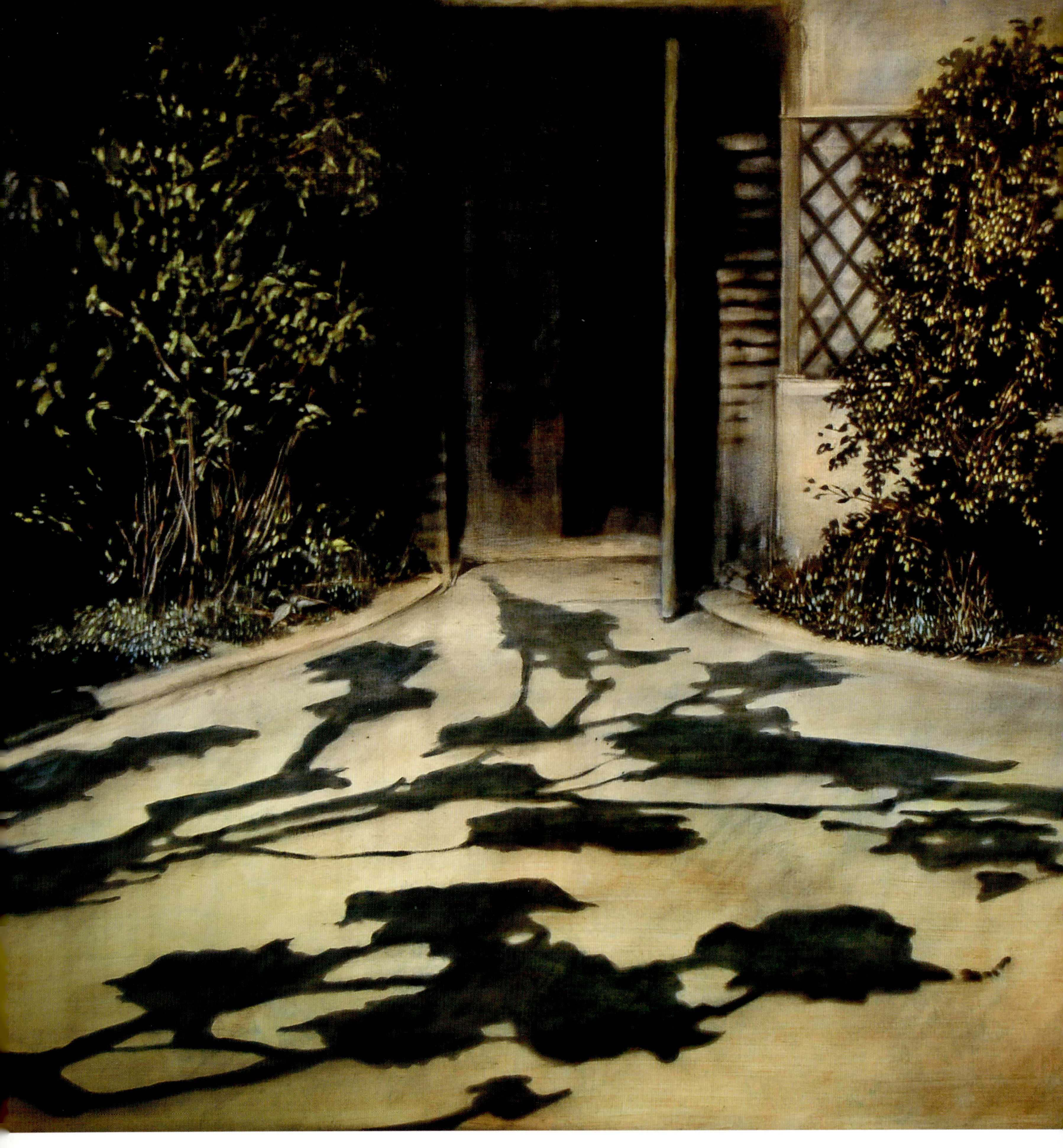

Foreshadows, 2007, oil and charcoal on canvas, 72" x 72"

the nineteenth and the beginning of the twentieth centuries. Its adherents varied widely in their practices, but they shared in common the aim of bringing to photography aesthetic and emotive means of expression that they felt had been left behind in painting. Reacting against the technical, empirical nature of the camera, many Pictorialists invented new ways of making photographs by using lens coatings and filters and different papers and emulsions for printing.[10]

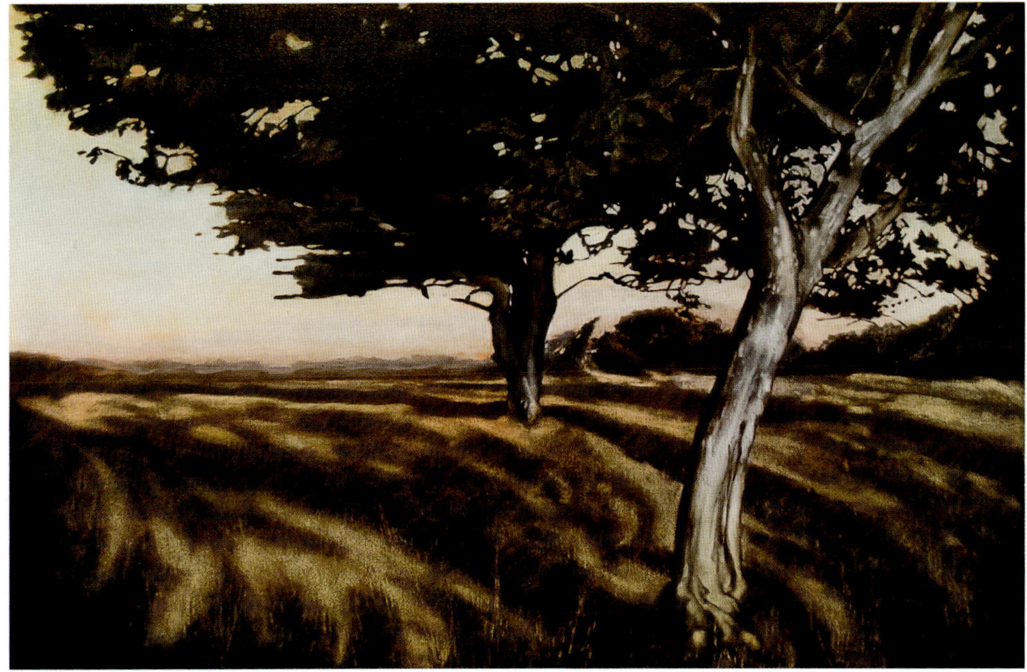

Despite their inventive methods to attempt to elevate the status of photography as a new, modern art medium, Pictorialism was a nostalgic, anti-modern movement that relied on traditional genres and subjects. In their landscapes, a sense of harmony with nature is often evoked by romanticizing the labourers on the land, and by recalling picturesque and idealized landscapes from the past. Borrowing from Symbolist painters, and in tune with the general interest in mysticism of the time, Pictorialist photographs often show a withdrawal from the outer world into an inner one of peace and harmony.[11] Details in the landscape are easily washed away in gum bichromate prints, or made less distinct through out-of-focus camera settings, resulting in a more generalized, abstracted image. Without the specific context of the photograph, as Pictorialism scholar Kristina Lowis remarks, "its singular relationship to time [is] denied."[12] The documentary character of the photograph as an index of a unique moment in time and space becomes veiled in an aesthetic of fusion of subject and object, turning the indexical quality of the photograph into a Romantic symbolism that had developed slowly over the course of the nineteenth century.

The tension between the desire for divine infinity and finite human existence, which created the dynamism of early Romanticism, was

Orchard (after Coburn), 2007, oil and charcoal on canvas, 32" x 48"

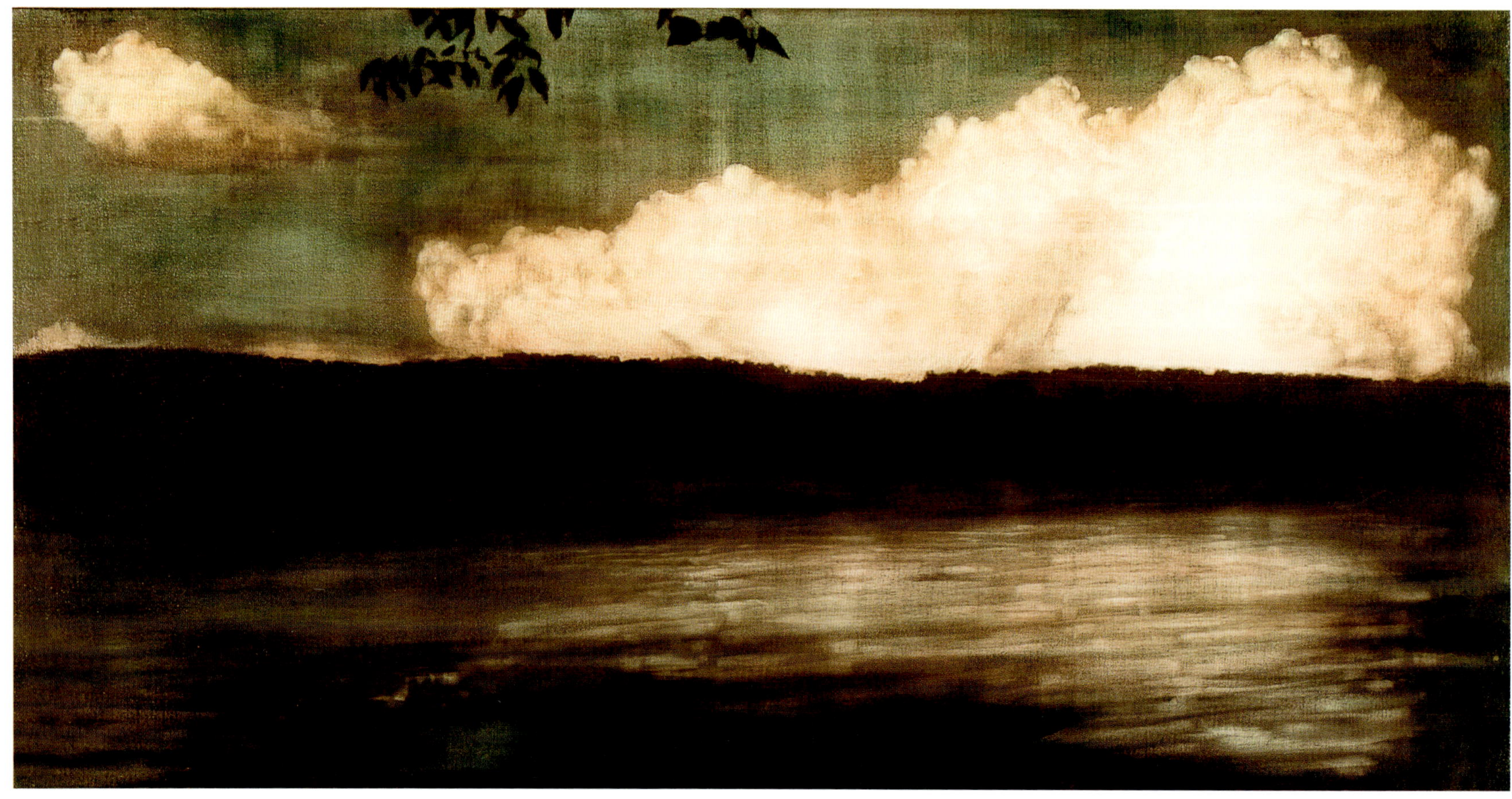

generally lost in these photographs, where everyday reality and nature itself are traded in for a dream state of mind — a static, languorous feeling of oneness with the external world from which there is no return, no connection to everyday life.[13] In some of these pictures, light dissolves form, and with it, the precision of reason and the pain of division between self and other. In others, darkness suggests a dimming of the light of reason to allow for a contemplation of the absolute end of difference in death. The Pictorialists dwell on death as the desired final unity. In this they come close to allegorical

art of the past such as Durer's *Melancholia*: the instability of meaning in the world instigates a contemplation of a transcendent spirit and an abjection of the finitude of nature and culture.[14]

Such fatalism and morbidity may be attractive again in a twenty-first century already marked by terror and visions of the end of the world. This might explain the renewed interest in symbolism and the Pictorialists. But Hutchings's allegorical tactics turn away from melancholia, and stay within the dynamic ambitions of modern allegory. In *Landscapes for the End of Time*, Hutchings depletes Pictorialist

Old cloud (after Steichen), 2007, oil and charcoal on canvas, 36" x 72"

imagery of its fatalism and absolutism and re-injects it with a dialectical tension between the desire for divine infinity and the desire for finite human existence. Setting up an active dialogue between the old and the new, he salvages the underlying utopian desire of Pictorialist landscapes and lets it loose within his charcoal-black natural imagery.

Gathering Storm Clouds, Sheltering Trees: Transcendental Longing

While Hutchings turns to Romanticism as a means to resist an objectifying scientific world view, he does not shy away from technology in this resistance. *Sky* (2010) (see image on pages 24–25) has its origin in a digitally manipulated photograph, as do all other paintings of this series. From high-tech Photoshop, he proceeds to a low-tech process and traces the image onto canvas with the aid of an overhead projector. Then he begins the painting process, starting with charcoal, which he rubs into the canvas to create large, solid forms. These are modified and shaped with erasers, bringing light into the darkness, specks at a time. The drawing is then overlaid with layers of thin, slightly coloured oil glazes. Hutchings's unique process creates an uncertain surface, where the apparent seamlessness of the scenes falls apart.

Hutchings's unorthodox painting methods correspond to the Pictorialists' unusual pho-

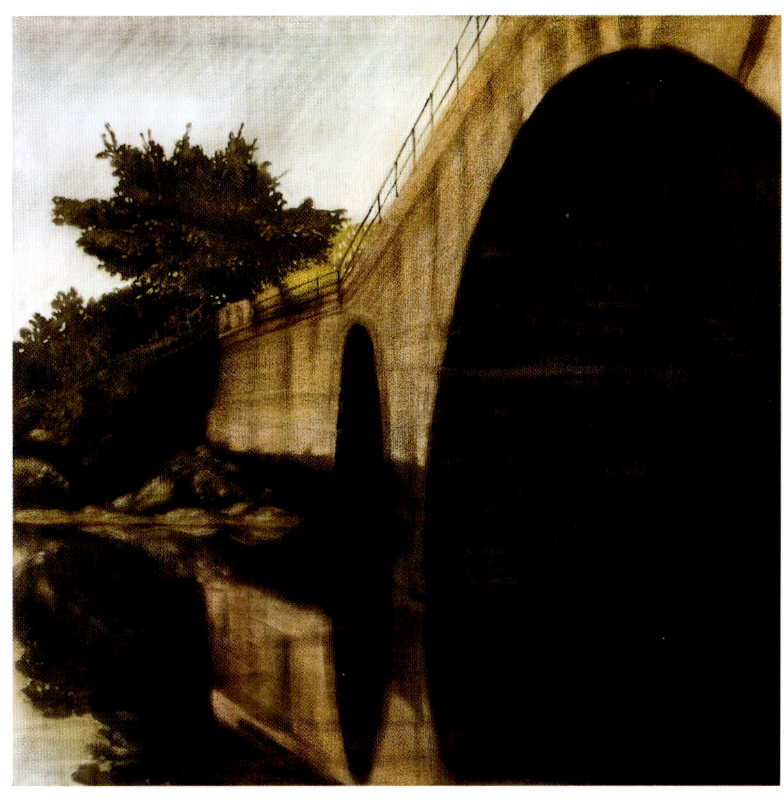

tographic inventions. Many Pictorialists used special lenses, rough-textured paper, light-sensitized gum arabic and pigment — any material and technique that came their way. [15] But while the Pictorialists used their inventions often to create a more abstract reality, an illusionary, idealistic "truth," Hutchings's use of technology helps him appropriate historical imagery and oversaturate it with Romantic effects to bring out the artificiality of its symbolism. Where the Pictorialists washed away details, and hand-marked and painted their surfaces to dilute photography's indexical qualities, Hutchings's scratching, rubbing and overlaying of paint returns a sense of time-

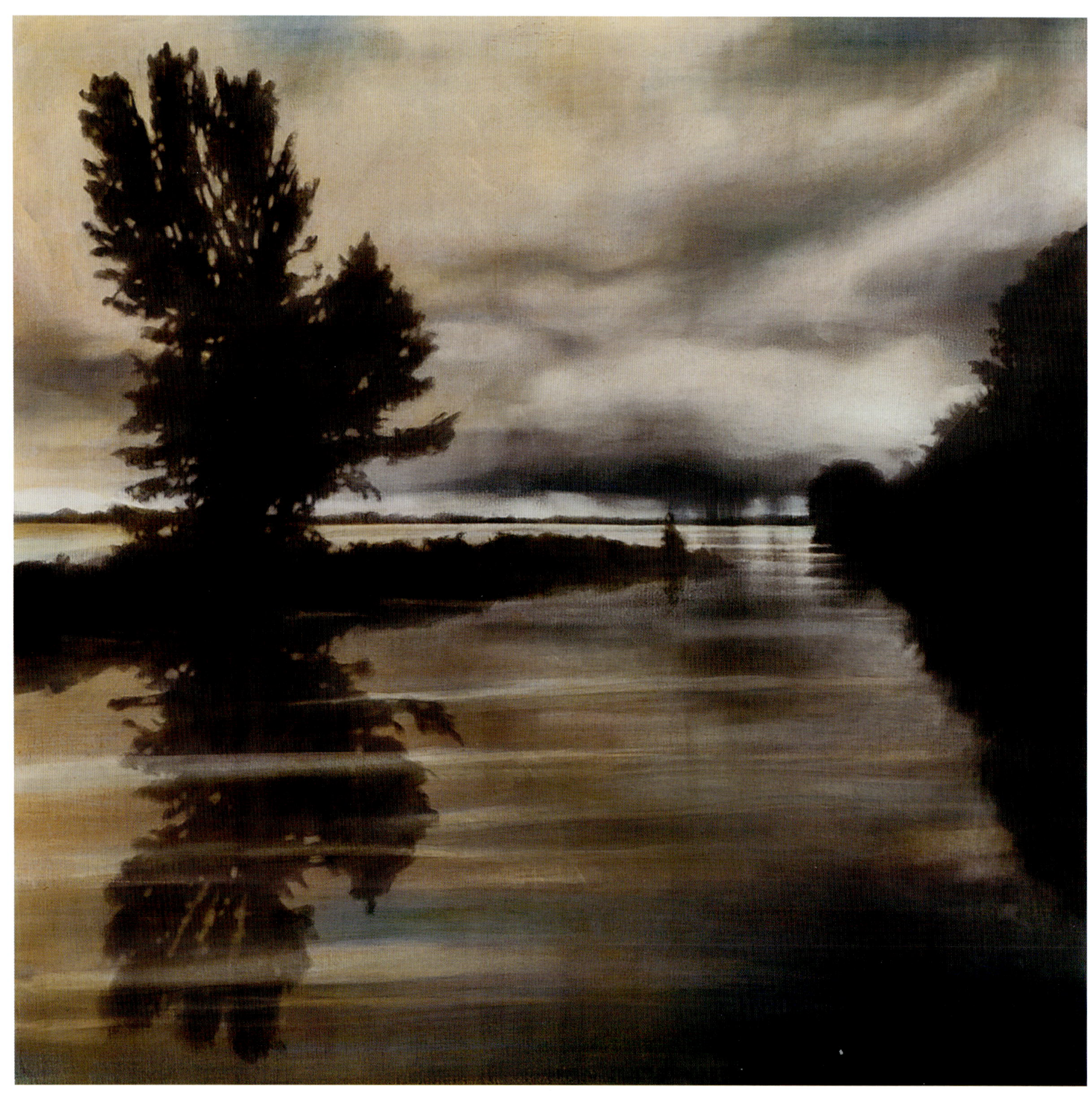

Distant storm, 2008, oil and charcoal on canvas, 42" x 42"

bound process to Romantic, timeless imagery, and underlines the *cultural*, human construct of Nature that these paintings represent.

There is, perhaps, no image of nature more suited to the idea of a loss of self into eternity than the image of sea, sky, and sun. No matter how many millions of snapshots and department-store paintings show us the sun setting in the sea, a seascape still manages

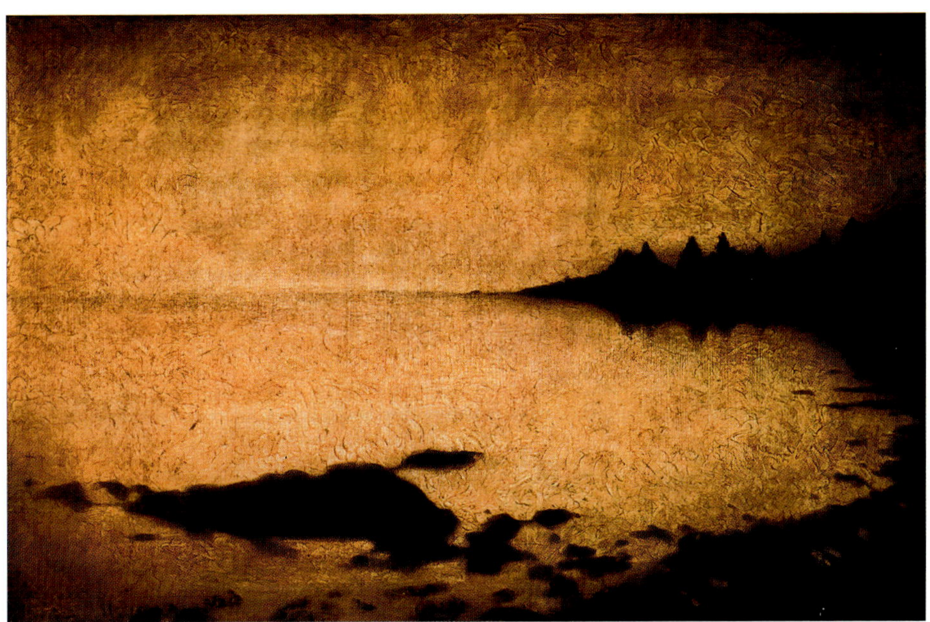

to provoke a longing for a communion of self and world. As Dominic Willsdon writes about Hiroshi Sugimoto's series of seascapes, such an image can convey "a sense that the possibility of that communion is somehow lost to us, but that both the belief and the loss can be communicated in art."[16] Where the loss in Sugimoto's photographs is expressed in a dark minimalist abstraction, Hutchings appropriates a photograph, Gustave Le Gray's *Sky*, that shows a surplus of effects. The mid-nineteenth-century image shows a low horizon over dark, shimmering water that opens up to a seemingly infinite space of the sky.[17] Ragged dark clouds are rimmed with a saturated colour that gains its luminosity from the setting sun.

Le Gray's seascapes were constructs. Due to technical limitations in the lenses, the skies

in most nineteenth-century photographs were overexposed and printed as white backdrops. To get around this, in the darkroom Le Gray fused a properly exposed sky with a properly exposed sea image, thereby creating a hybrid photograph that showed a correct exposure in both its upper and lower sections.

Le Gray's small-format photograph facilitates a withdrawal of the mind into an inner, disembodied landscape. It answers to a desire to transcend the real world's boundaries of forms and constrictions of time into a world that is as aleatory as clouds, as formless as water. Hutchings's intervention exists in the blow-up of this image to the scale of 8 ×18 feet. The elements become large as life, oversaturated and unstable to the point of disintegration. At the same time, the painting addresses the viewer's embodied presence — *implicates* the viewer in a process of decay.

John Ruskin, the Victorian social thinker and art critic, observed how colours and patterns of clouds seemed to change over the years, and surmised that these changes had something to do with pollution of the atmosphere created by heavy industry. He spoke of his findings, which for him symbolized the degradation of nature by industry in the nineteenth century in general, in two lectures delivered at the London Institute in 1884, which were later published as *The Storm-cloud of the Nineteenth Century*. The importance of Ruskin's proto-environmentalism lies not in its scientific accuracy or inaccuracy, but in the expression of his fear that nature is vulnerable and historic, rather than unvanquishable and timeless.[18]

Despite its beauty, Hutchings's *Sky* depicts a threatened and threatening nature. Other works in the series, however, express the Romantic desire to address nature as a more powerful, sheltering order. *Grove*, 2010, (see image on pages 22–23) is a painting of a dense forest that finds its origin in photographs Hutchings took in Dorset, England. Altered and rearranged in Photoshop, the resulting image is reminiscent of an 1897 photogravure by Edouard Hannon, *The Clearing*.[19]

In Hannon's photograph we observe straight, bare trunks of pine trees, like the col-

umns of a cathedral, that flank a central, shining path moving towards a penetrating light beyond the forest. The viewer is drawn in, invited to contemplate an all-encompassing, mystical luminescence that promises to gradually dissolve the individual forms of the trees. Where the unifying light in Hannon's *The Clearing* becomes a symbol for the divine, in Hutchings's *Grove* the light is dappled equally on the forest floor and on the pathway and breaks up in innumerable patches between the leaves and branches. The fused borders between light and dark in *The Clearing* become sharply demarcated silhouetted trees in *Grove*, whose rounded horizon seems to indicate a globe, the dark earth standing out sharply from the light of an unknowable cosmos. There is no clear path to reach this luminosity. The even, all-over pattern of

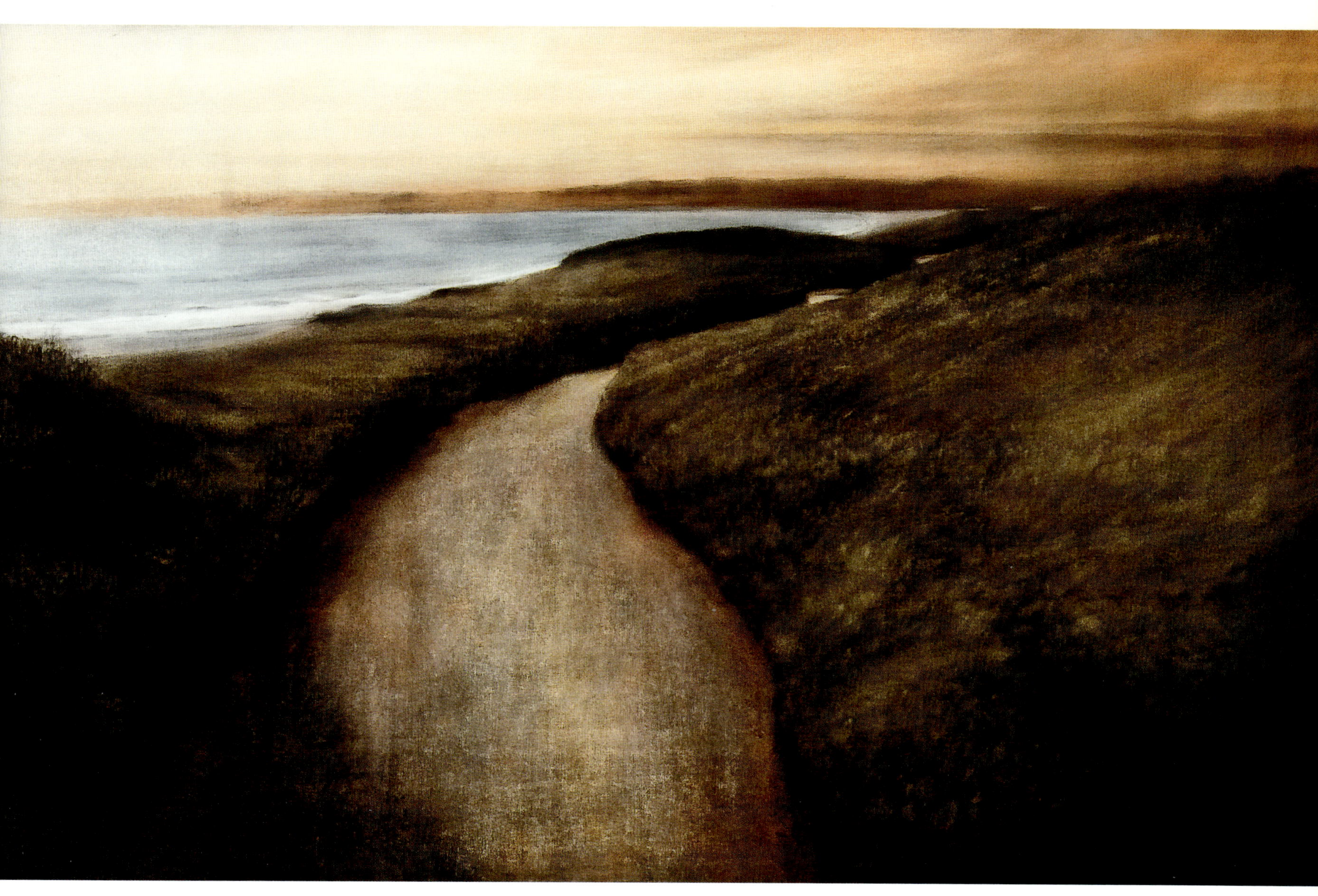

light and dark holds the search for a way out forever in suspense. *Grove* holds back the invitation to contemplate divine infinity in nature.

While *The Clearing* measures 8 × 6 inches, *Grove* measures 8 × 18 feet. Viewers, standing in front of Hutchings's life-sized trees, are not so much invited in as *apprehended* by this painting. Rather than feeling one with nature and the universe, they begin to feel like one of the trees, and sense the connection between the trees and themselves as living beings connected to the earth.

The path, 2010, oil and charcoal on canvas, 42" x 96"

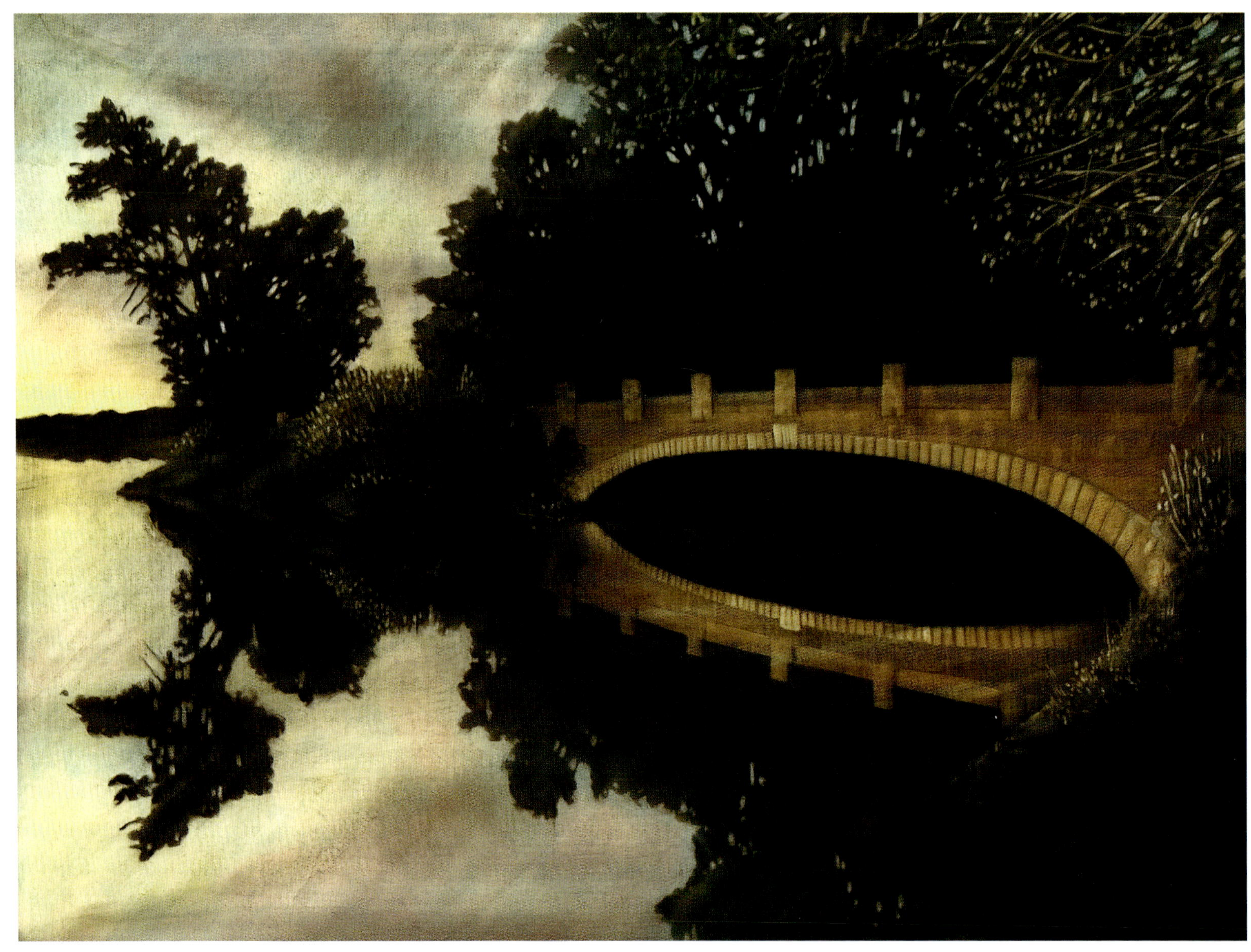

Towards the picturesque, 2007, oil and charcoal on canvas, 36" x 48"

Towards Arcadia: A Pastoral Dream

When Hutchings's trees and bushes become more isolated, they begin to take on human characteristics. Like Caspar David Friedrich's famous *Wanderer above the Mists* of 1818, the five bushy trees in *Roads* (2006-2010) (see image on pages 12–13) are perched on the "edge of the world" as multiple "wanderers" contemplating the ungraspable, divine infinity before them. Like Friedrich's wanderer, who, dressed in his city clothes and isolated on the top of a mountain, seems far removed from the mysterious, formless world before him, the trees in *Roads* appear ill at ease in this scene, awkwardly plunked as they are on a threshold between earth and sky.

Despite its un-gracefulness, *Roads* adheres to elements of the pastoral, to picturesque views that were invented in the seventeenth century and kitschified through innumerable clichéd representations of the landscape ever since.[20] While many Pictorialists clung to the rural landscape's elements of composition, in *Roads* picturesque characteristics lose their effects through the strange shapes and positions of the trees.

A tree in the foreground of a landscape painting conventionally functions as a *repoussoir*, contrasting the near with the far and leading the eye of the viewer into the space that unfolds in the picture plane. In *Roads,* however, the tree on the left deflects the eye to a sky that

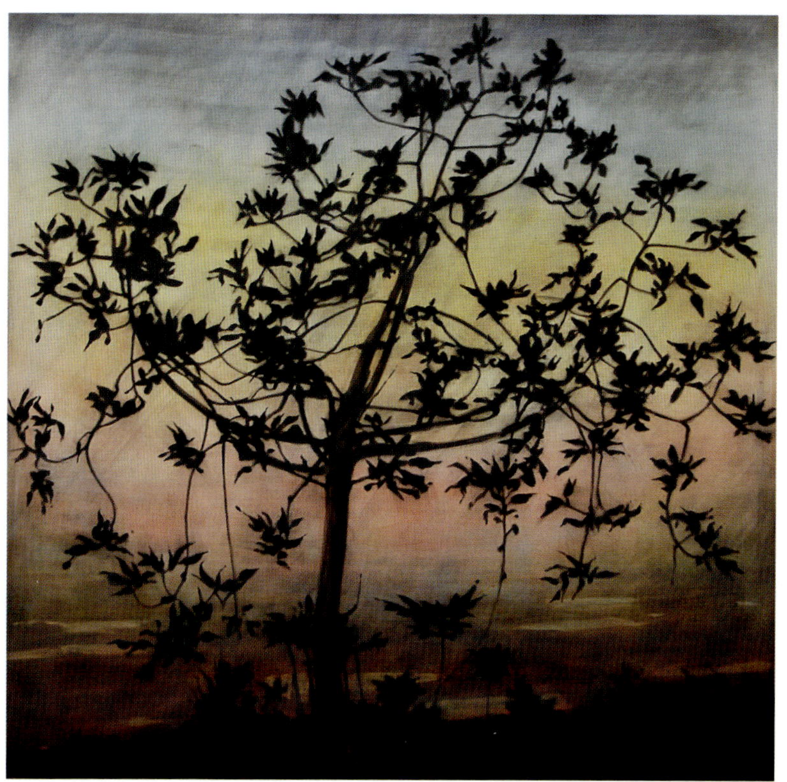

is cluttered with trees and to a shallow foreground that appears to be a steep ridge, providing little space to roam.

Traditionally, a road in the landscape signifies life's journey and functions as a formal device to create space. The doubling of the roads in many of Hutchings's painting appears to underline the importance of this pastoral element through reiteration. But in this work, the roads lead only a short distance into the picture plane, then abruptly drop off at the rim. The tree on the right, which we could expect to be another framing device, veers away strangely, towards the frame, as if pointing to a space outside the painting.

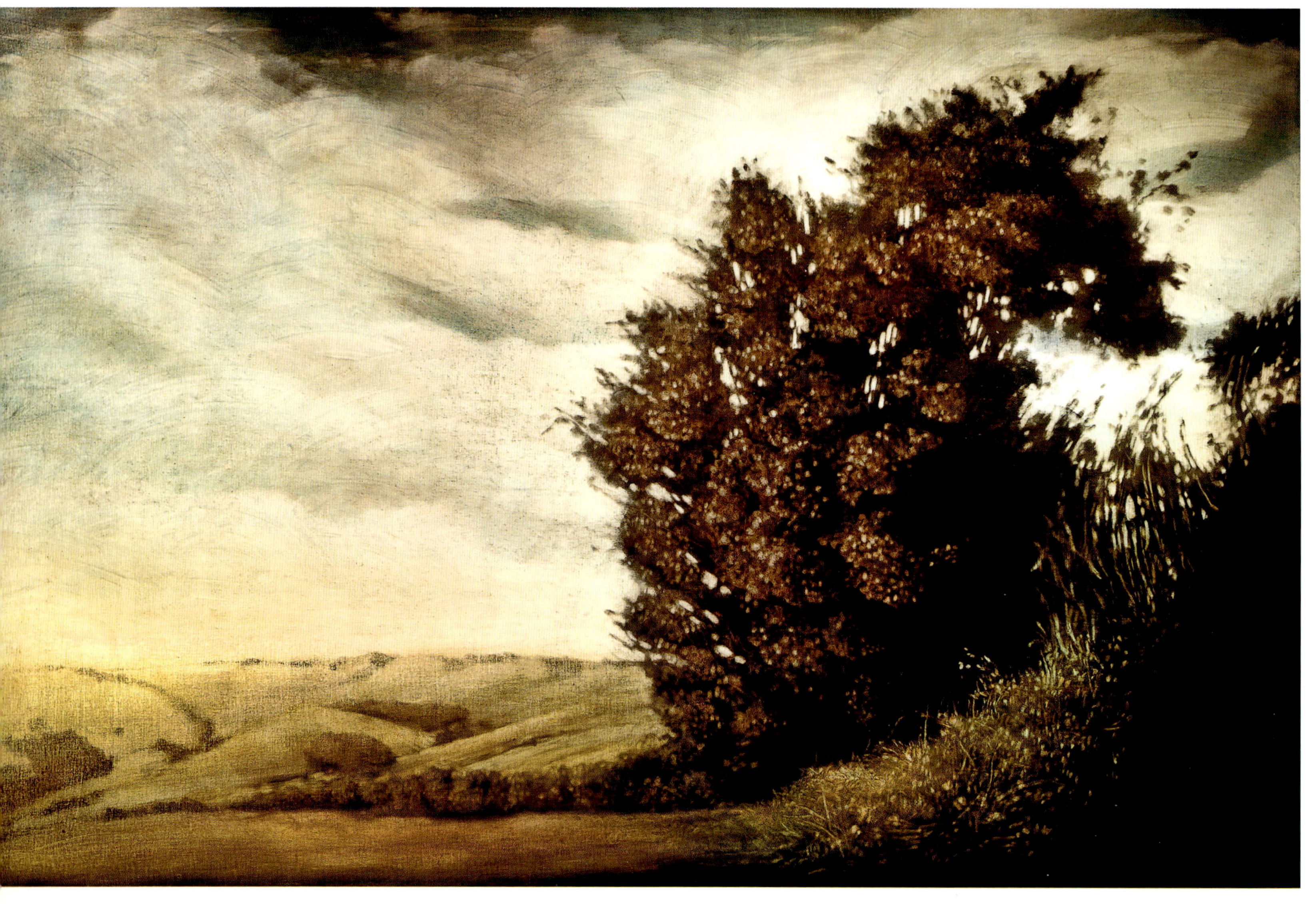

Finally, the luminous sky, a conventional device used to stir thoughts of unity and infinity, no more unifies this painting than does the ground below. Yet the personified trees seem turned towards the heavens as if in expectation of transcendence — an expectation that remains but a yearning.

Roads, and paintings such as *Plantation* (2009), *The Path* (2010), and *The Road into the Bush* (2010) show signs of human interaction with the land: a rutted road, planted saplings. The pastoral elements conjure up a dream of picturesque harmony in the landscape that are contradicted by dramatic effects that convey a restless mood: sharp contrasts, highlights, haziness, and dark, brooding colours. The overall

Tree with transformed landscape, 2010, oil and charcoal on canvas, 34" x 48"

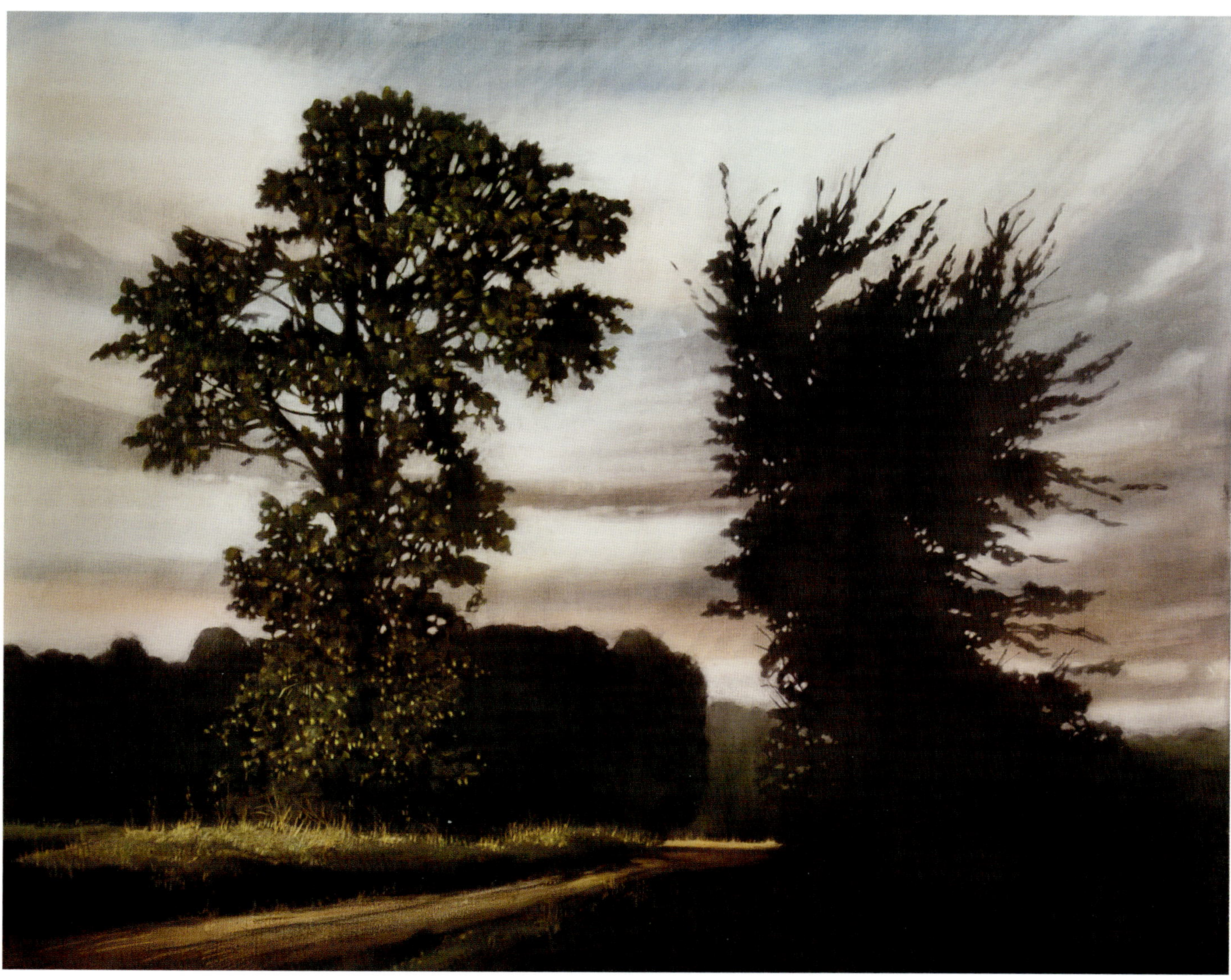

seamlessness of the scene in *Hill* (2010) (see image on pages 18–19) almost fools the viewer into ignoring the signs that disrupt its consolidation — the worked-over surface and the telltale doubling of motifs that point to Photoshop's technological interference.

Conclusion

Landscapes for the End of Time was inspired by Olivier Messiaen's *Quartet for the End of Time.* Writing in a prison camp, while facing the possibility of death, the composer turned to the Revelation of St. John to create his famous quartet. Ironically, it was the work itself, performed at the camp in 1941, that led to the

Landscape with two trees and path (towards the divine), 2008, oil and charcoal on canvas, 48" x 60"

release of Messiaen and the other musicians. Thus, *Quartet for the End of Time* is marked as much by a contemplation of the end of time as it is by the reality of time ticking away in life.

Hutchings's paintings are self-consciously artificial *ruins* of Romantic landscape paintings. In the twenty-first century, our awareness of the earth's endangered ecology makes it difficult to see harmony between culture and nature, or to see nature as a timeless order more powerful than the human, finite one that always ends in death. In light of the fragile ecological state of the earth, these "pastoral" paintings can only mourn the loss of Arcadia.

For centuries of Western culture, the pastoral dream of harmony between nature and culture has served as a model for a harmonious world. Rosalind Williams, in *Notes on the Underground*, suggests that the pastoral dream remains pertinent only if it can still somehow be projected onto the phenomenal reality of the landscape. She asks whether "destruction of the natural environment might be culturally as well as physically harmful to human life" and suggests that perhaps the ideal of a wholly man-made environment could take the place of the Arcadian dream by displacing nature completely rather than invading and degrading it.[21]

Displacing nature completely may be the unspoken aim of the hegemonic, technological culture of modernity, but a wholly technological model for society ignores the reality of our own nature and the nature we depend on. Hutchings the allegorist does not break with the reality of nature, nor does he break with history.

Landscapes for the End of Time retains a tension between the ephemeral and the infinite, a tension that is never resolved in a clean choice between the two. This body of work shows that the cosmos, in all its beauty, incredible vastness, and awesome intricacy, still offers an overwhelming sense of mystery. Science has revealed our deep connection to nature, but human language fails to reach the ultimate mysteries of the enchanted interconnectedness between human beings and their environment. And, as long as our individual lives are marked by a beginning and end of consciousness, the longing for the end of time continues, even in a world that is bound by historical time.

The allegorist's stance between desire and frustration saves the work from Pictorialism's stasis and from Romanticism's mysticism. But a penetrating light in even the darkest of pictures alludes to that unimaginable place without time, against which the fragility of the earth and the limitation of human endeavour stand out in sharp relief.

Notes

1   H. Masud Taj, "The Edge of the World," *Sentinel Poetry (Online) #51*, accessed October 14, 2009, http://www. sentinelpoetry.org.uk/0207/taj.html.

2   Petra Halkes, "The Allegorical Impulse in Stephen Hutchings's Plants, Bushes, and Hedges," in *Aspiring to the Landscape: On Painting and the Subject of Nature* (Toronto, Buffalo, London: University of Toronto Press, 2006), 73-106. Parts of this essay have been incorporated here.

3   H. Masud Taj, "The Edge of the World."

4   On the concept of time in allegory, see Azade Seyhan, *Representation and its Discontents: The Critical Legacy of German Romantics* (Berkeley and Los Angeles: University of California Press, 1992), 68-69.

5   Angus Fletcher, *Allegory: The Theory of a Symbolic Mode* (Ithaca, NY: Cornell University Press, 1964), 2.

6   See note 2.

7   Caspar David Friedrich (1774-1840), Philipp Otto Runge (1777-1810), and Carl Gustav Carus (1789-1869). See note 4.

8   Neil Evernden, *The Social Creation of Nature* (Baltimore: Johns Hopkins University Press, 1992), 93.

9   Robert Demachy (1859-1936) and his predecessor Gustave Le Gray (1820-1884), Alvin Langdon Coburn (1882-1966) and Edward Steichen (1879-1973). Hutchings's *Demachy's pines #1* (2007) is an appropriation of Toucques Valley (1906), a Robert Demachy photograph that is in the public domain and can be found on the Wikimedia Commons.

10   See Alison Nordström et al., *TruthBeauty: Pictorialism and the Photograph as Art, 1845-1945* (Vancouver, Toronto, Berkeley: Douglas & McIntyre; Vancouver: Vancouver Art Gallery), 2008.

11   Ulrich Pohlmann, "Symbolism and Pictorialism, The Influence of Eugène Carrière's Painting on Art Photography around 1900" in Patrick Daum et al., *Impressionist Camera: Pictorial Photography in Europe, 1888-1918* (London: Merrell Publishers, 2006.), 89.

12   Kristina Lowis, "European Pictorial Aesthetics," in Daum et al., 51.

13   See Sylvain Morand, "Imagination and Pigment: Archaism and Technique in Pictorialism" in Daum et al. Morand writes, "If the art photography movement was, from the beginning, at a distinct remove from the present world, it was even more so a few decades later." (254).

14   See Susan Buck-Morss, *The Dialectics of Seeing: Walter Benjamin and the Arcades Project* (Cambridge, MA: The MIT Press, 1989), 170-175, for Benjamin's analysis of Dürer's *Melancholia* and baroque allegory.

15   Sylvain Morand, in Daum et al., 251-269.

16   Willsdon, Dominic, "Hiroshi Sugimoto – Aegean Sea, Pilion" in Geoffrey Batchen et al., *Singular Images: Essays on Remarkable Photographs* (New York: D.A.P. Aperture Foundation, 2006), 101.

17   Le Gray's *Sky* is a combination of two of his photographs, *The Great Wave, Sète* and *Mediterranean Sea, Sète*, both from 1857, and both reproduced in Sylvie Aubenas, *Gustave Le Gray, 1820-1884* (Los Angeles: J. Paul Getty Museum, 2002).

18   Keith Hanly, in "The Discourse of Natural Beauty," writes: "If the atmospheric effects that Ruskin observed were arguably the result of the 1871-72 eruption of Vesuvius rather than the mills of South Lancashire, they did represent a prophetic enlargement of the results of industrially caused pollution." Michael Wheeler (ed.), *Ruskin and Environment: The Storm-cloud of the Nineteenth Century* (Manchester: Manchester University, 1995), 36.

19   Reproduced in Daum et al., 175.

20   See Malcolm Andrews, *Landscape and Western Art* (Oxford: Oxford University Press, 1999), 97.

21   Rosalind Williams, Notes on the Underground (Cambridge, MA.: The MIT Press, 1990), 2-11.

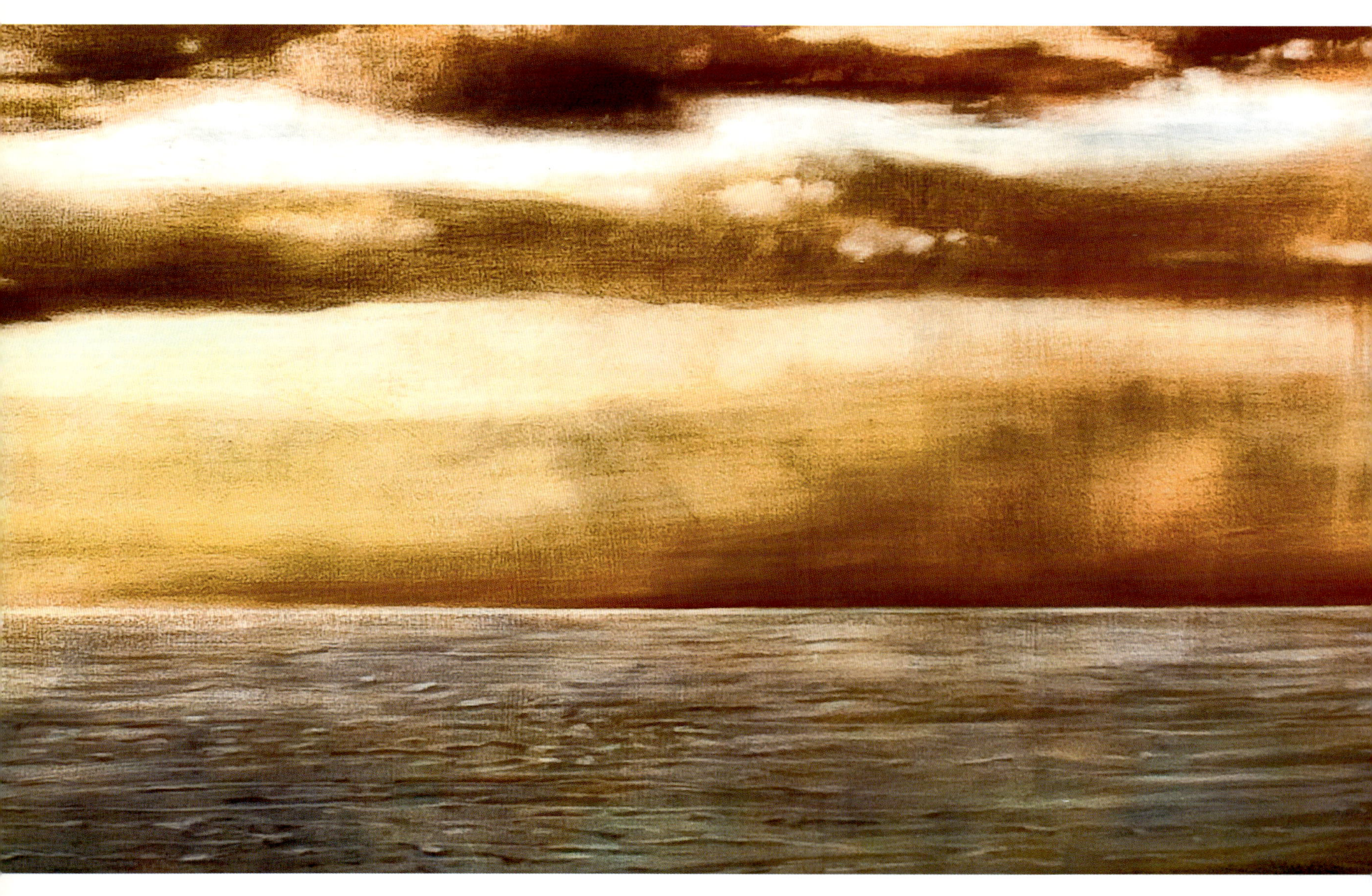

Close-up
Details of the *Landsapes for the End of Time* paintings

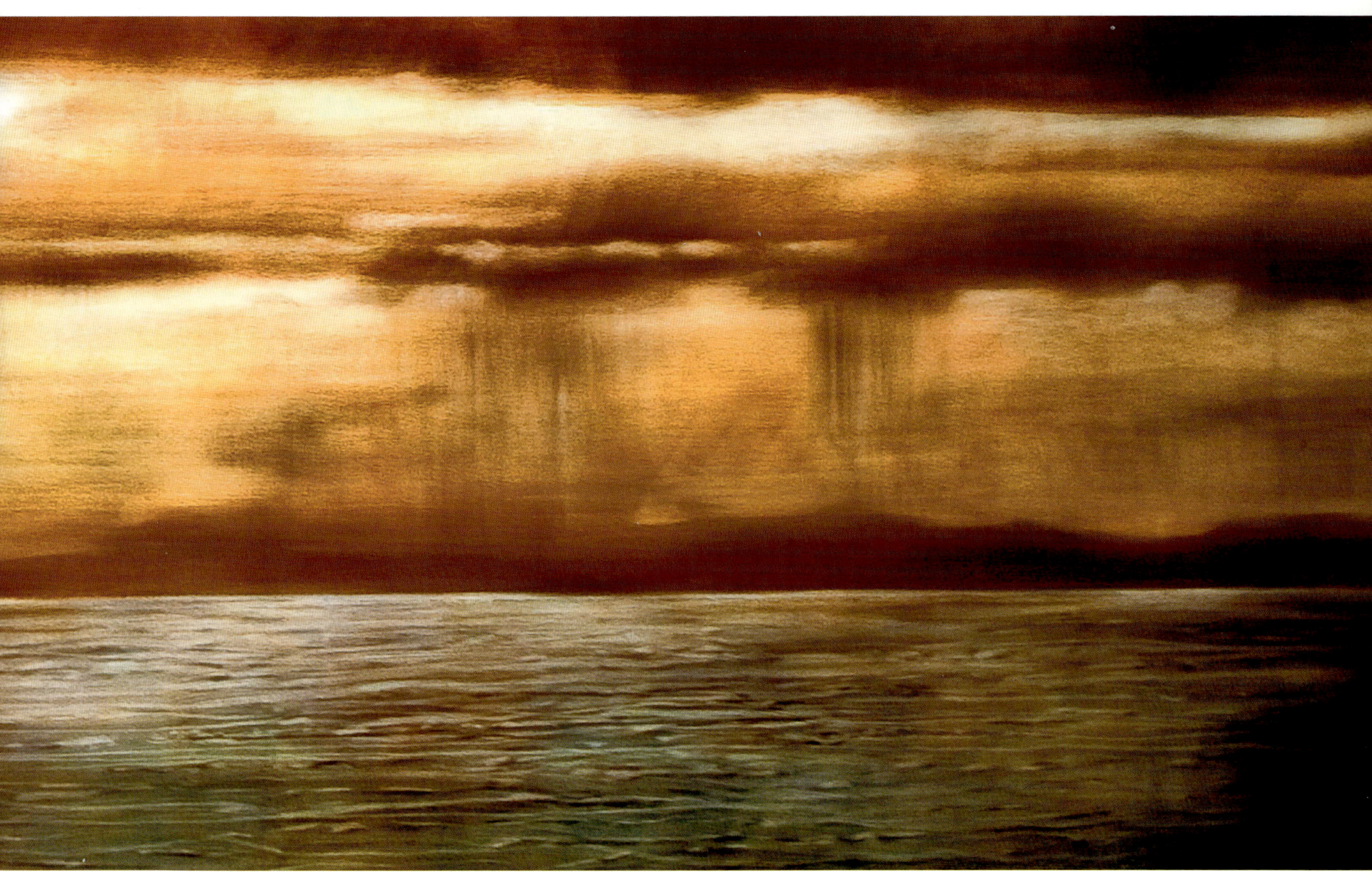

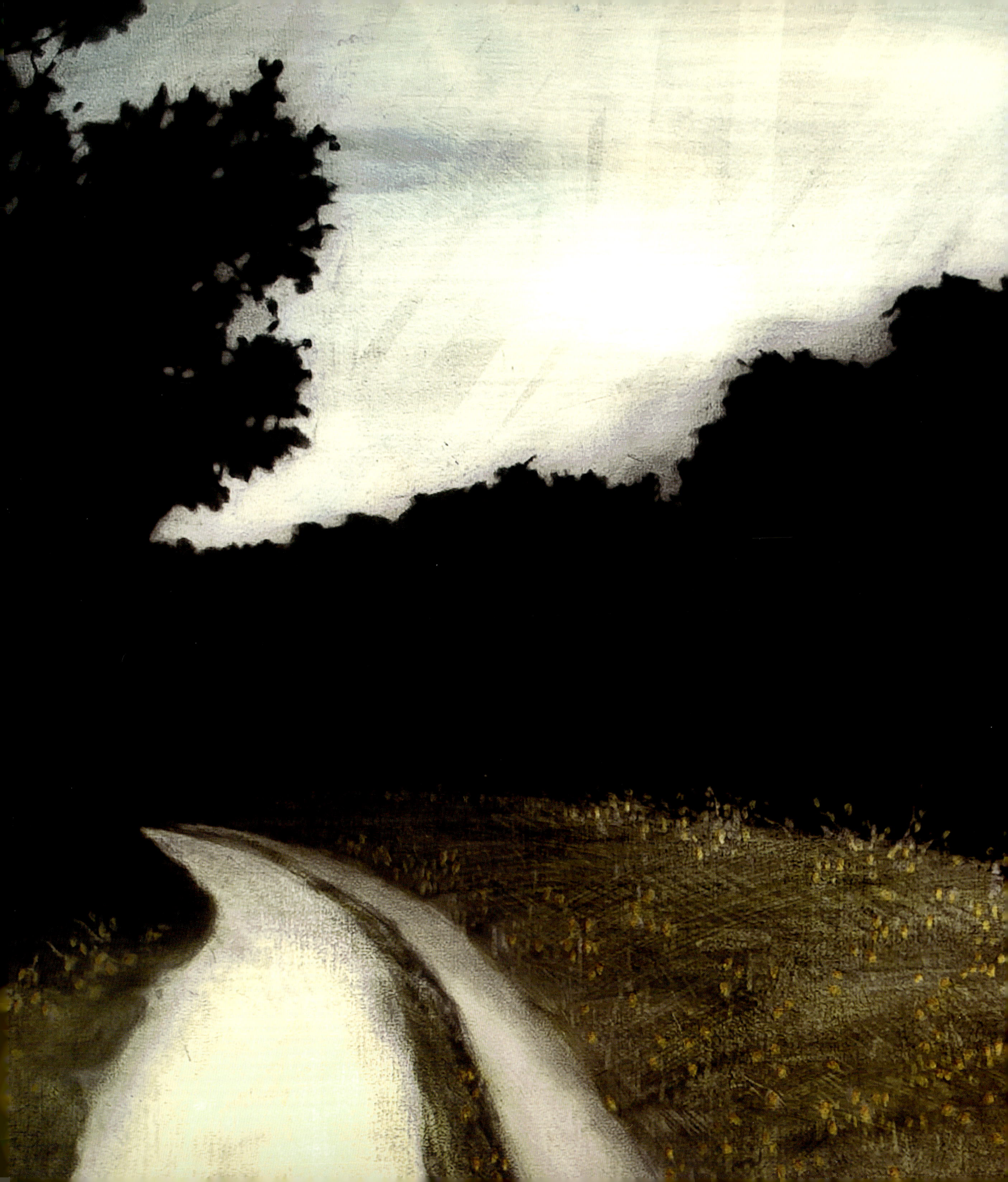

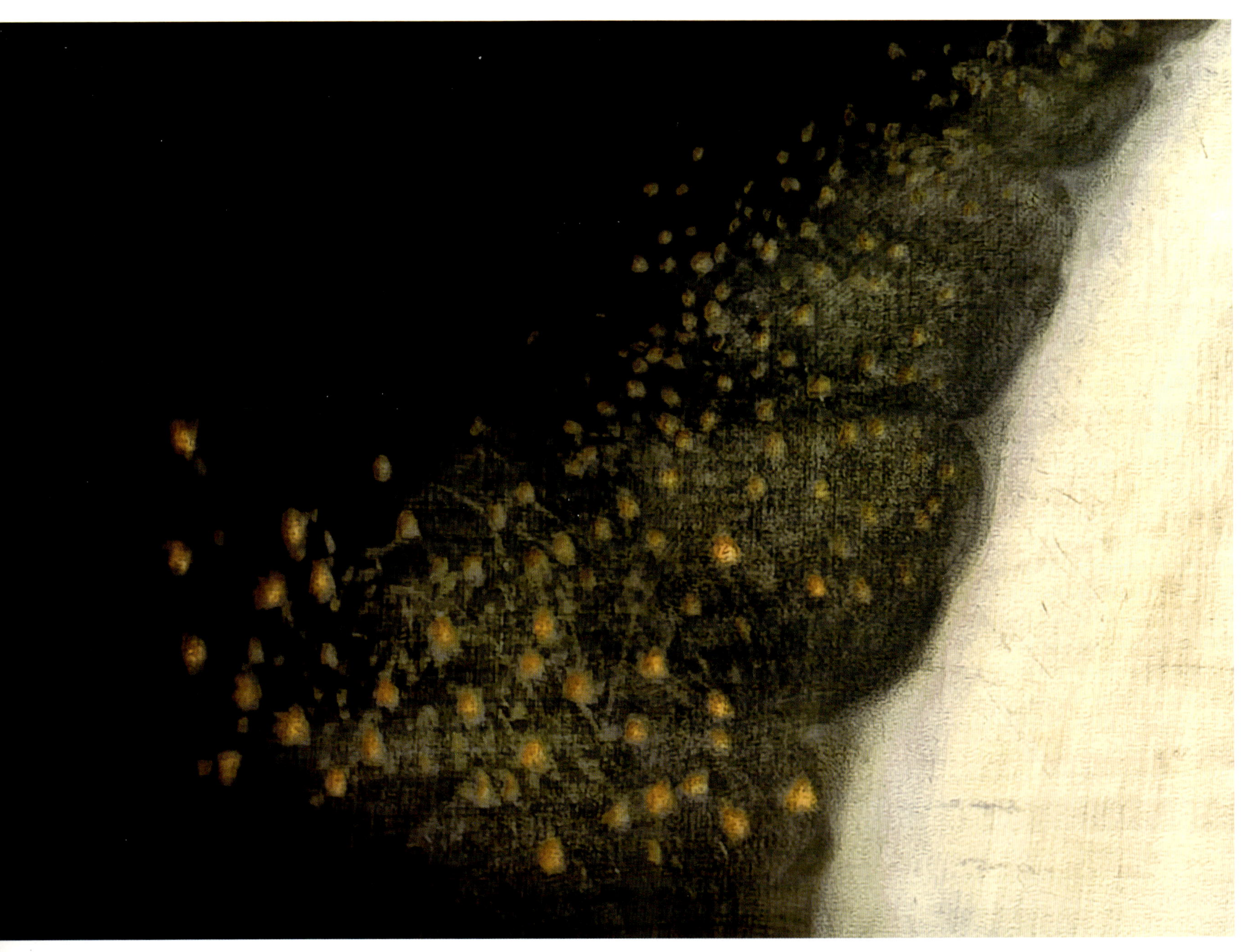

previous, above, and right:

Approach (details), 2010, oil and charcoal on canvas, 4' x 9'

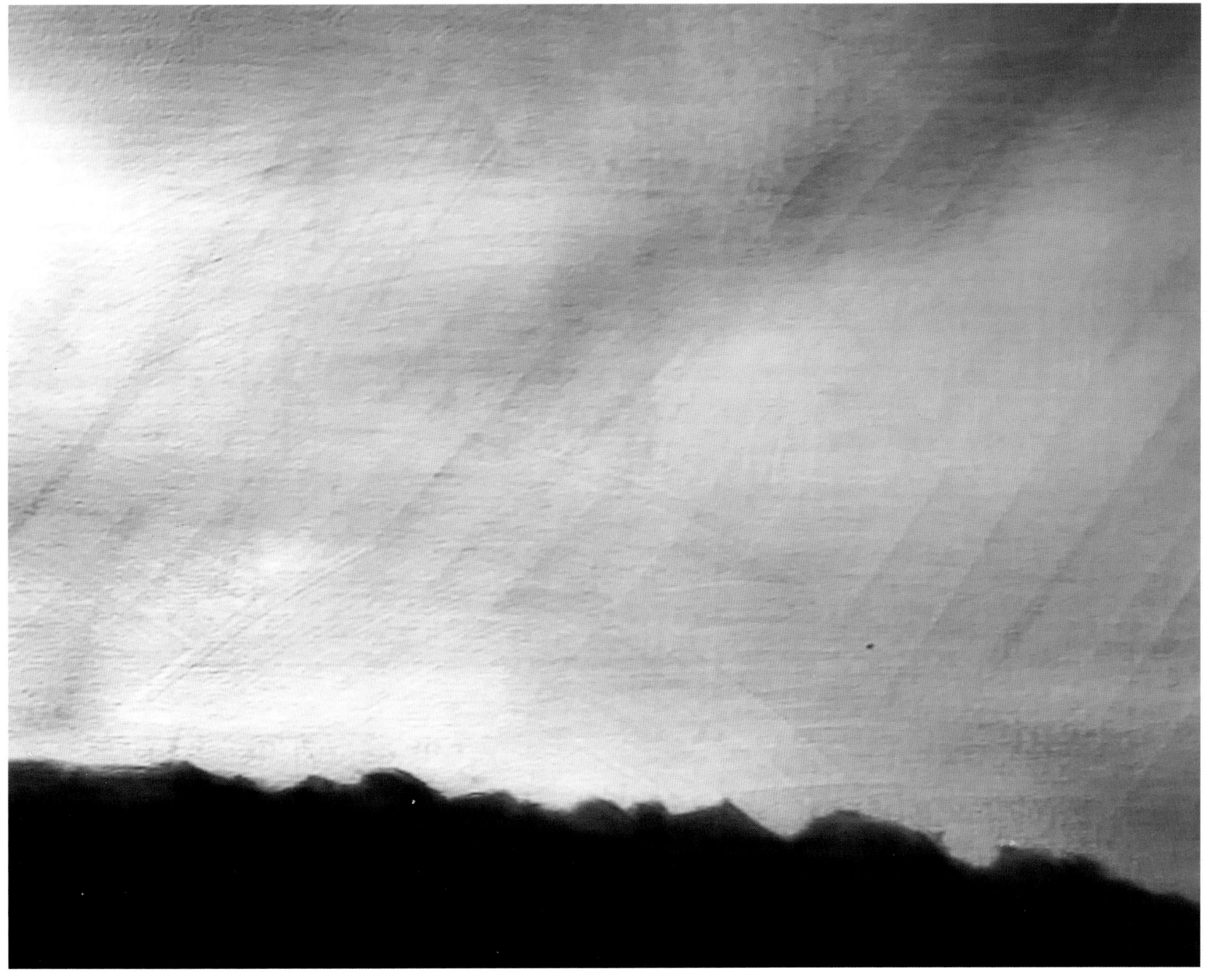

above: ***Title,*** 2010, oil and charcoal on canvas, 8'x 18'

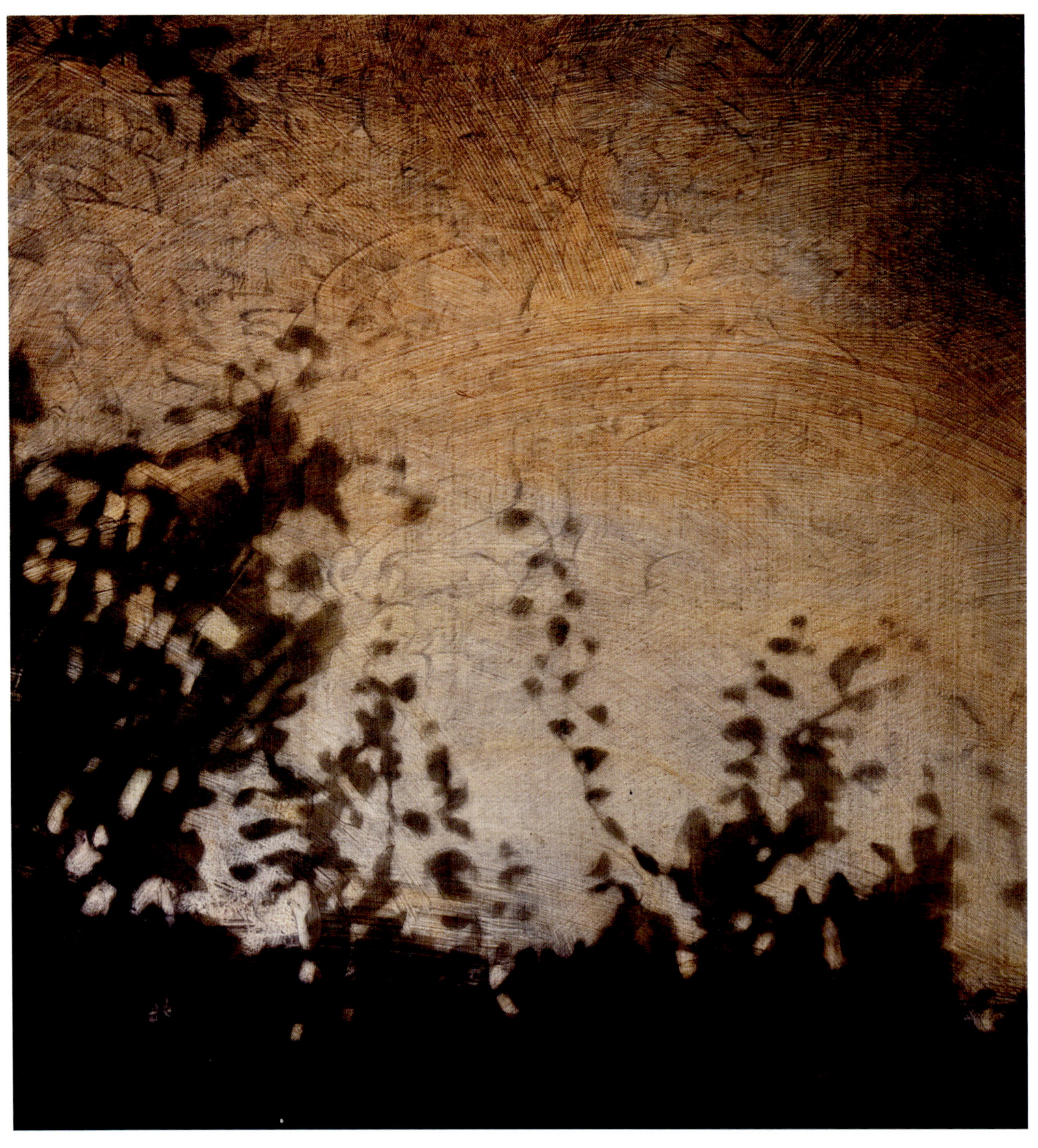

above, right and following spread:

Roads (details), 2010, oil and charcoal on canvas, 8' x 18'

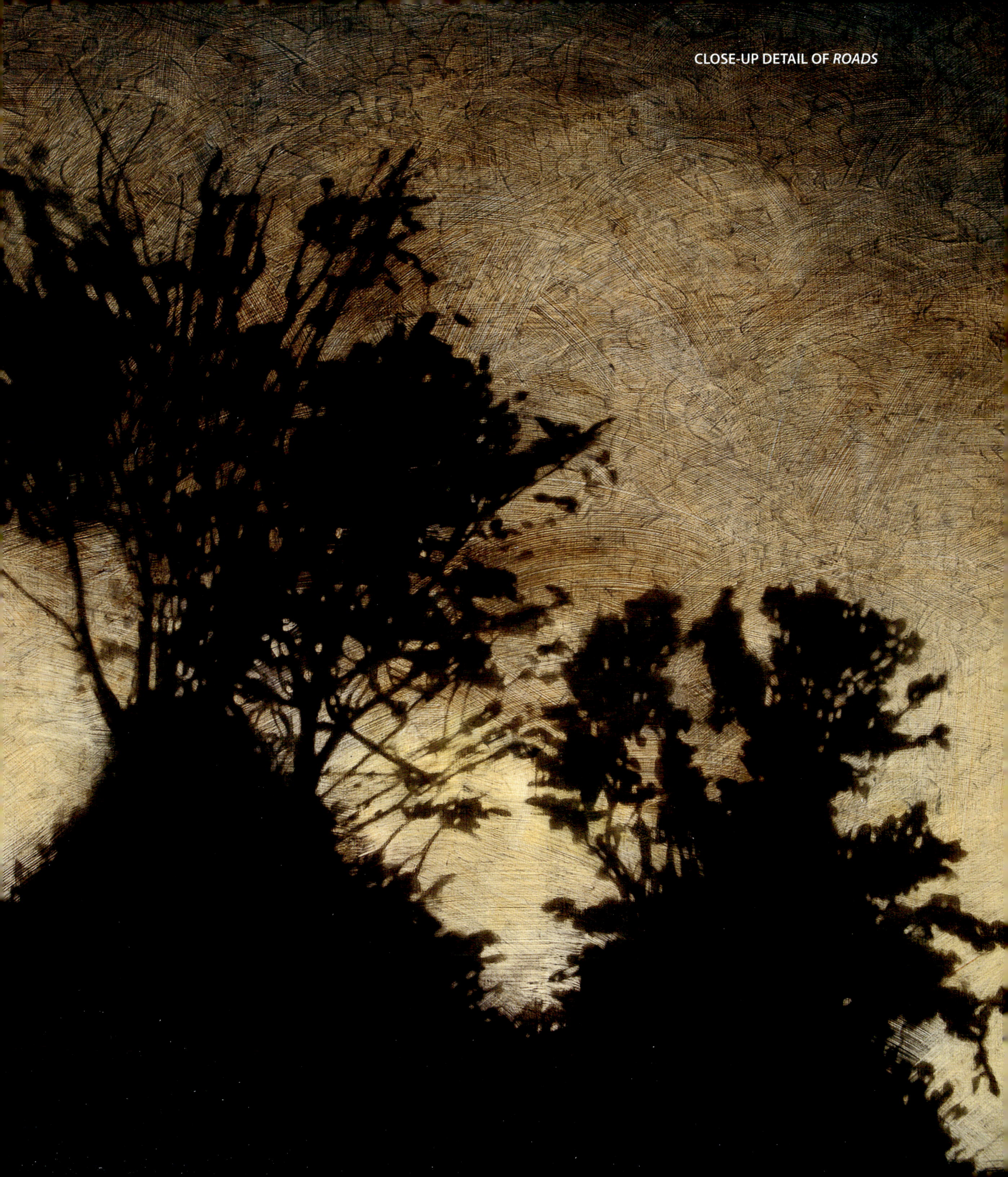
CLOSE-UP DETAIL OF ROADS

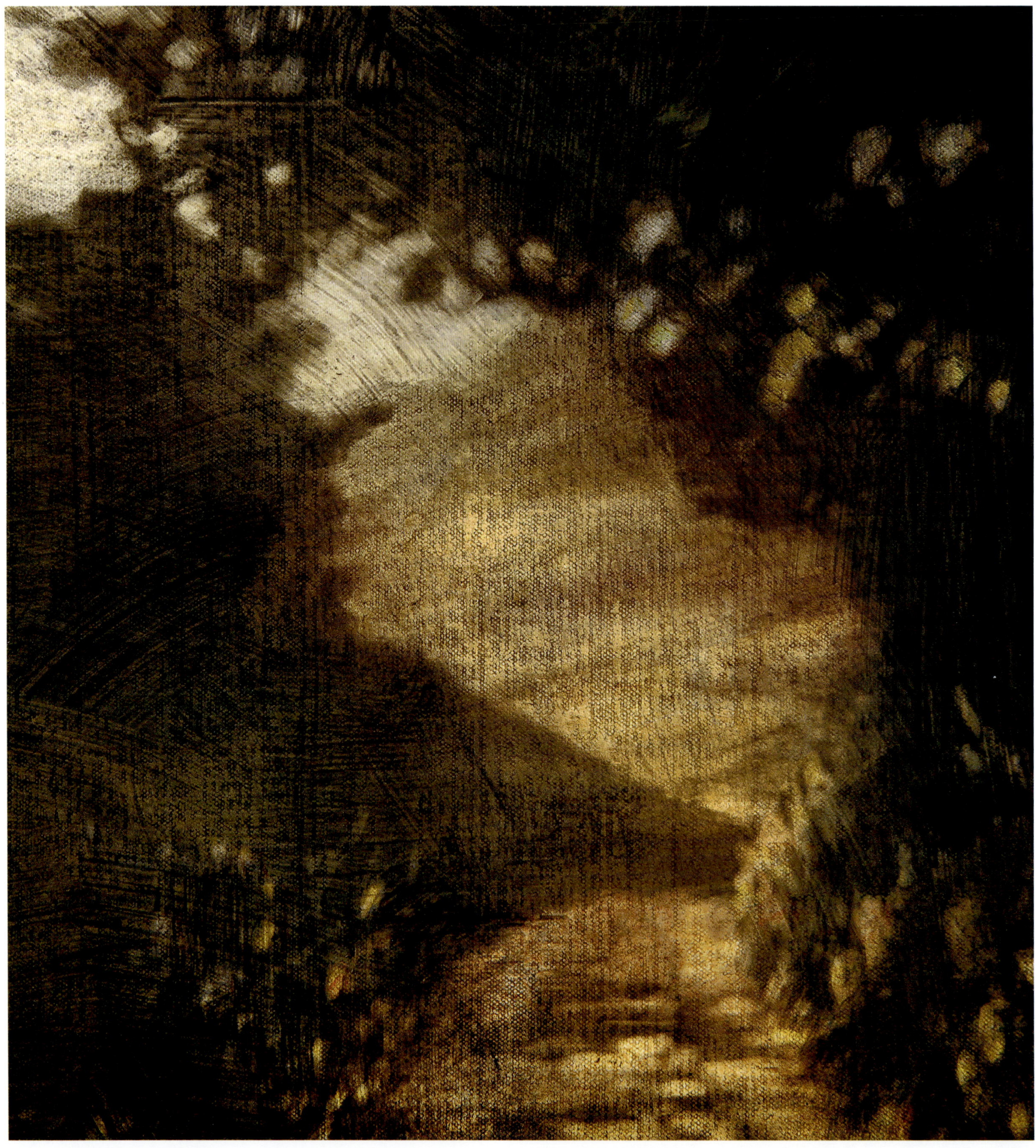

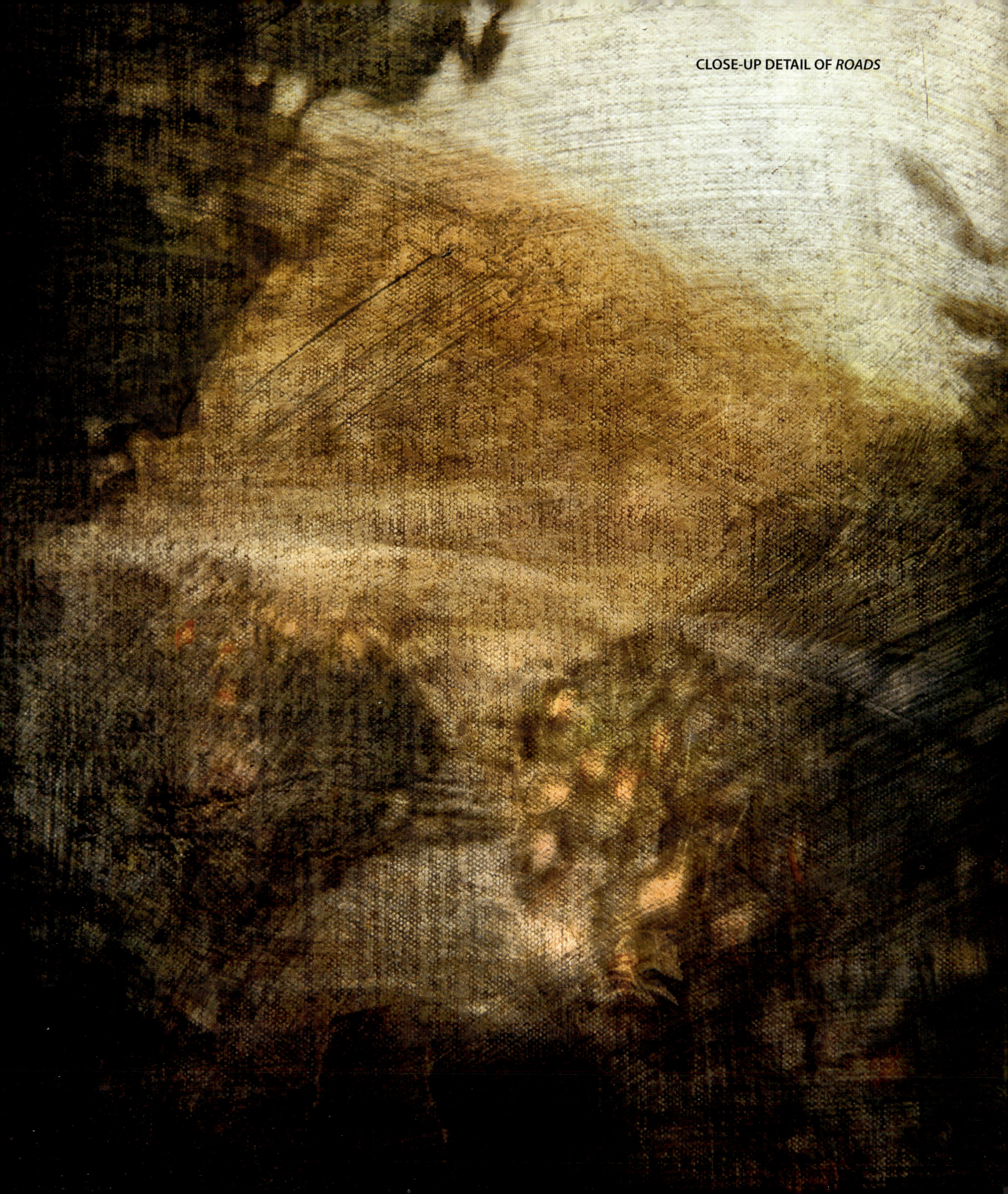
CLOSE-UP DETAIL OF ROADS

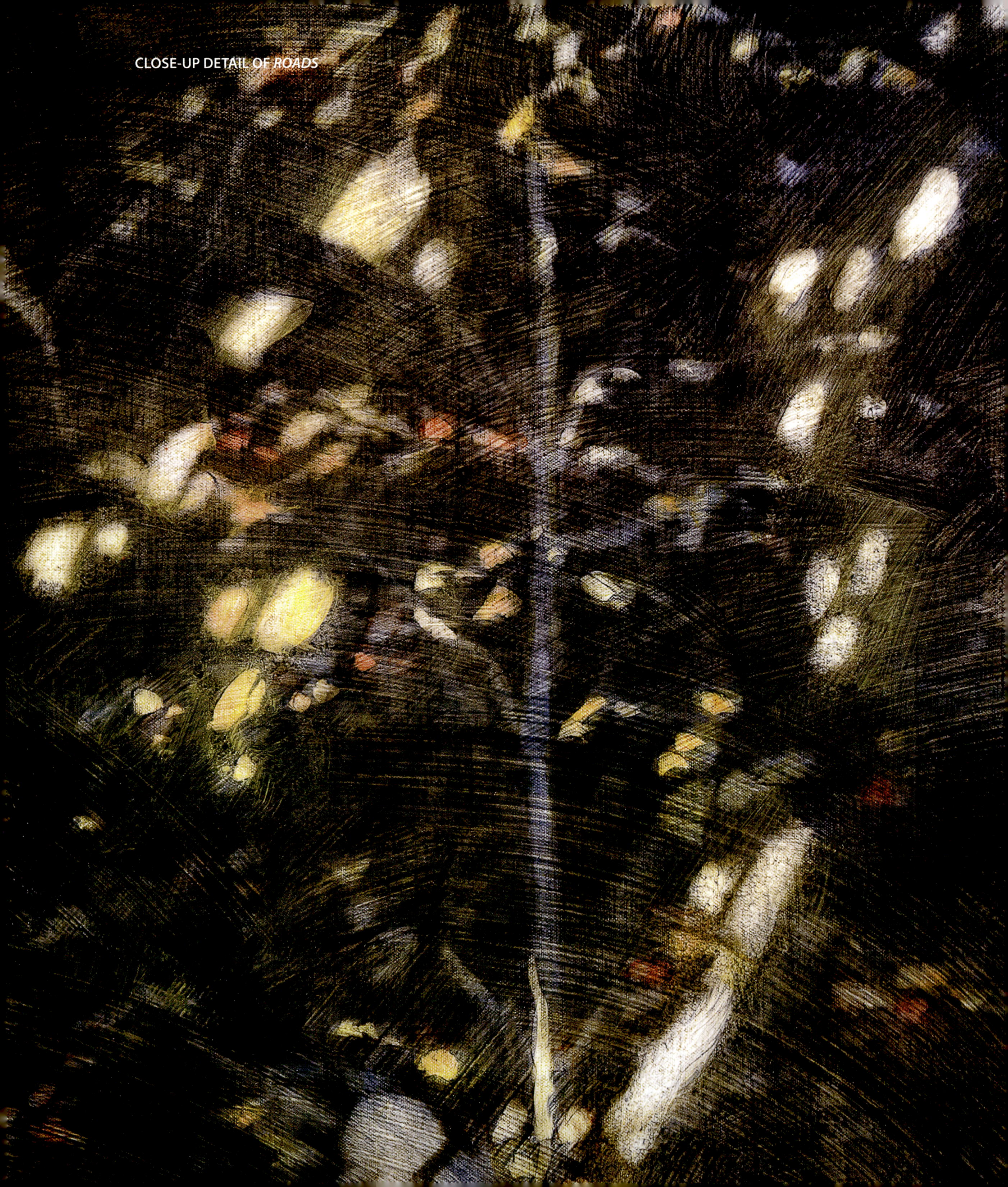

CLOSE-UP DETAIL OF ROADS

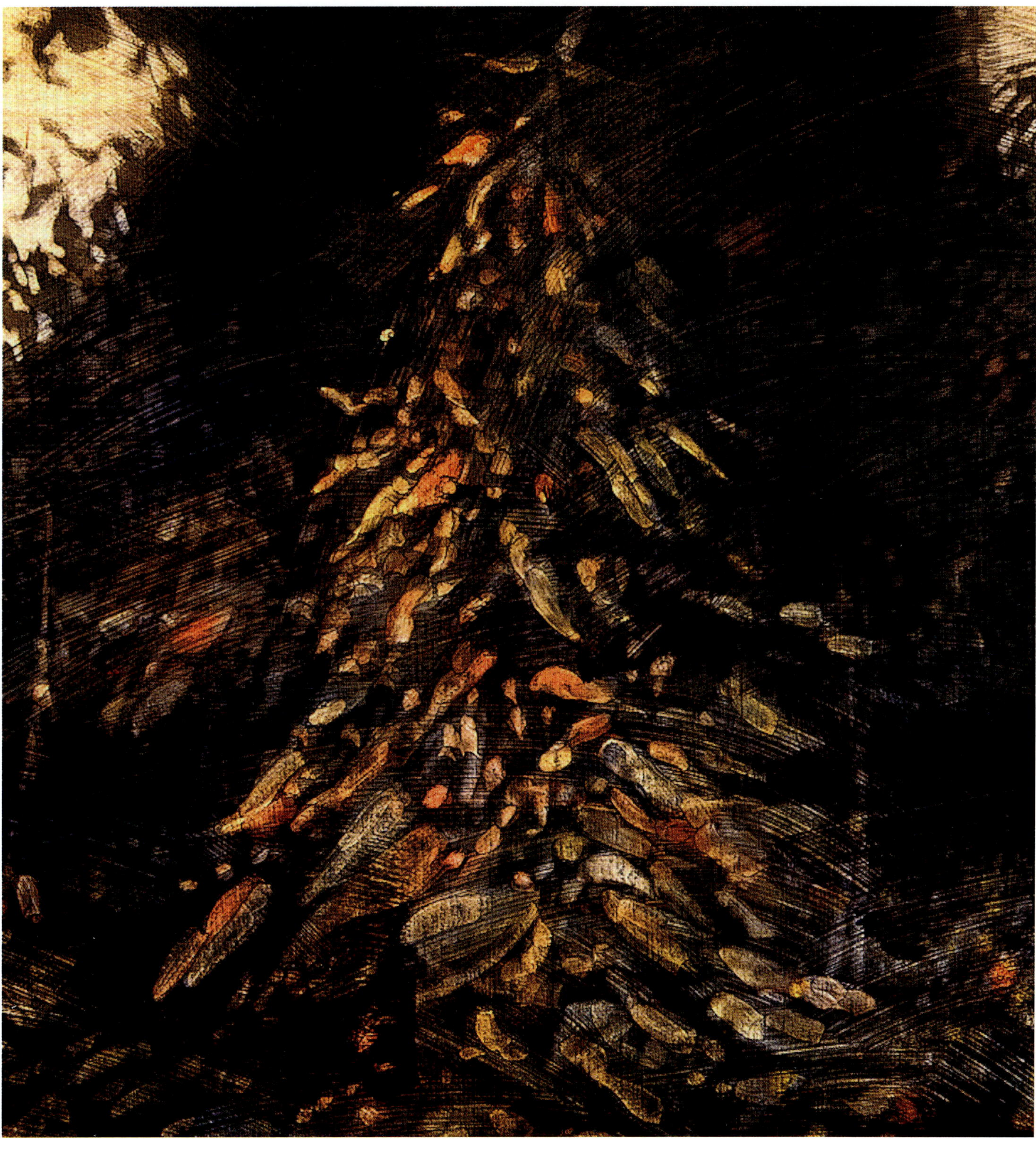

above and left: ***Roads*** (details), 2010, oil and charcoal on canvas, 8' x 18'

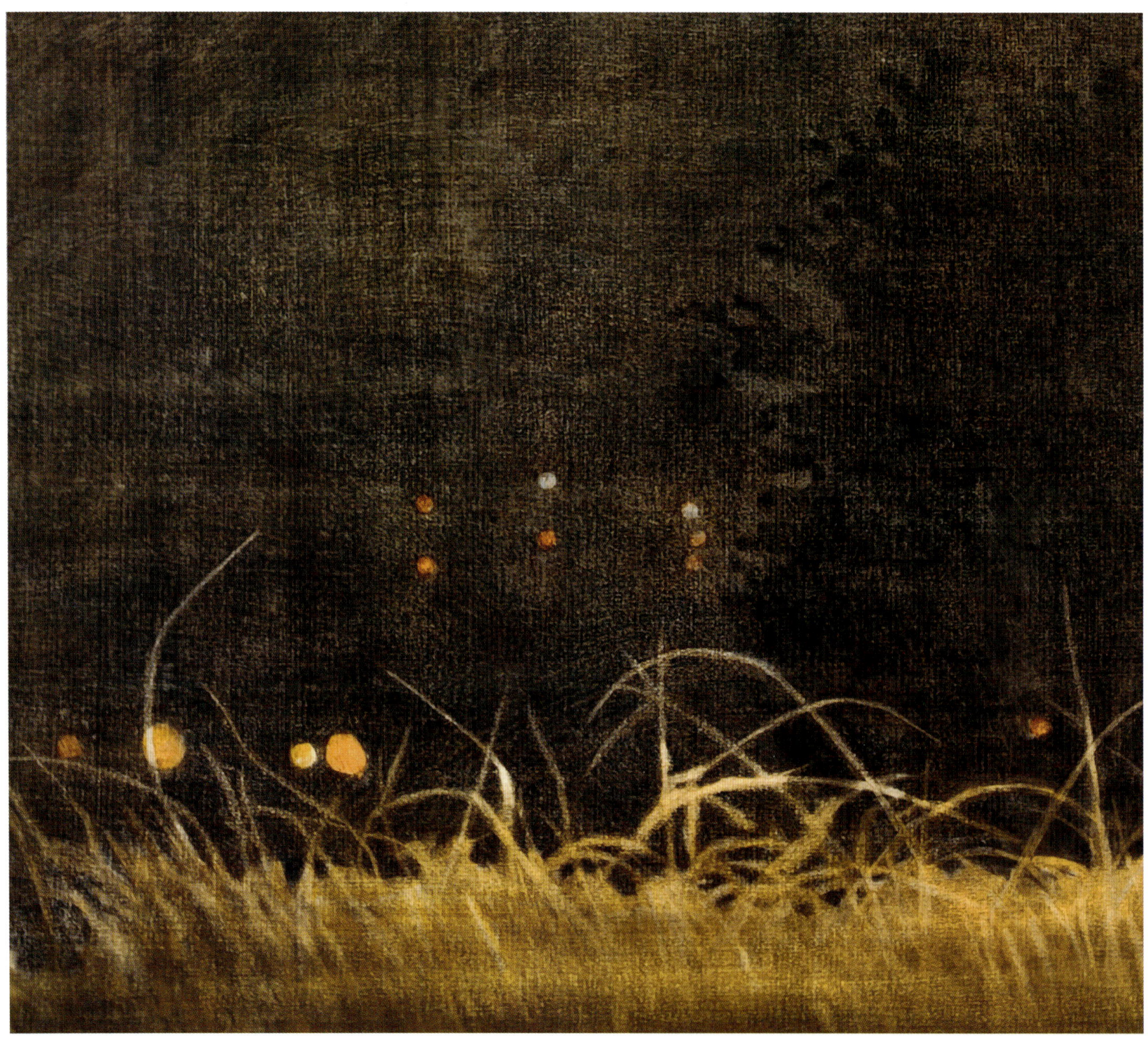

above and right: ***Abyss*** (details), 2010, oil and charcoal on canvas, 4' x 9'

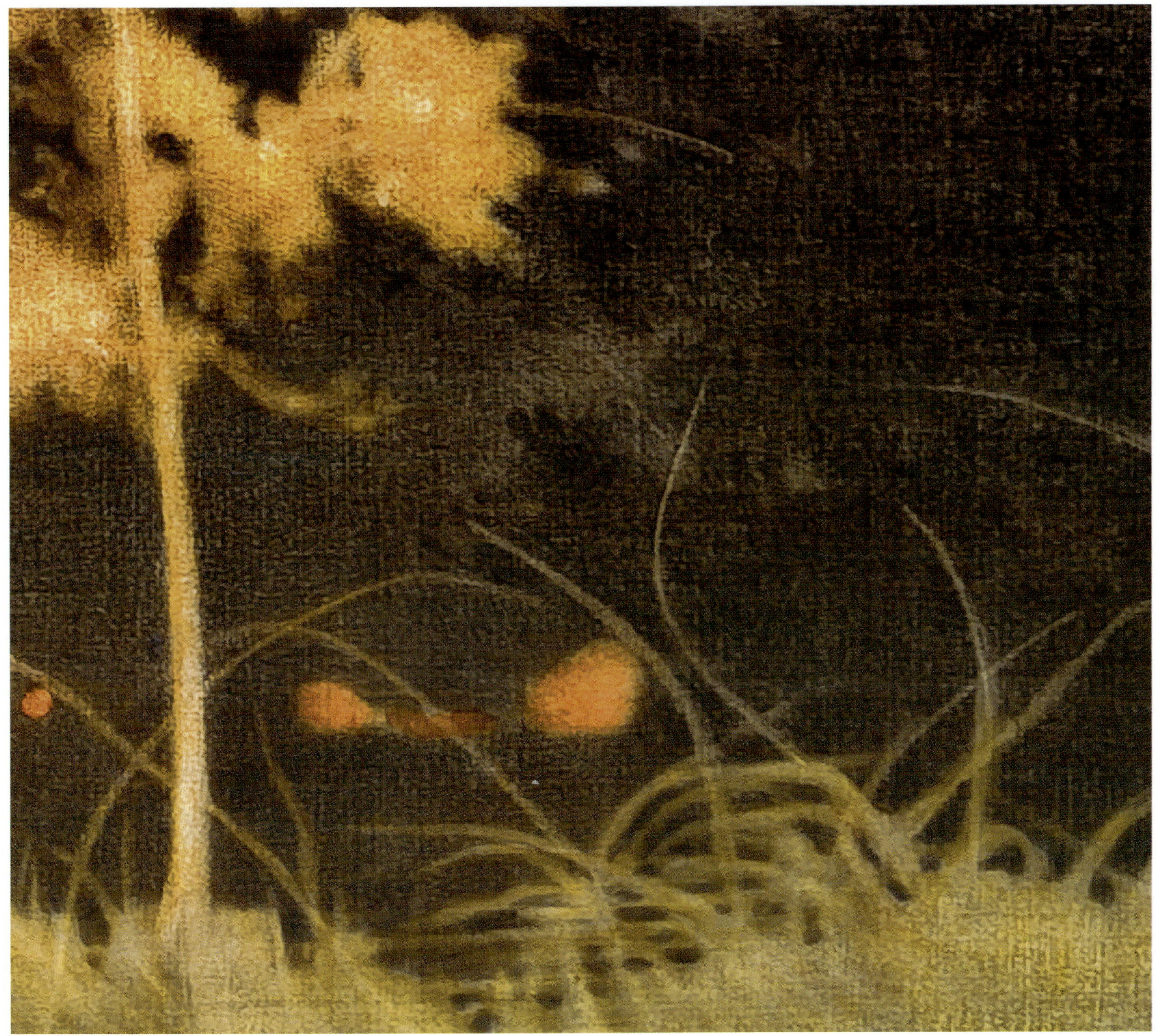

above: ***Title,*** 2010, oil and charcoal on canvas, 8'x 18'

CLOSE-UP DETAIL OF BRANCH

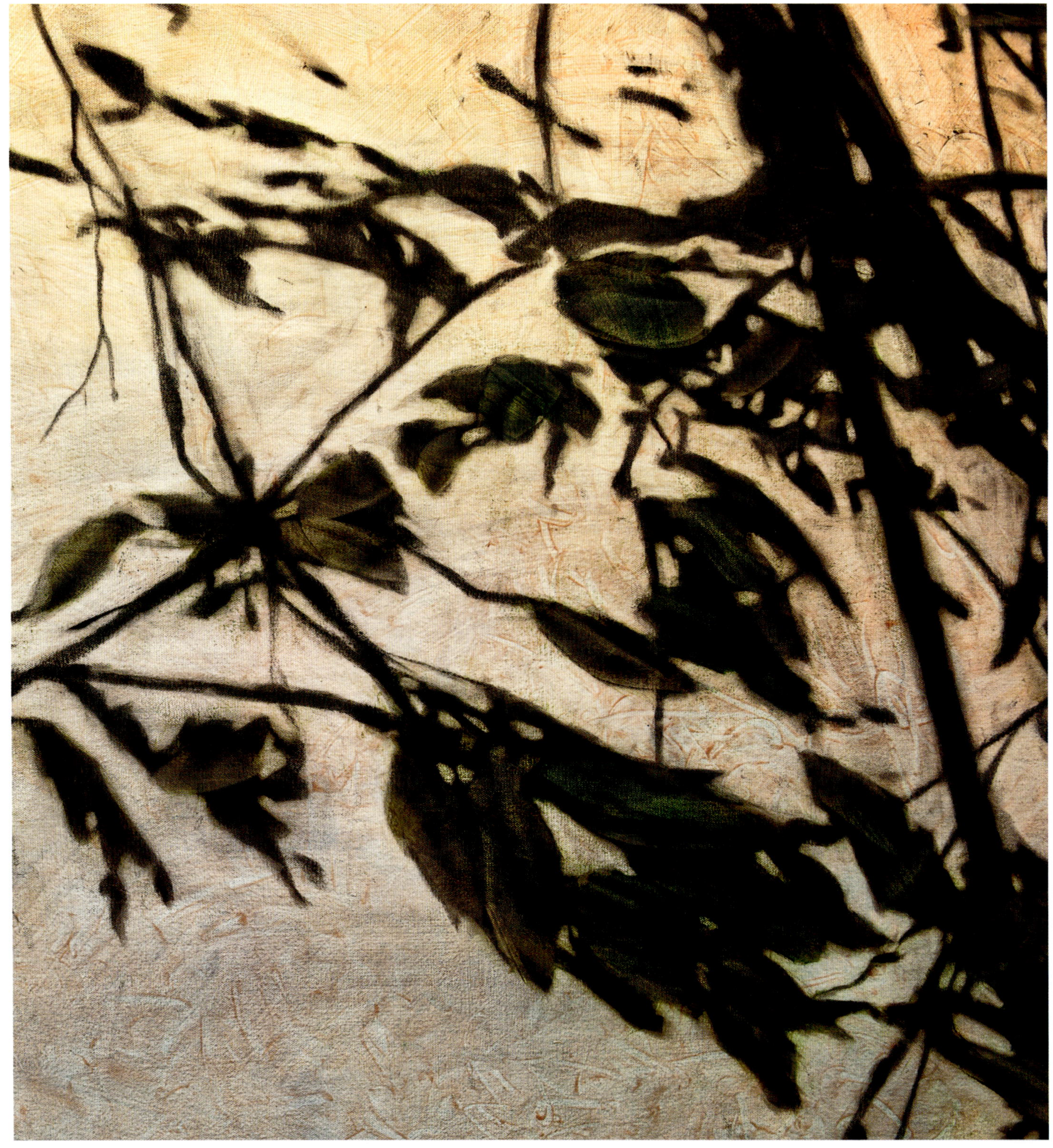

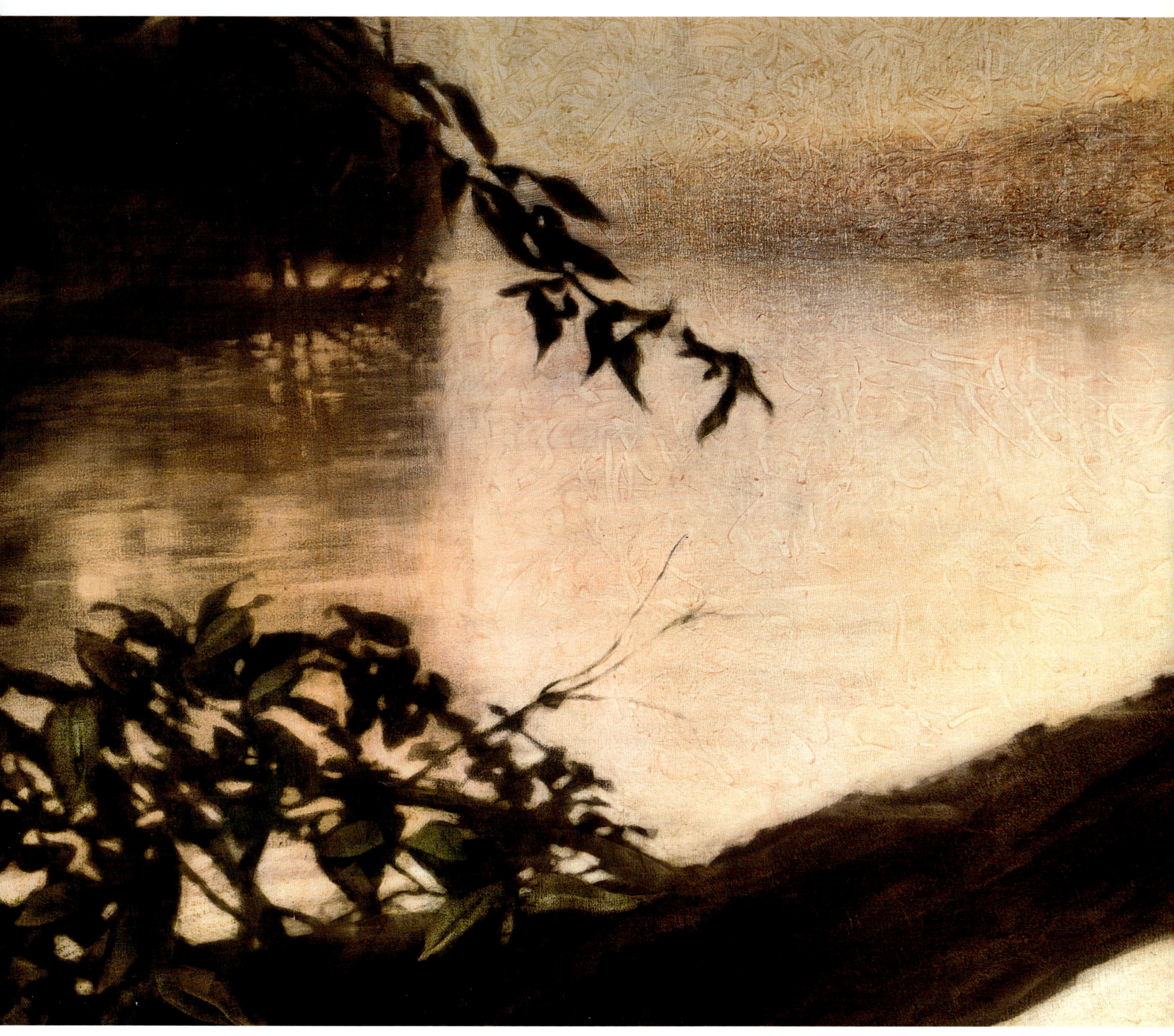

previous, above, left, and following spread:

Branch (details), 2010, oil and charcoal on canvas, 8' x 18'

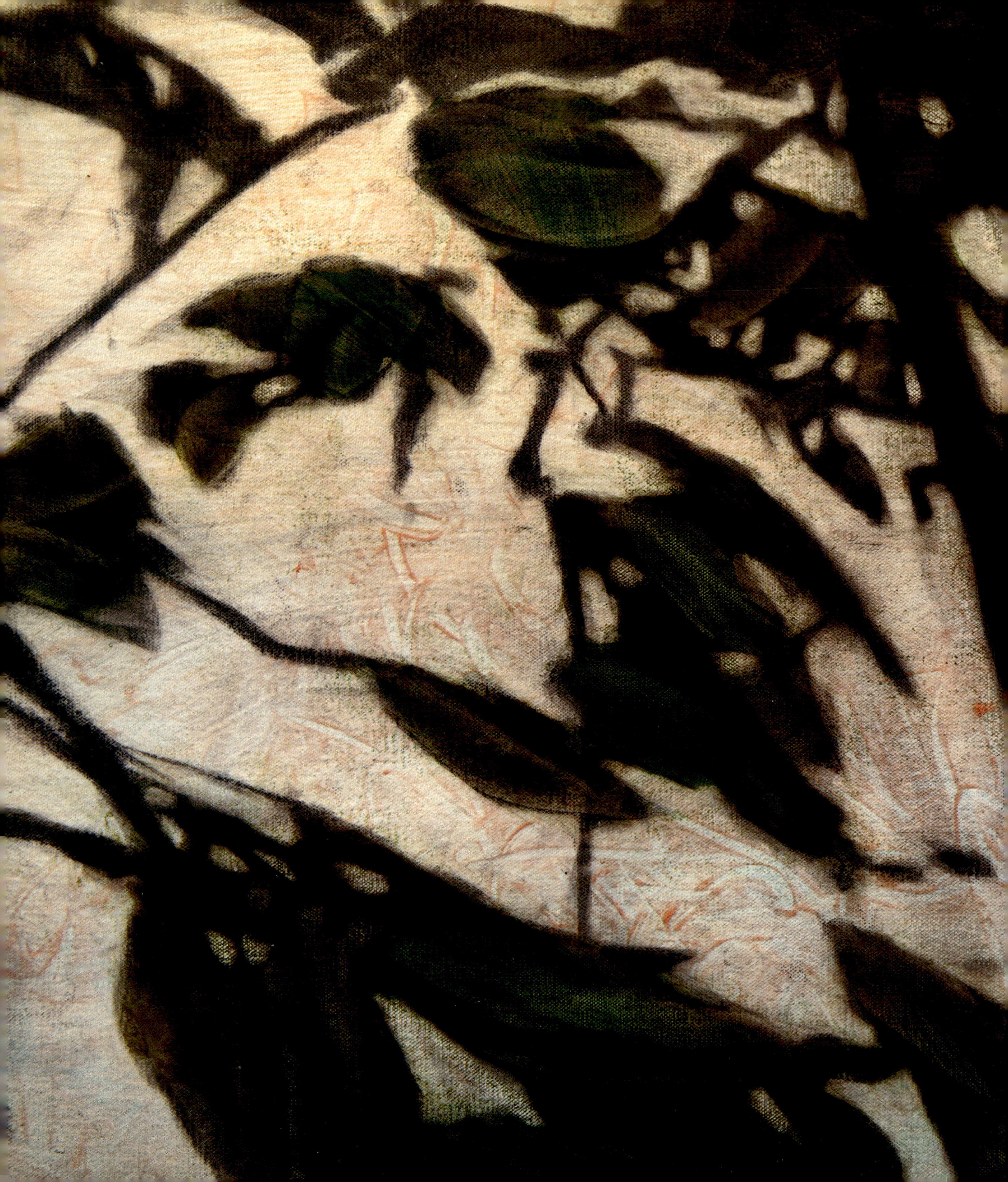

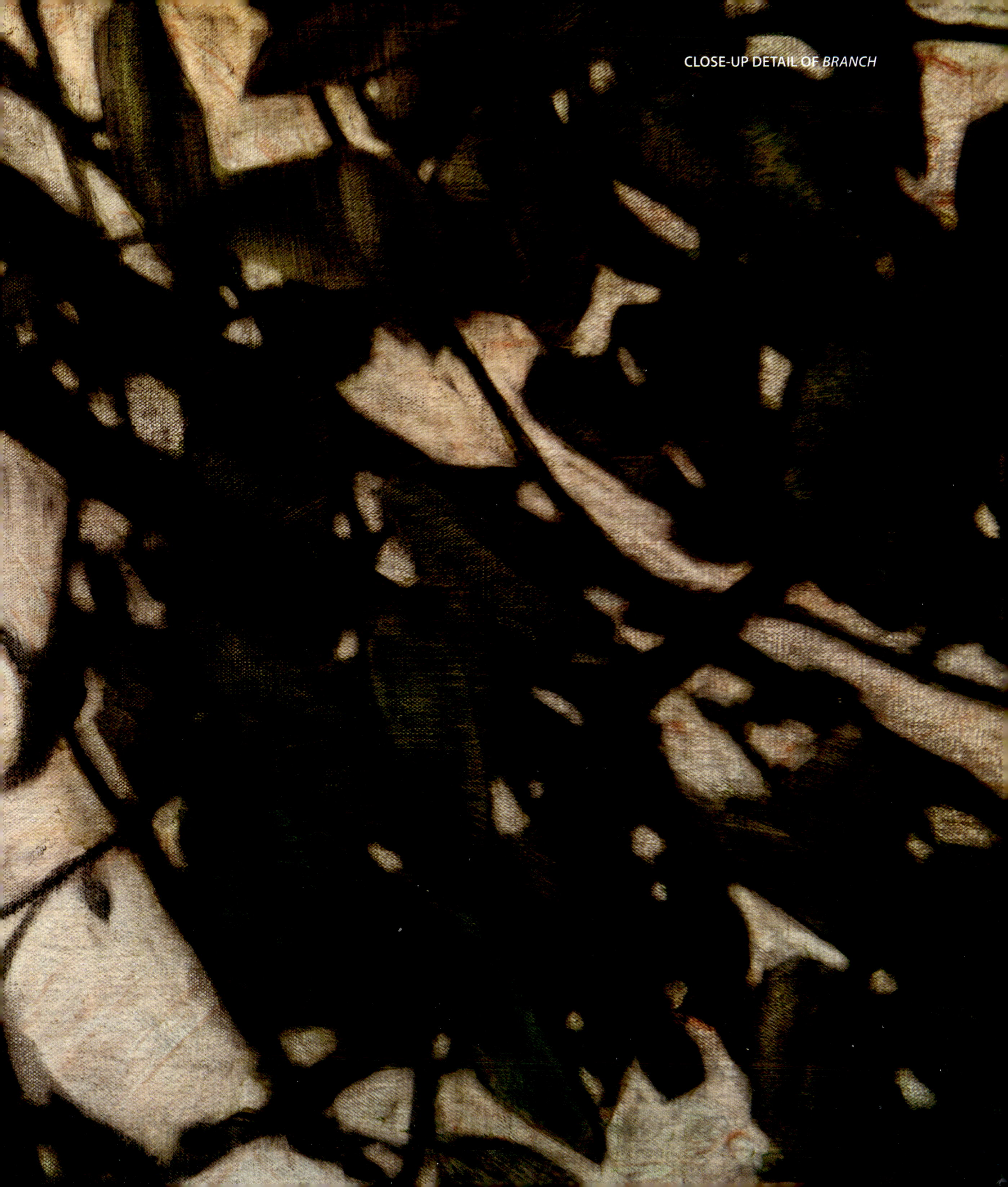
CLOSE-UP DETAIL OF BRANCH

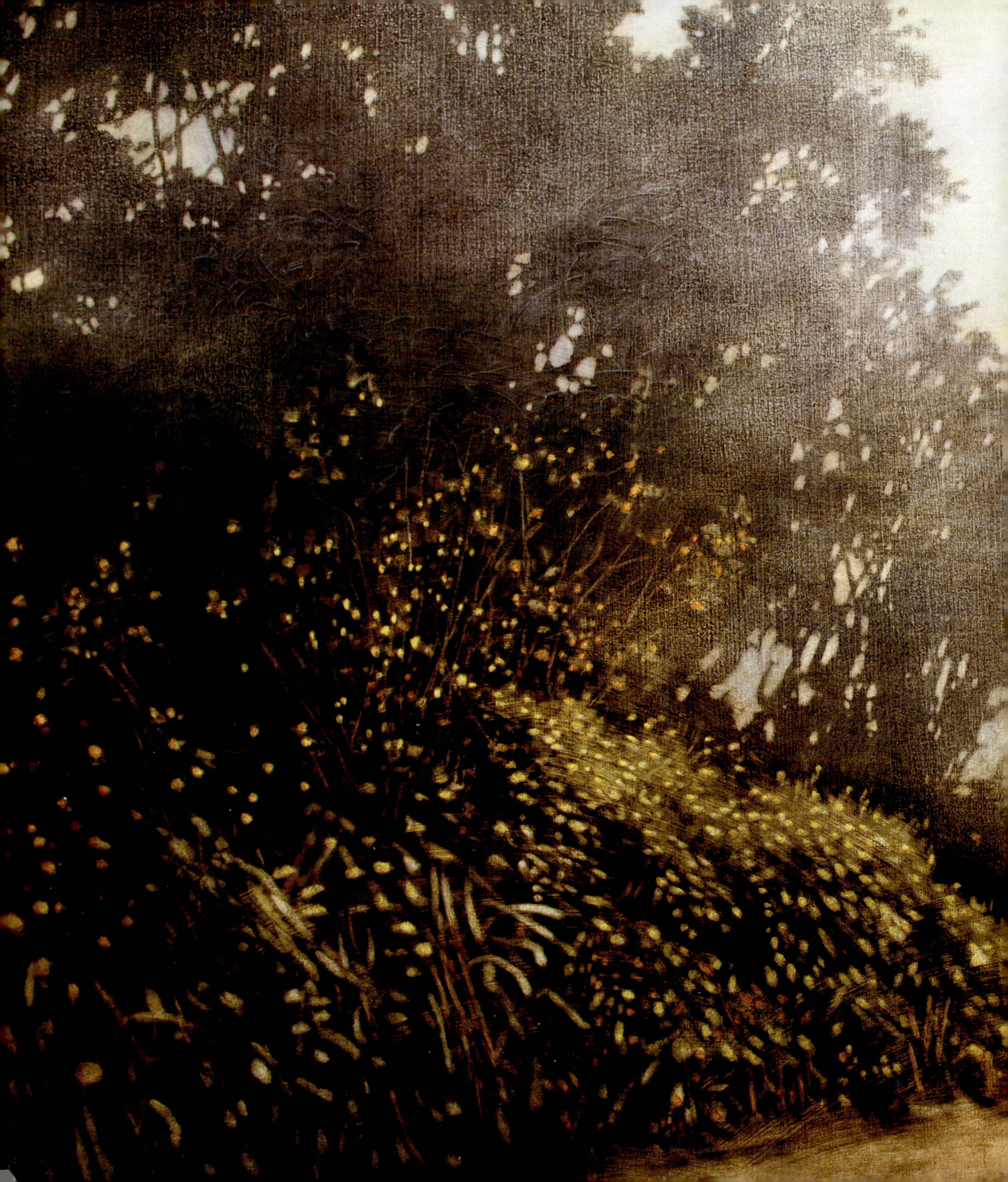

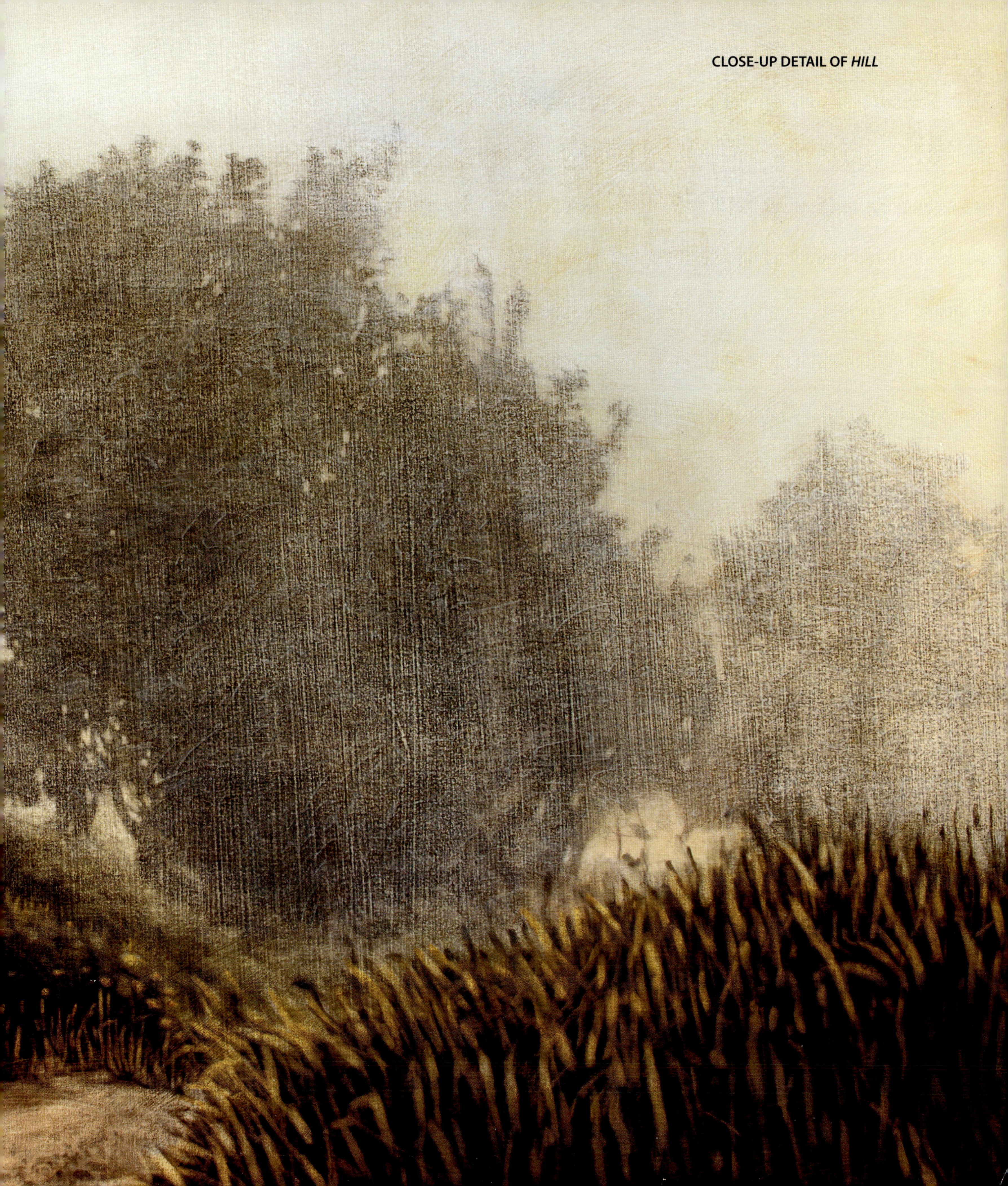

CLOSE-UP DETAIL OF HILL

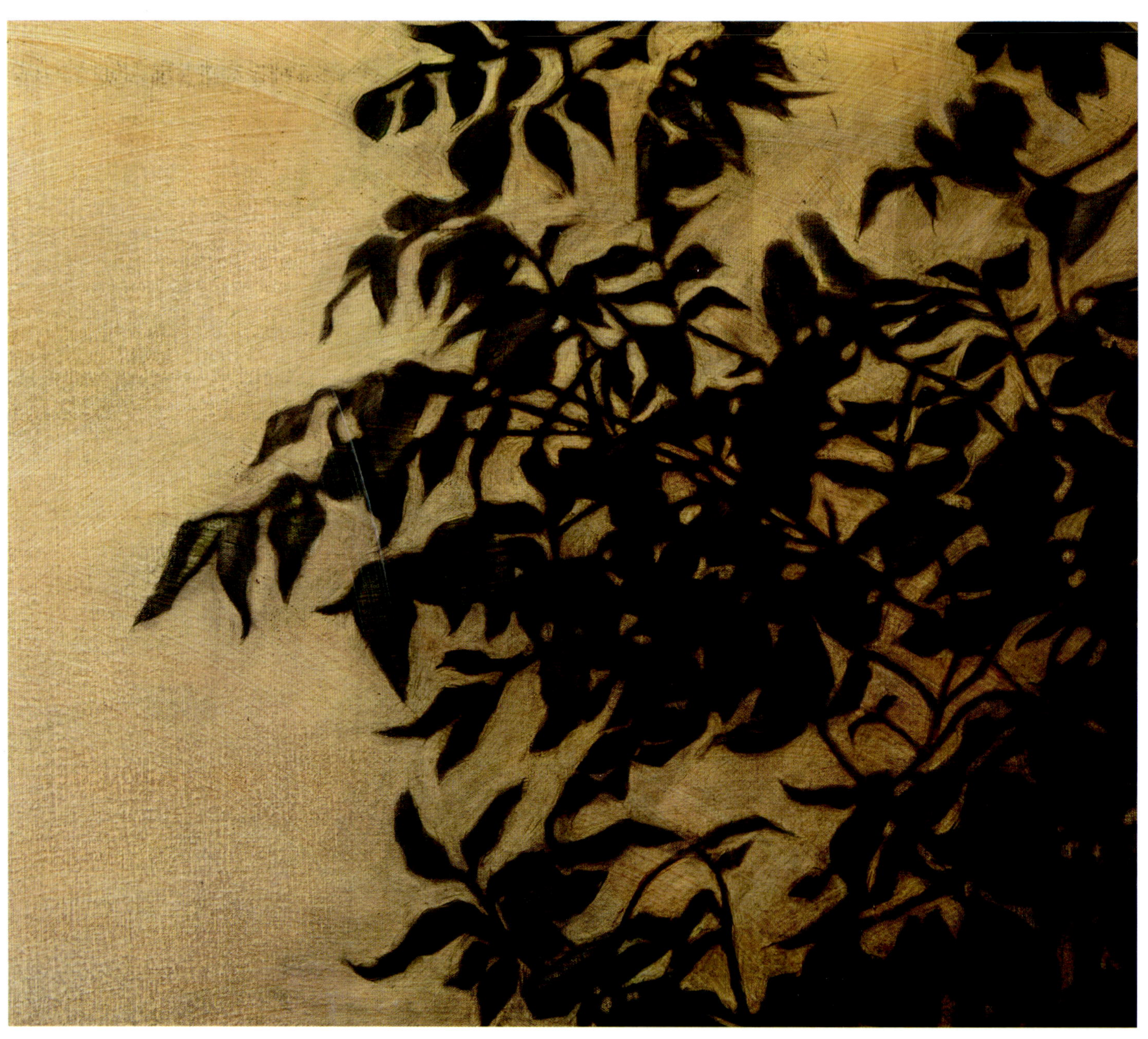

previous, above, right and following spread:
Hill (details), 2010, oil and charcoal on canvas, 8' x 18'

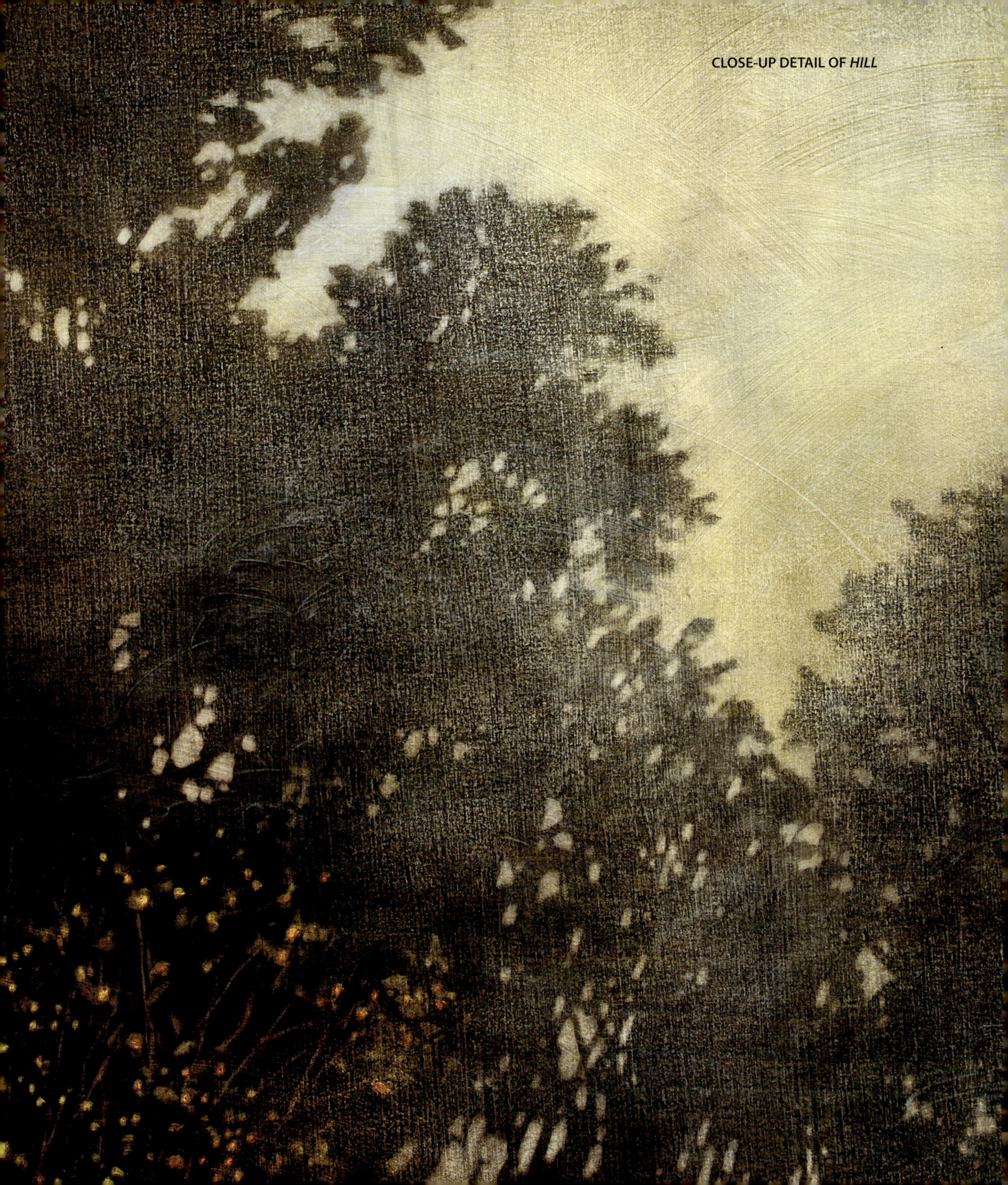
CLOSE-UP DETAIL OF HILL

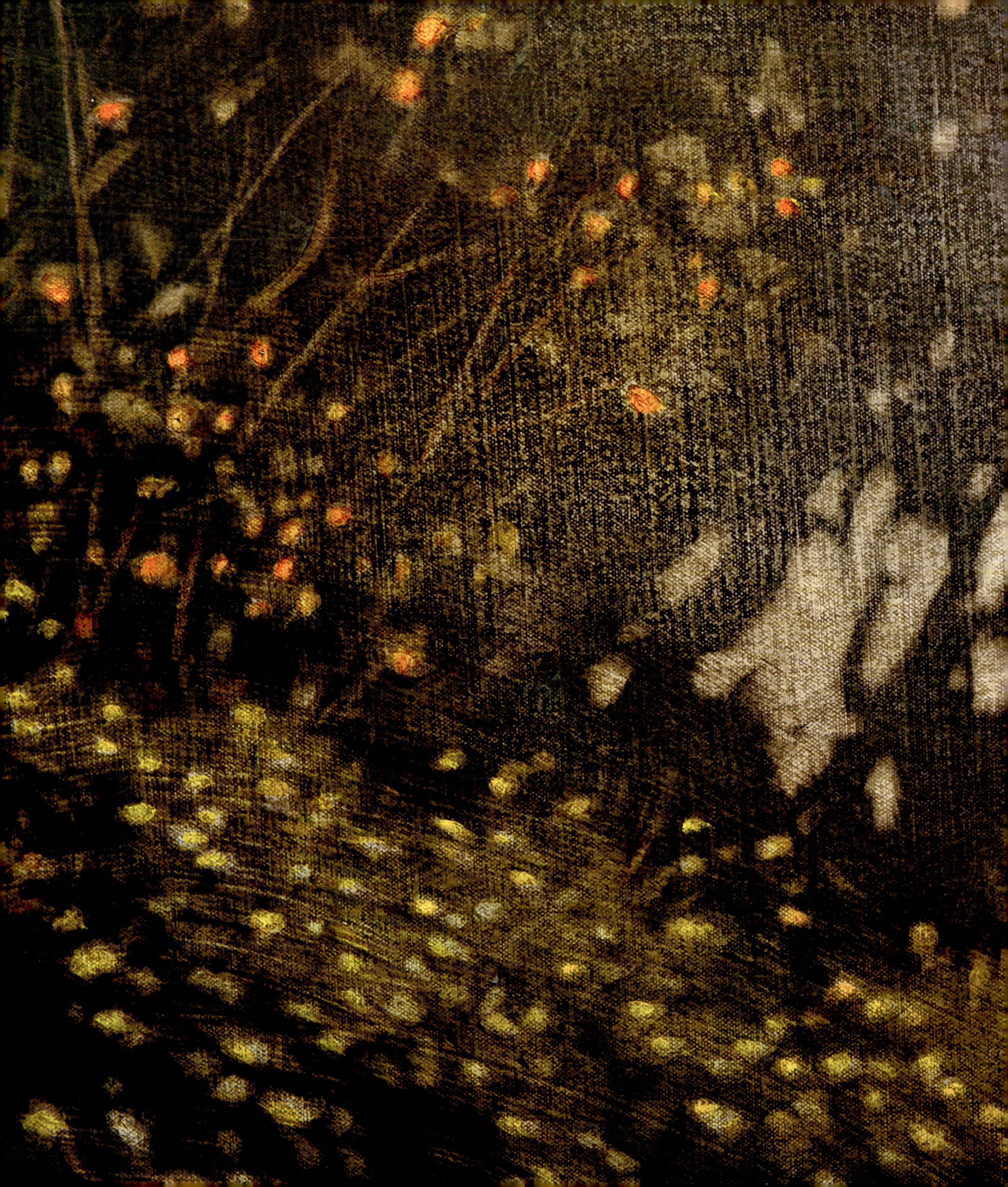

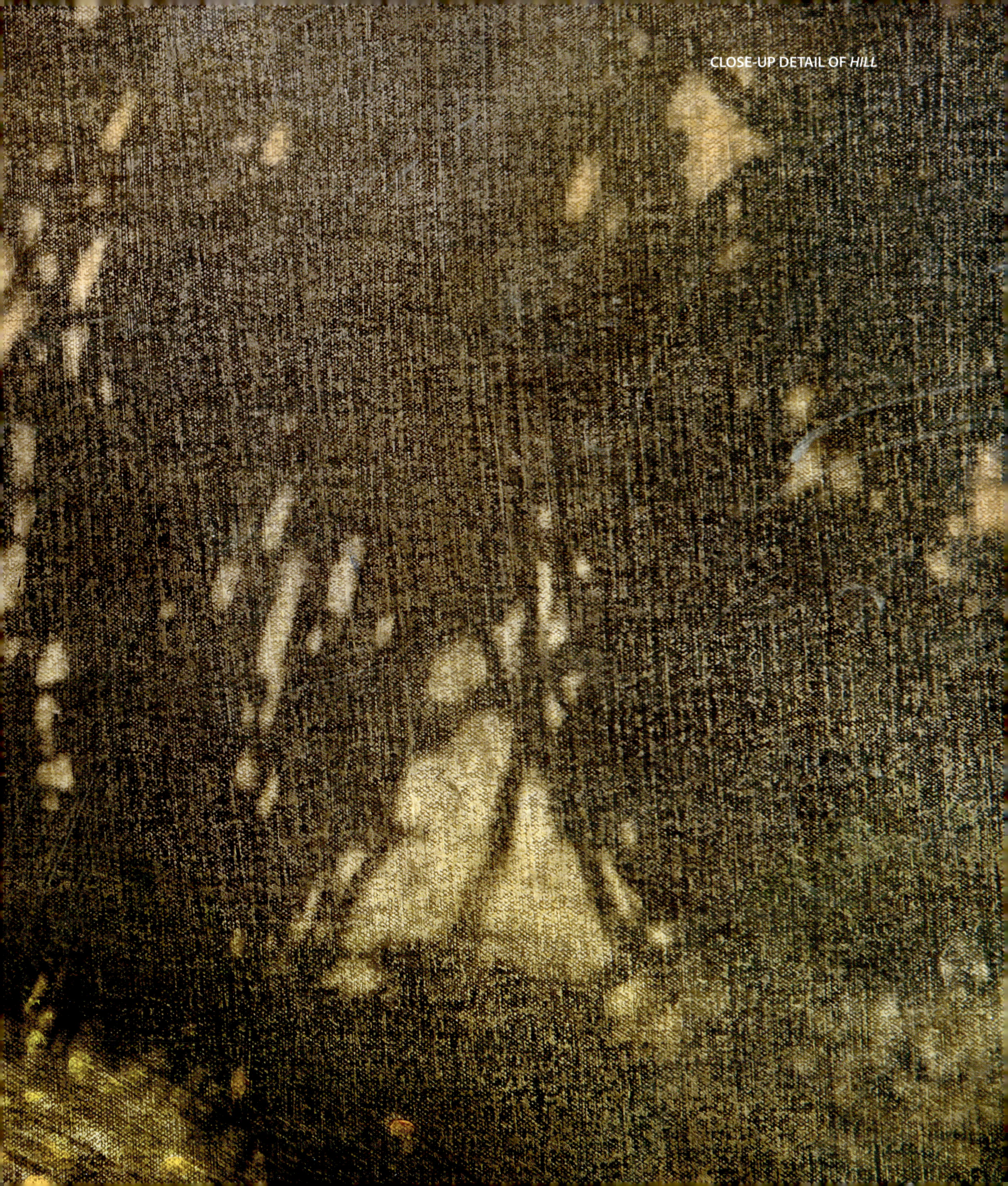
CLOSE-UP DETAIL OF HILL

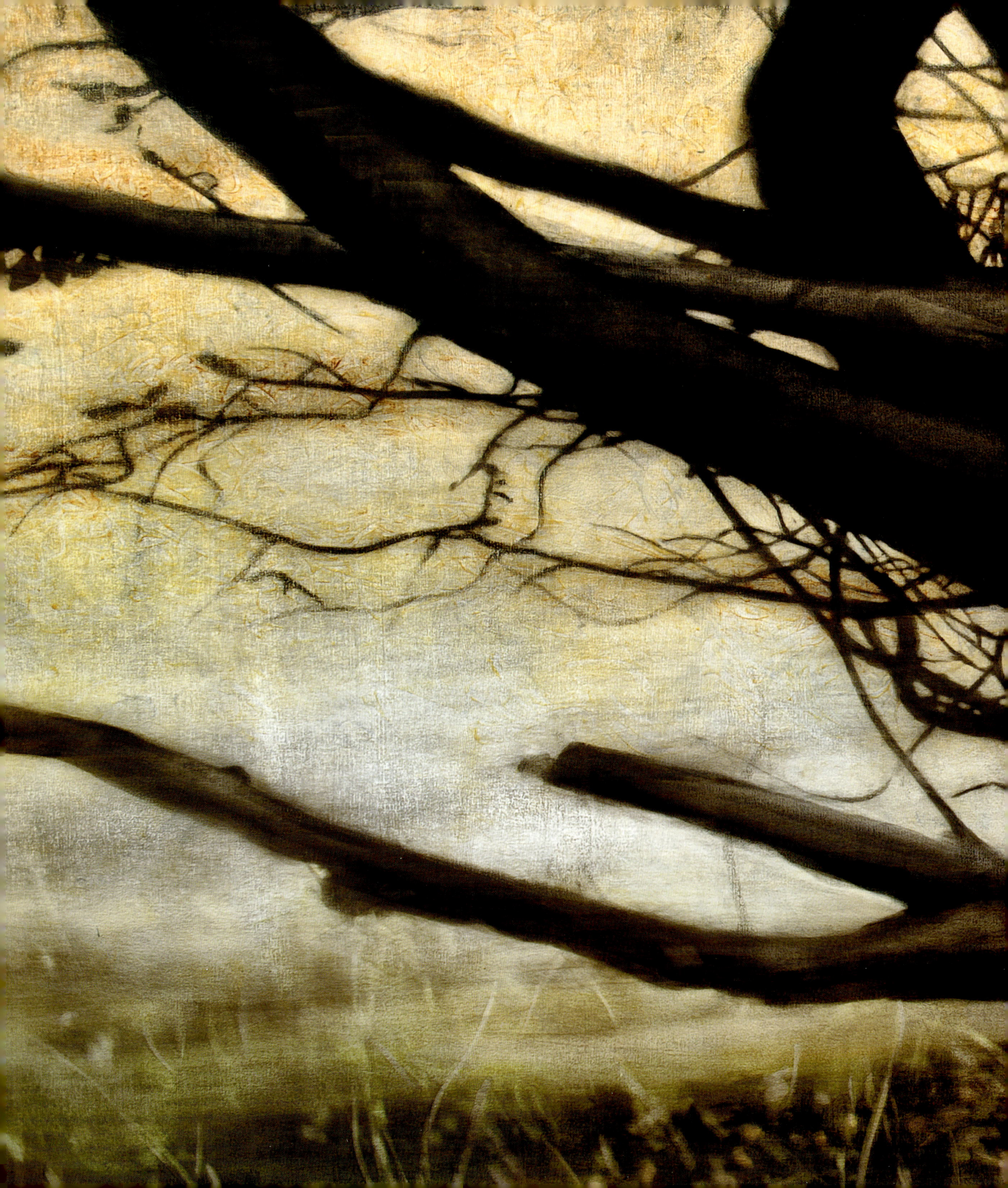

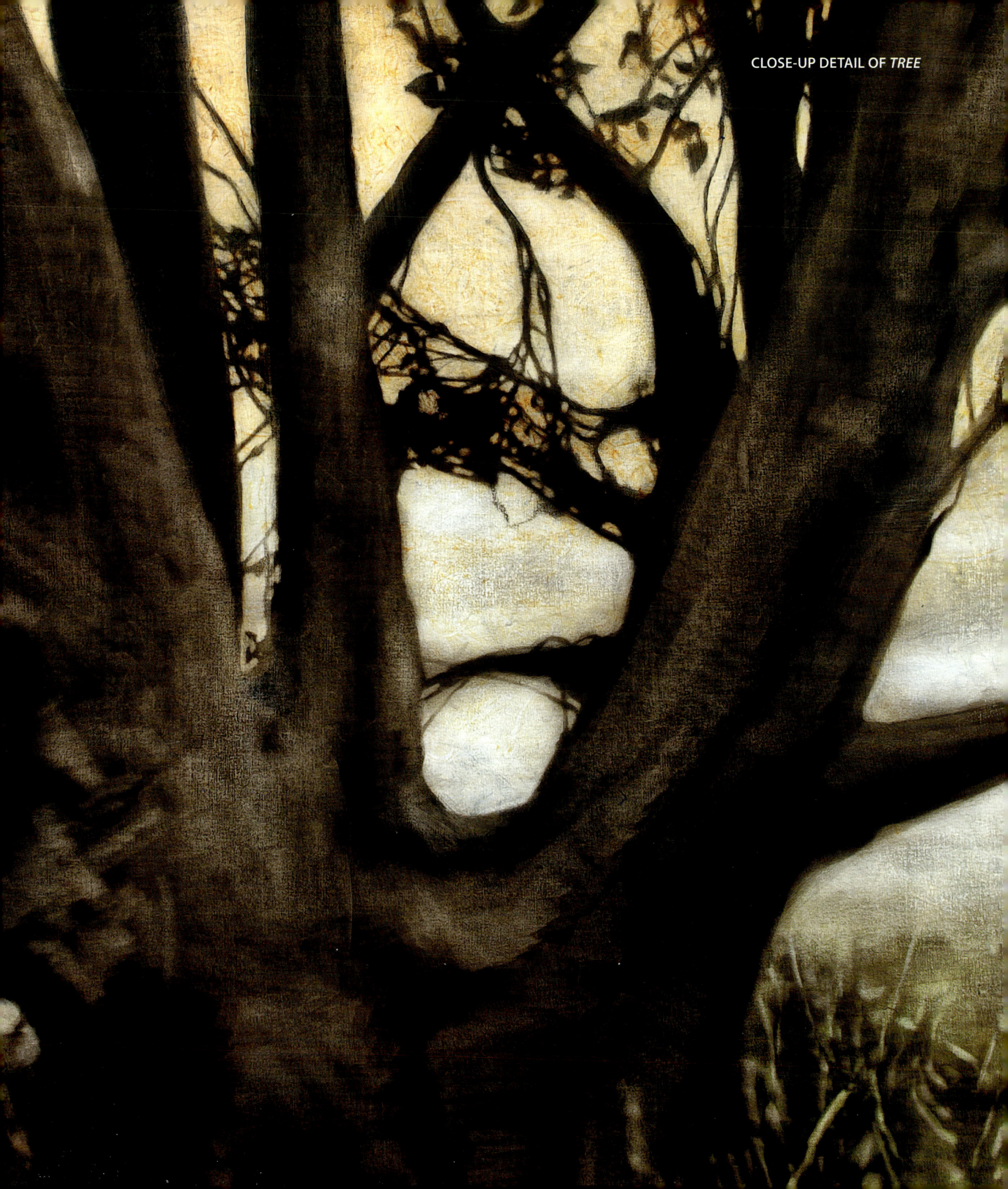
CLOSE-UP DETAIL OF TREE

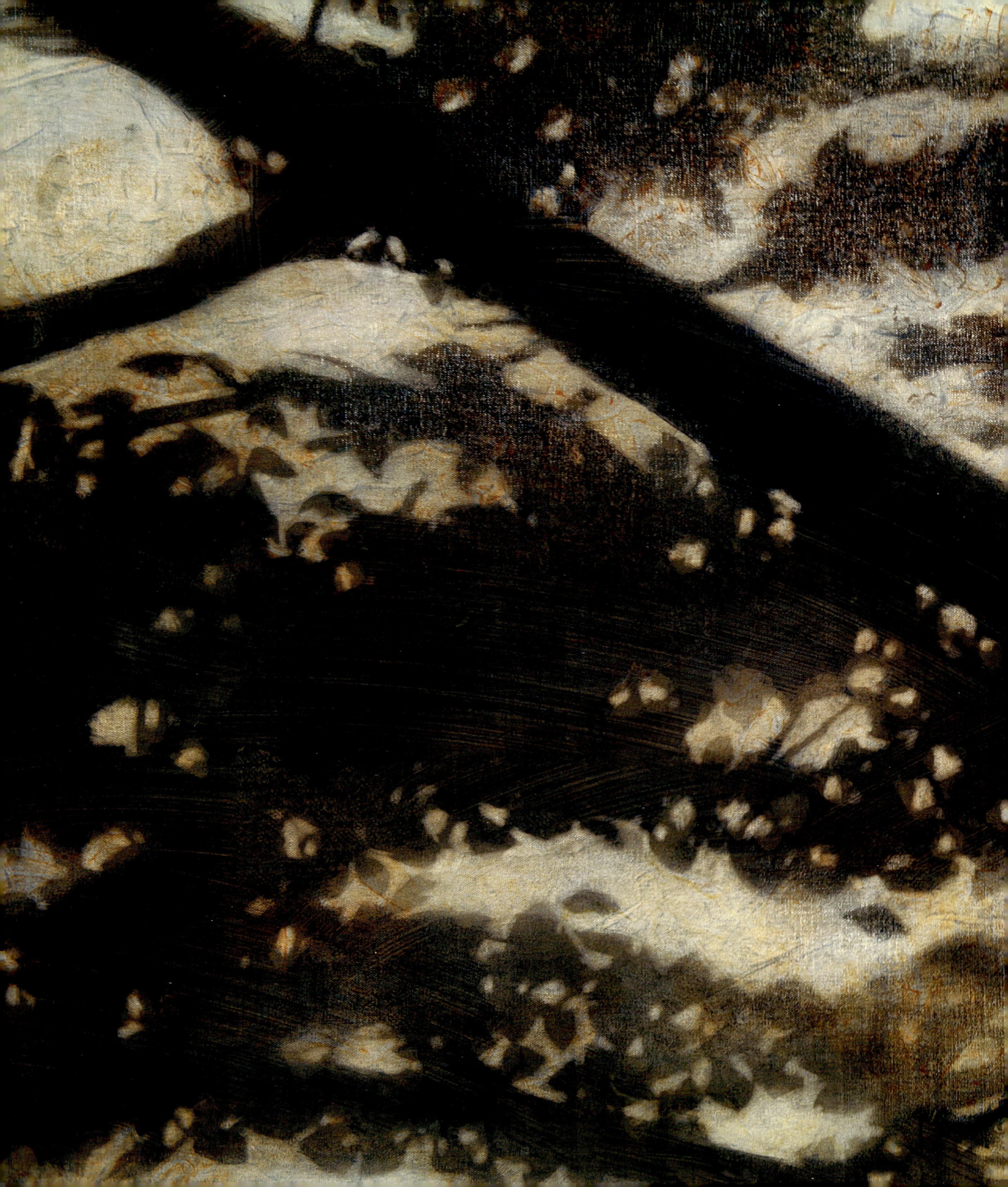

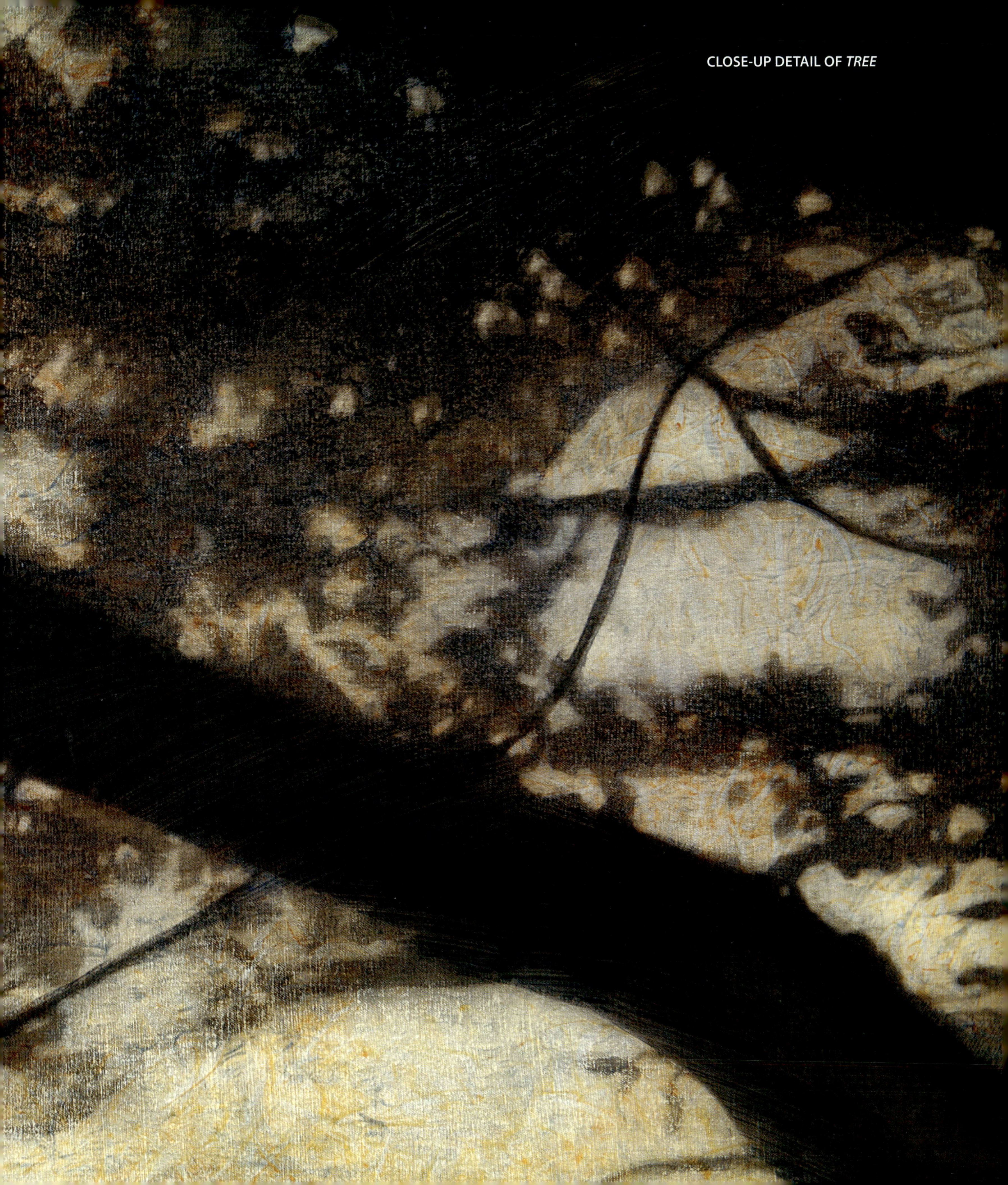
CLOSE-UP DETAIL OF TREE

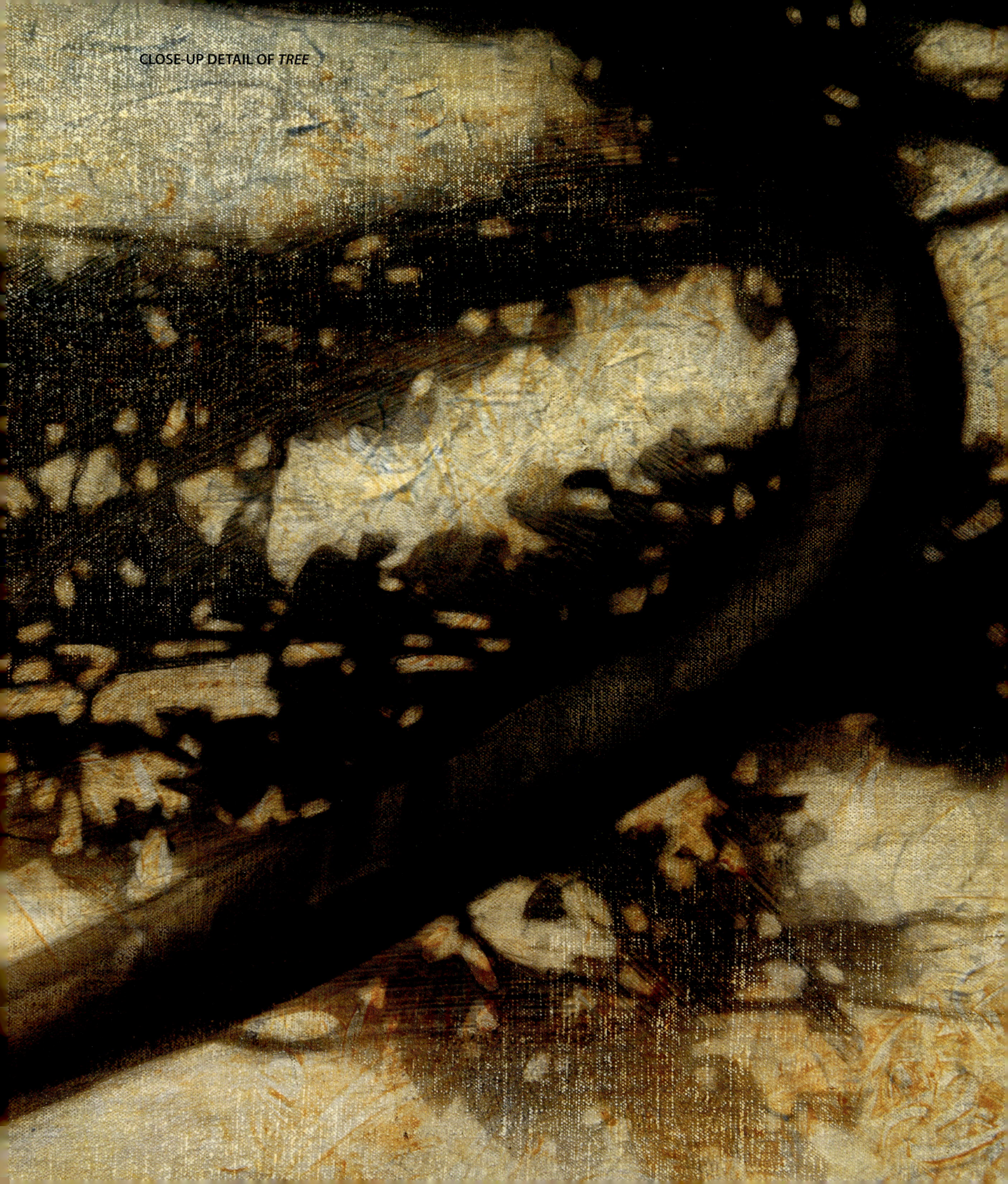
CLOSE-UP DETAIL OF *TREE*

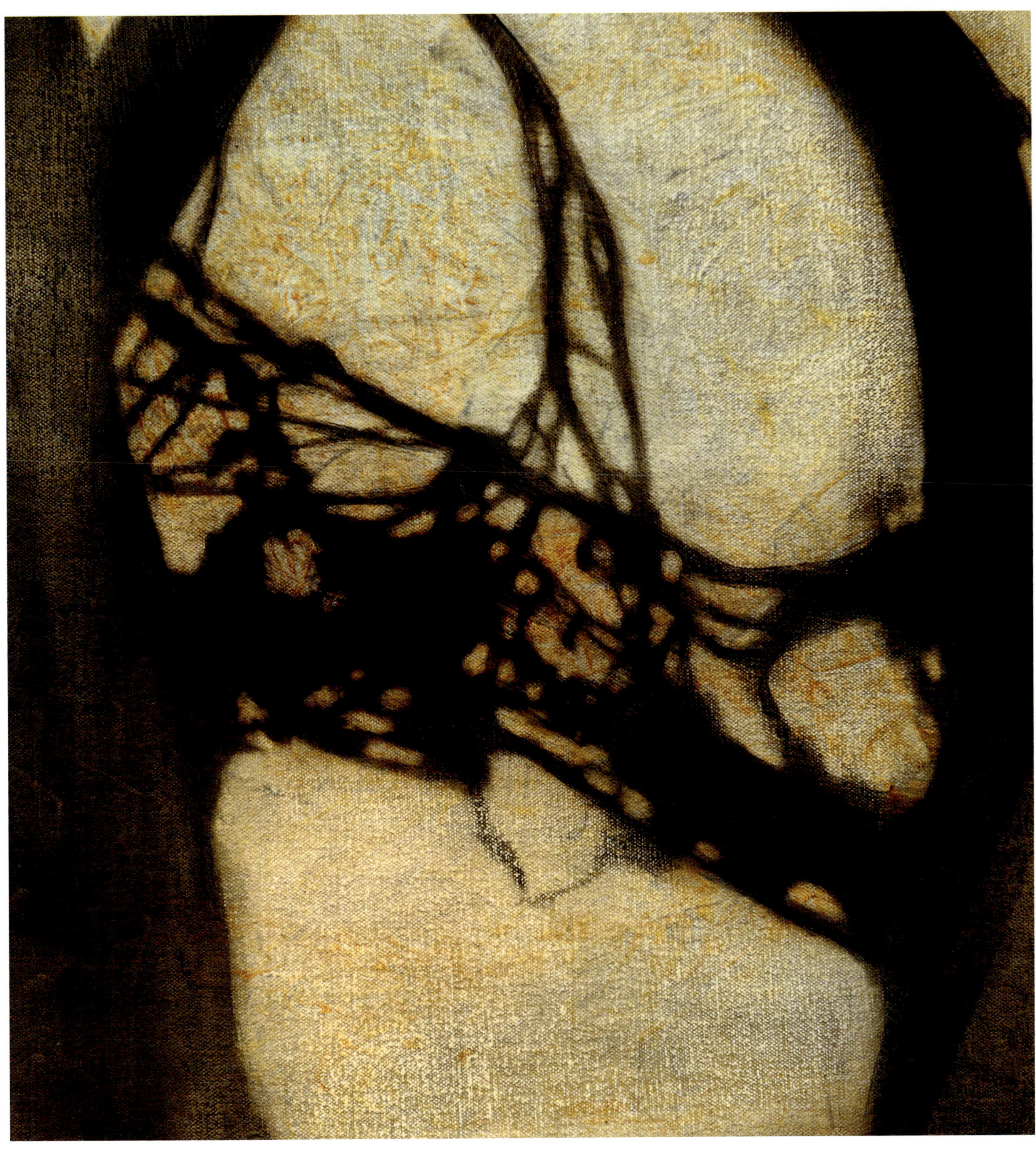

previous two spreads, above, and left:
Tree (details), 2010, oil and charcoal on canvas, 8' x 18'

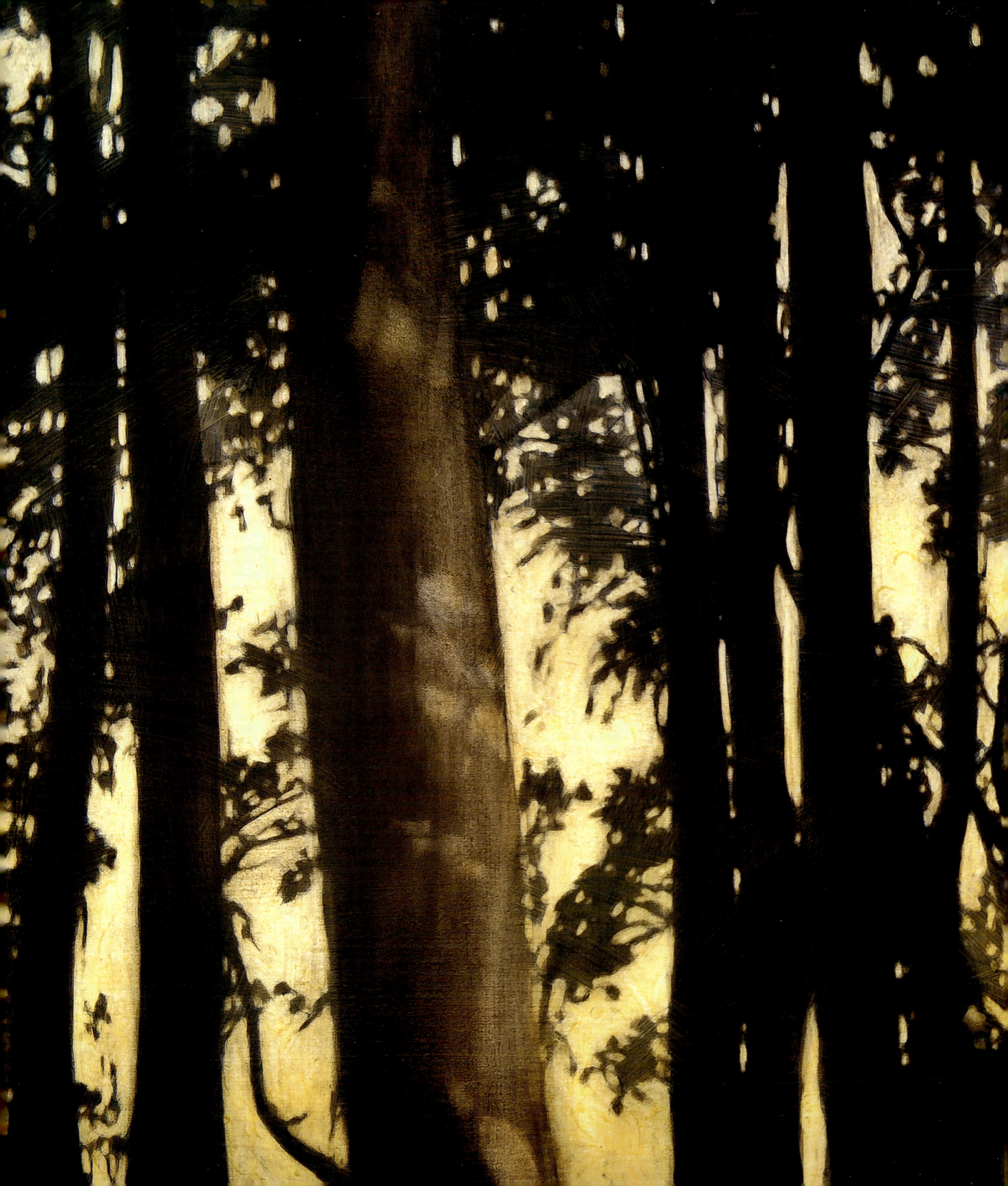

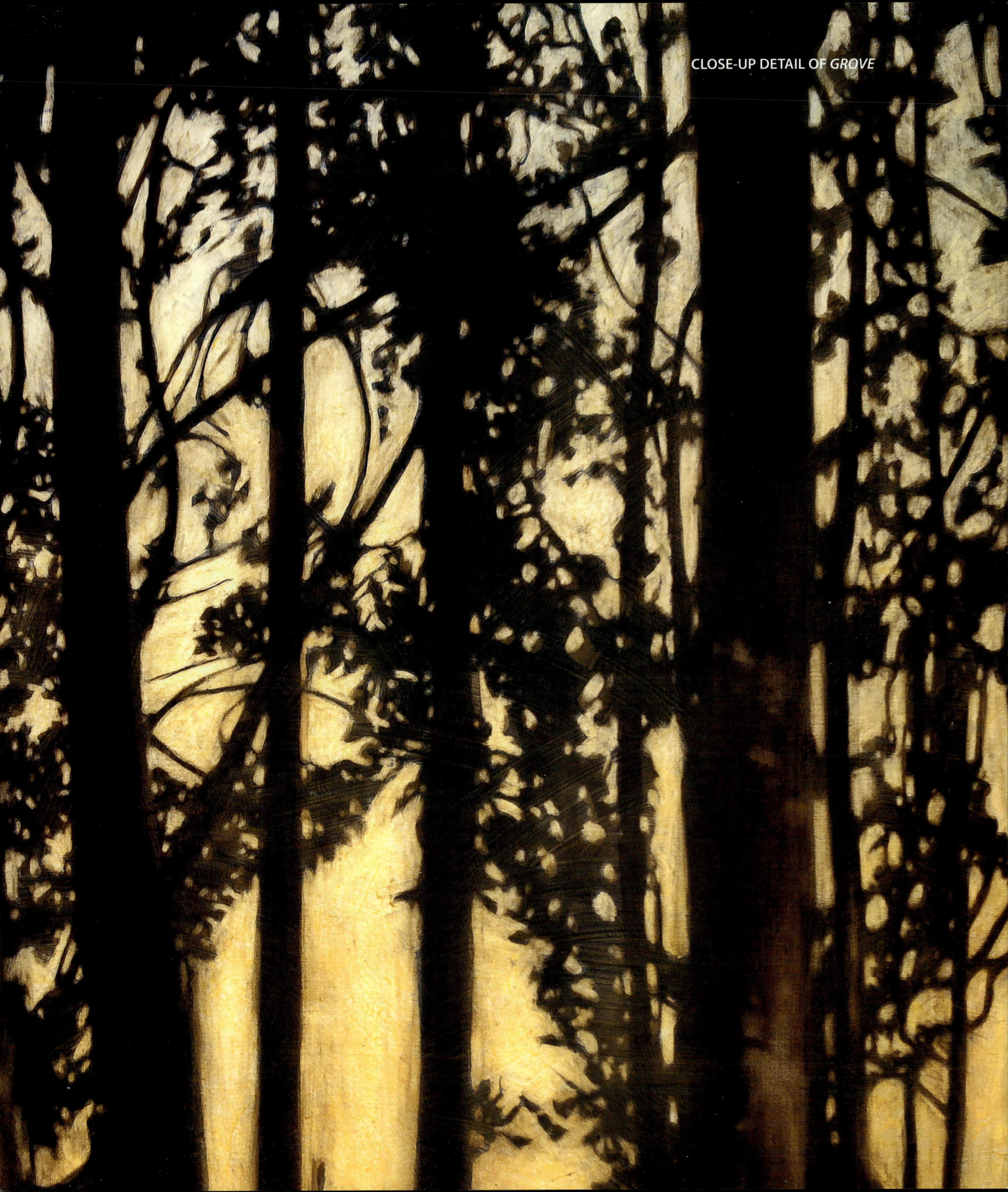
CLOSE-UP DETAIL OF *GROVE*

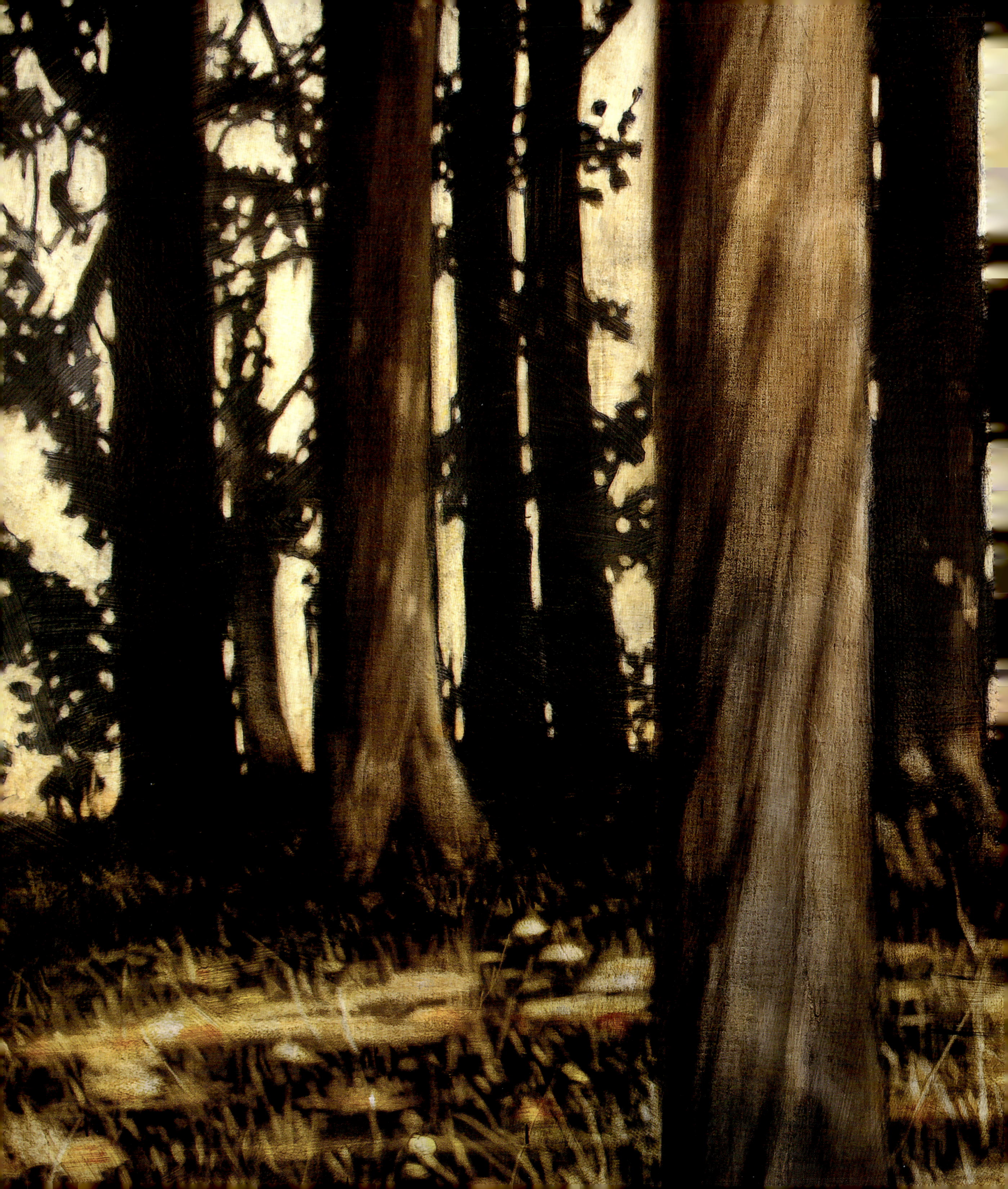

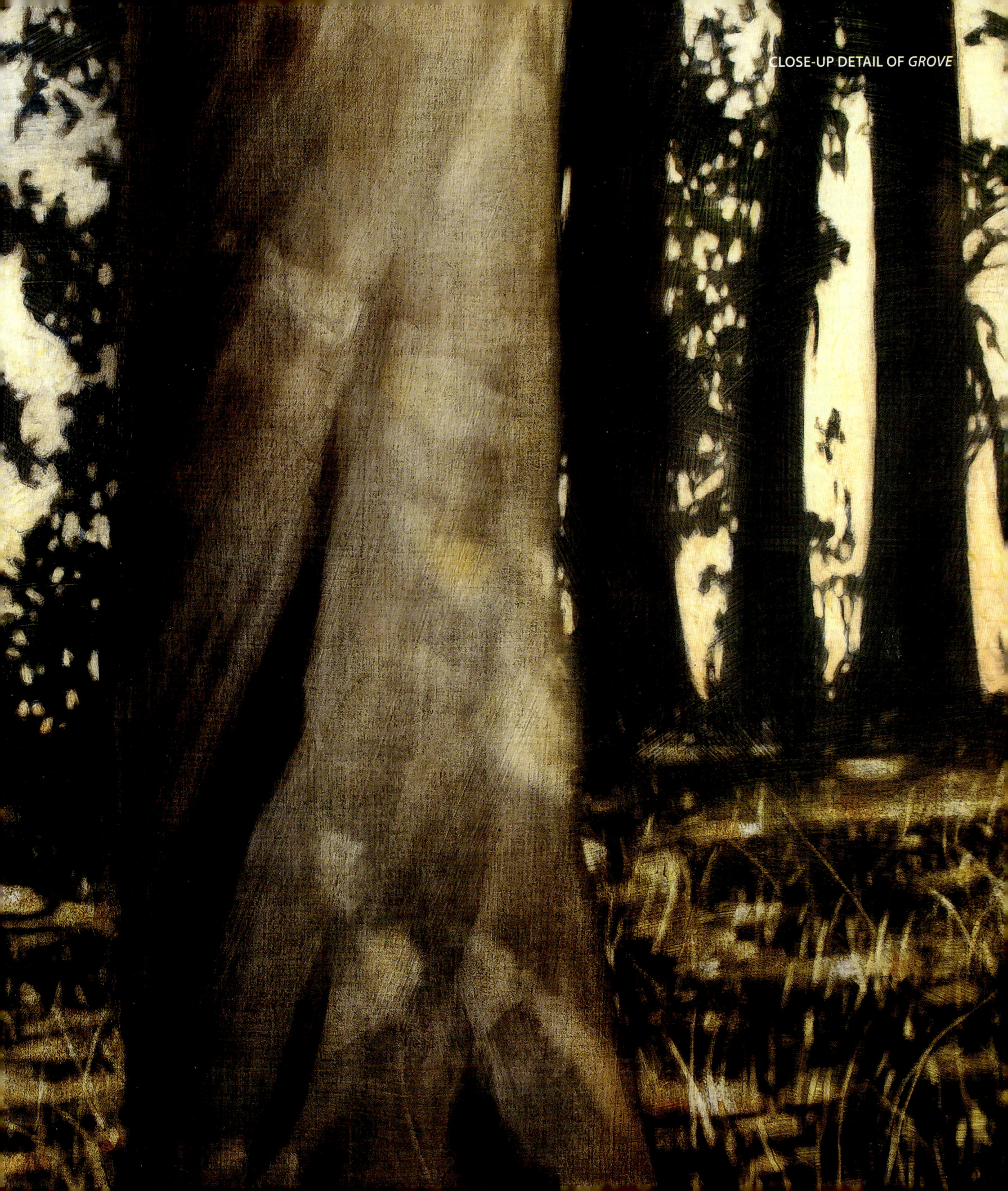
CLOSE-UP DETAIL OF GROVE

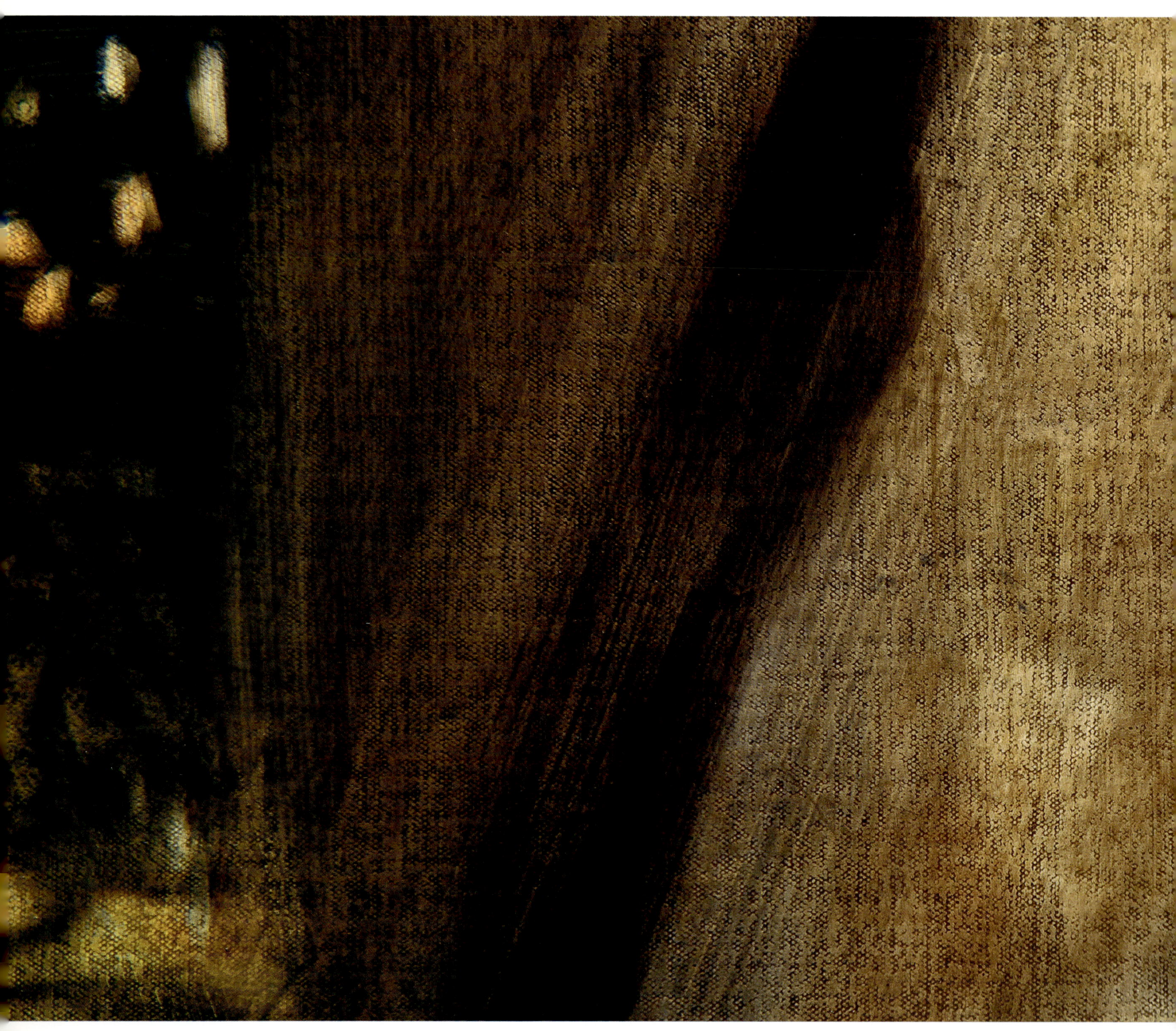

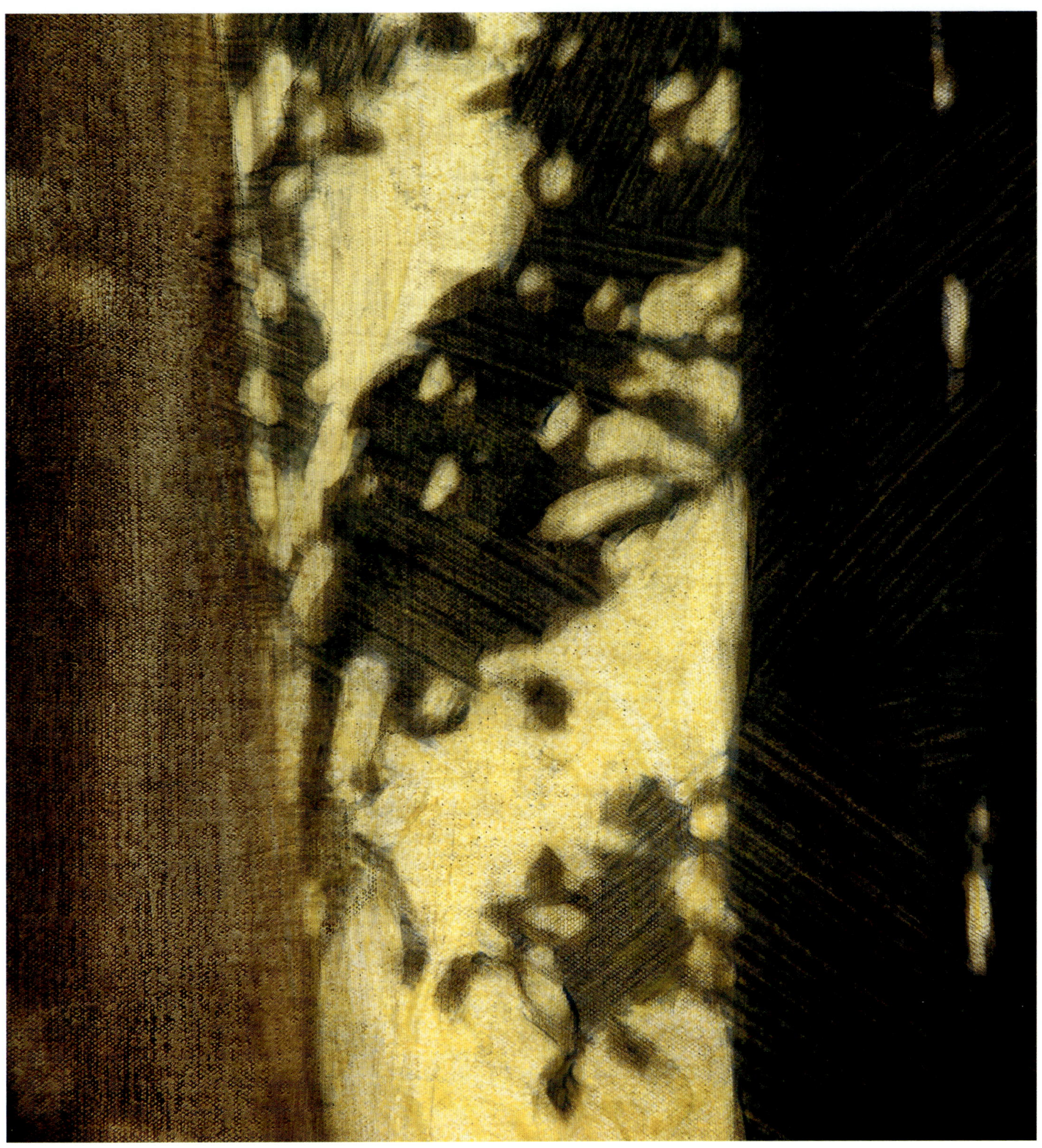

previous two spreads, above and left:
Grove (details), 2010, oil and charcoal on canvas, 8' x 18'

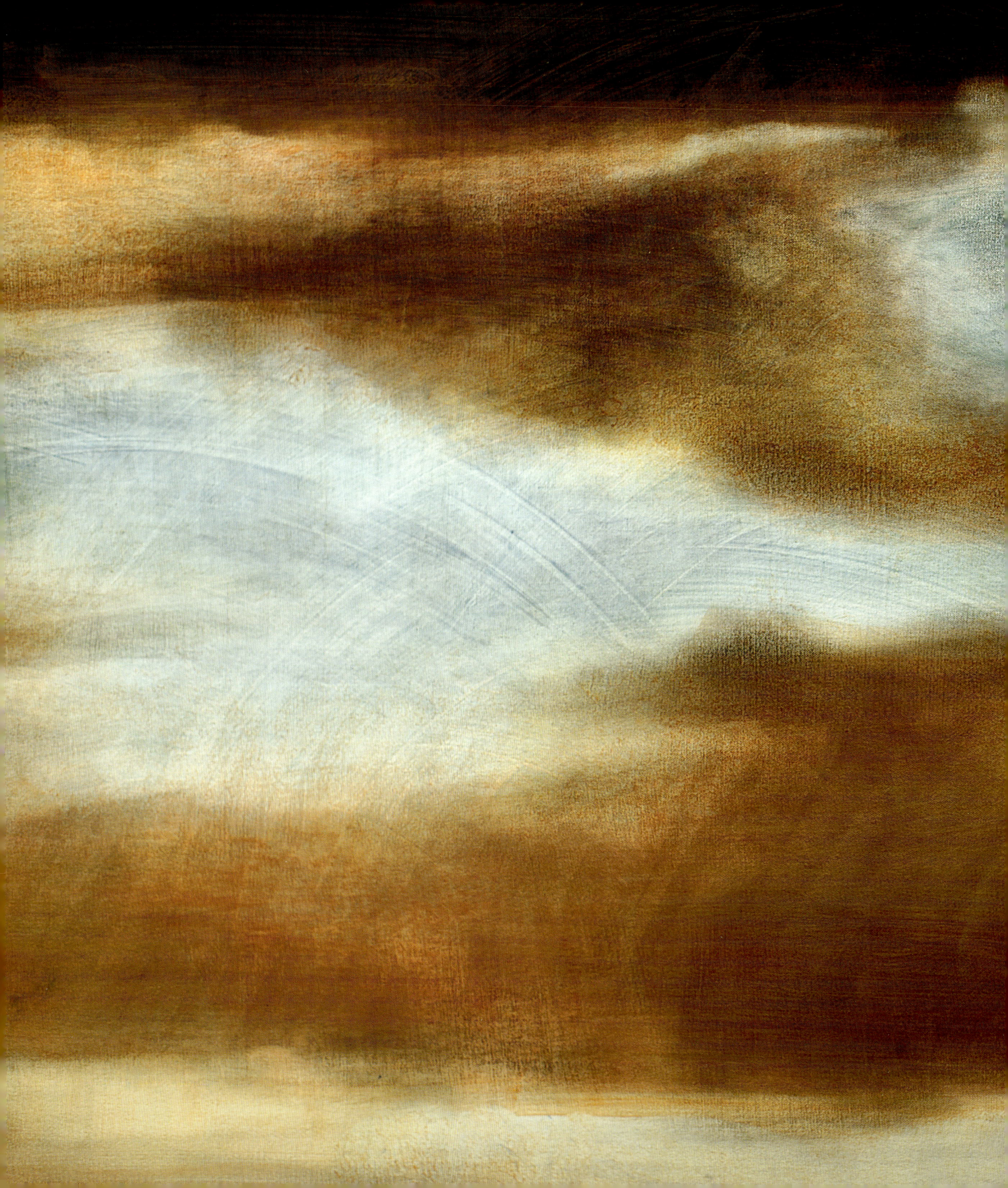

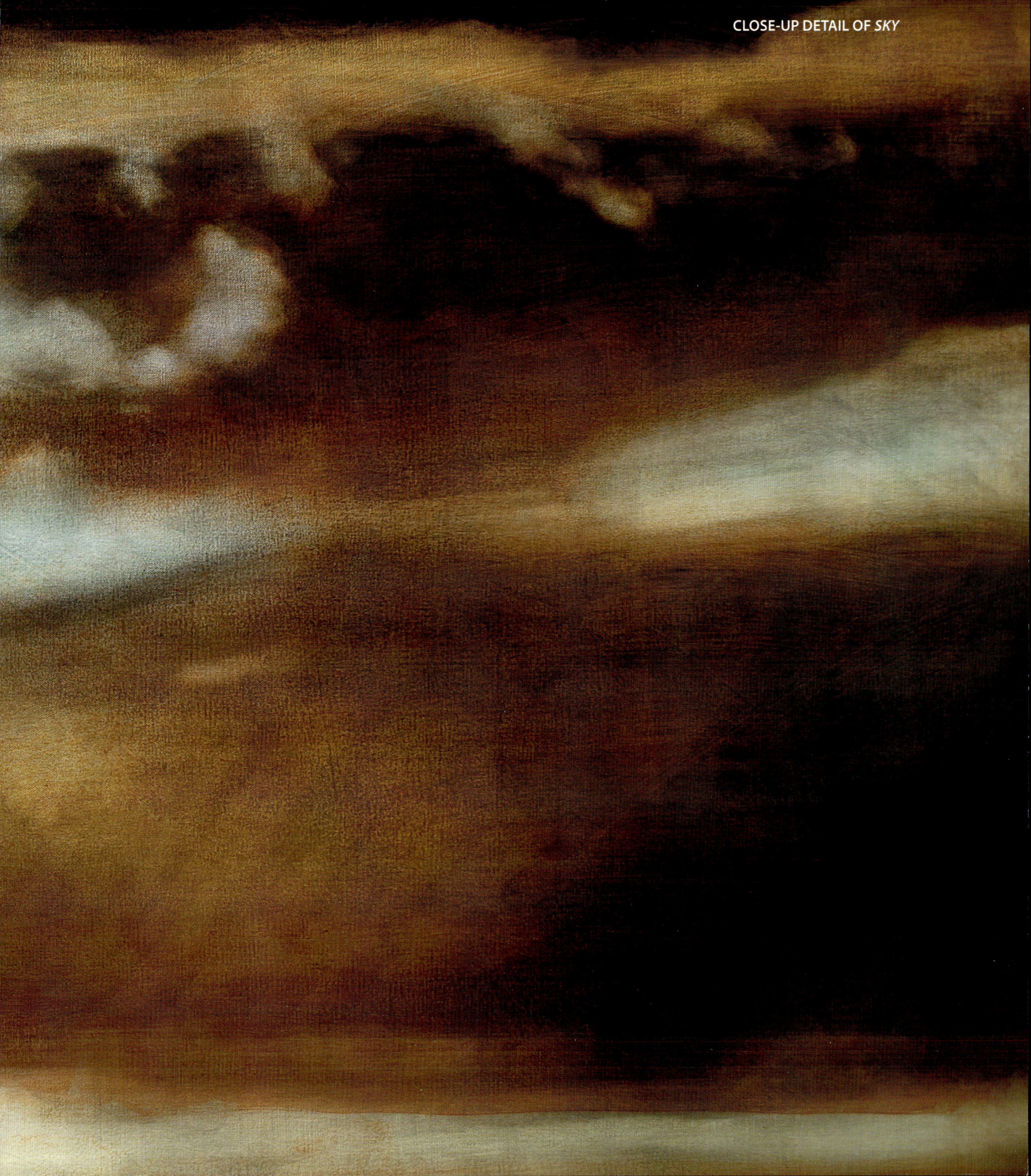
CLOSE-UP DETAIL OF SKY

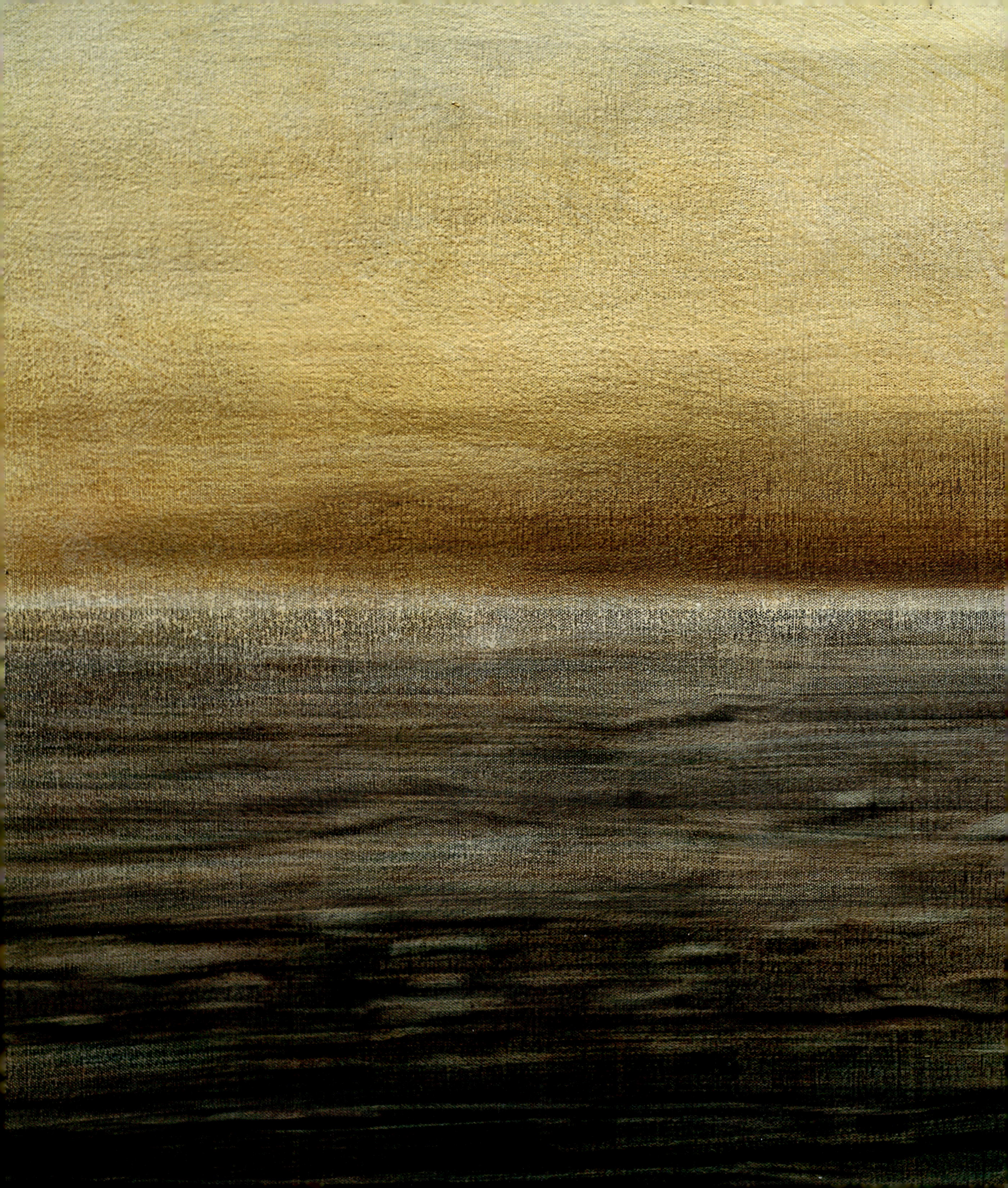

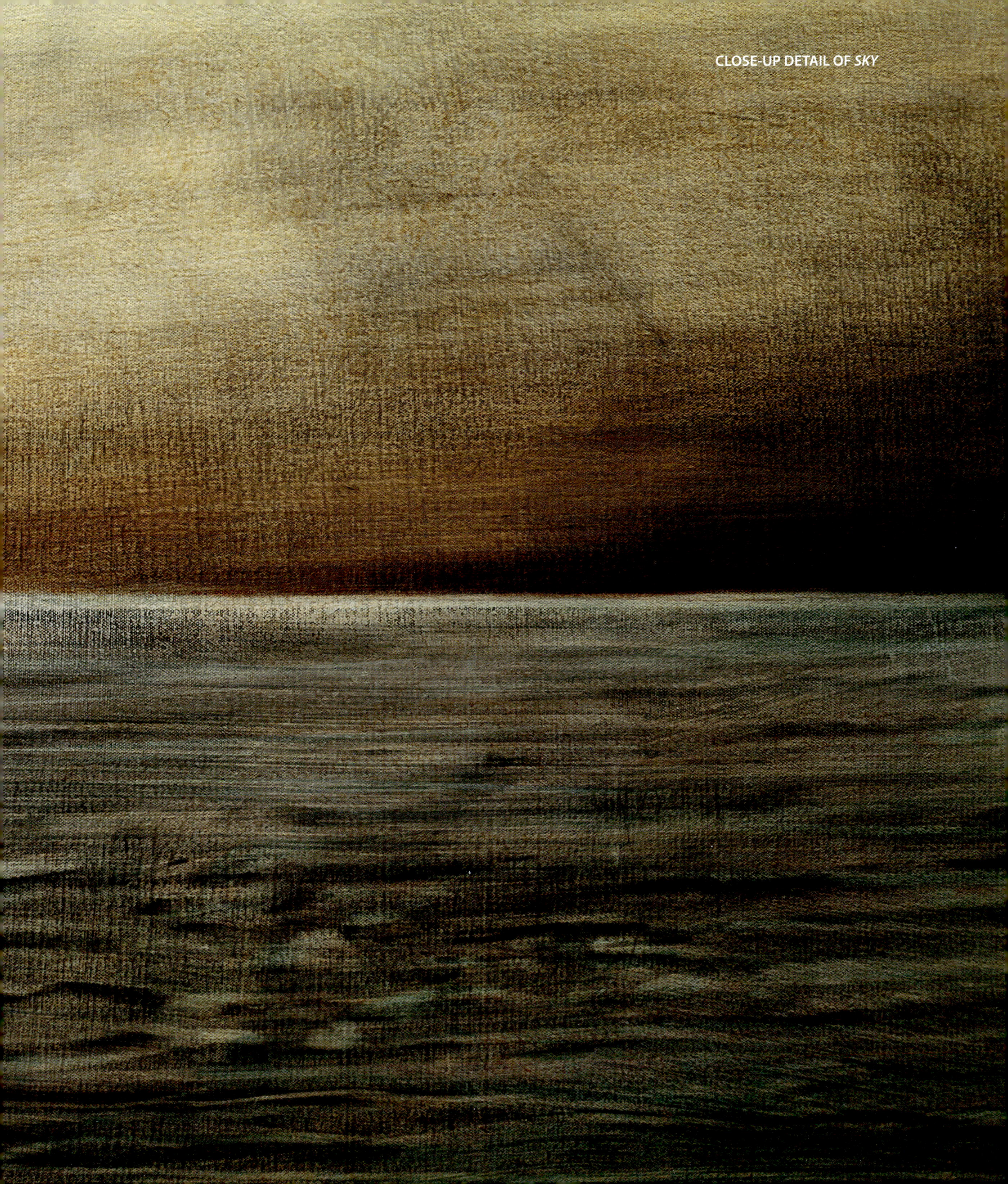
CLOSE-UP DETAIL OF SKY

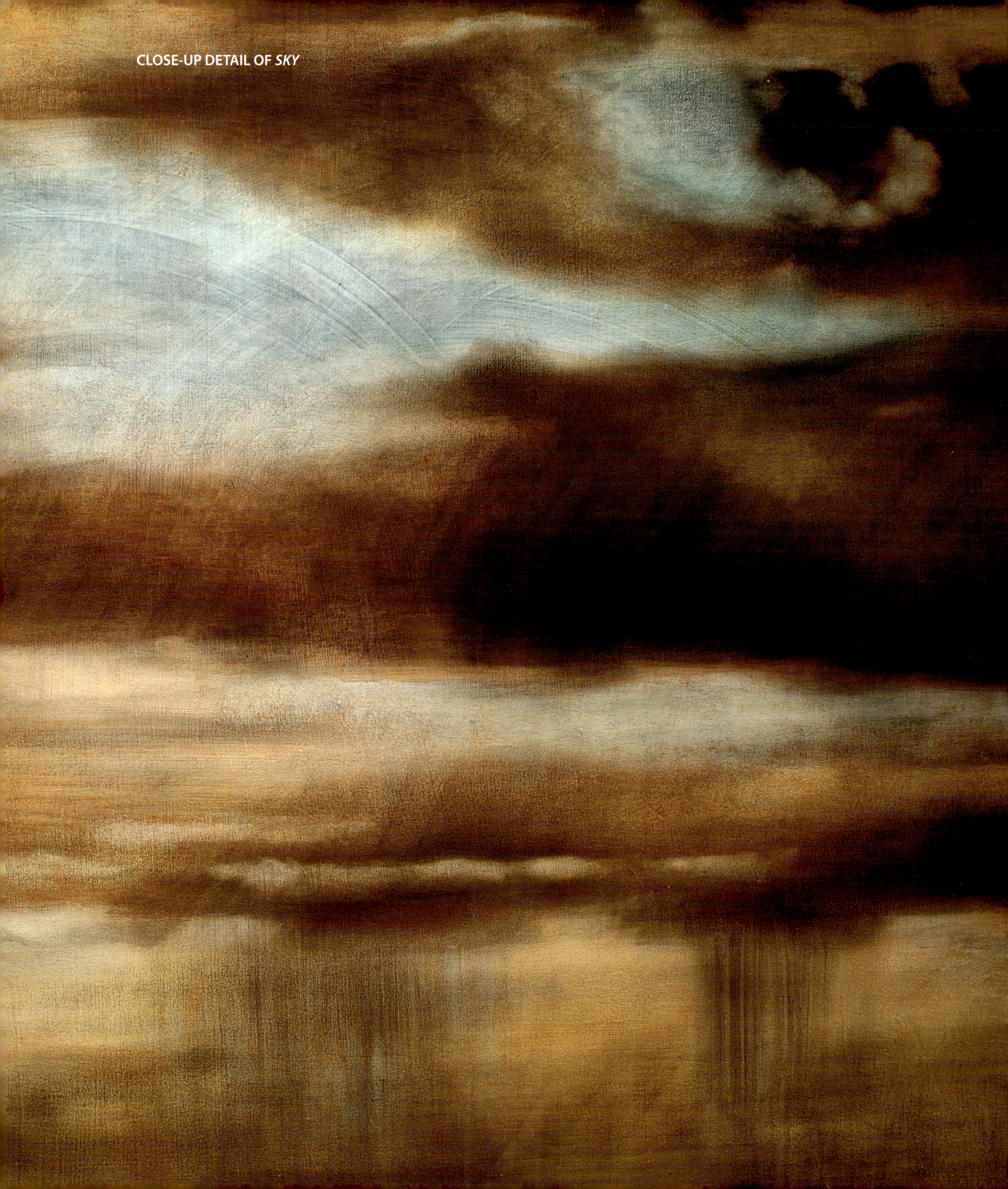
CLOSE-UP DETAIL OF SKY

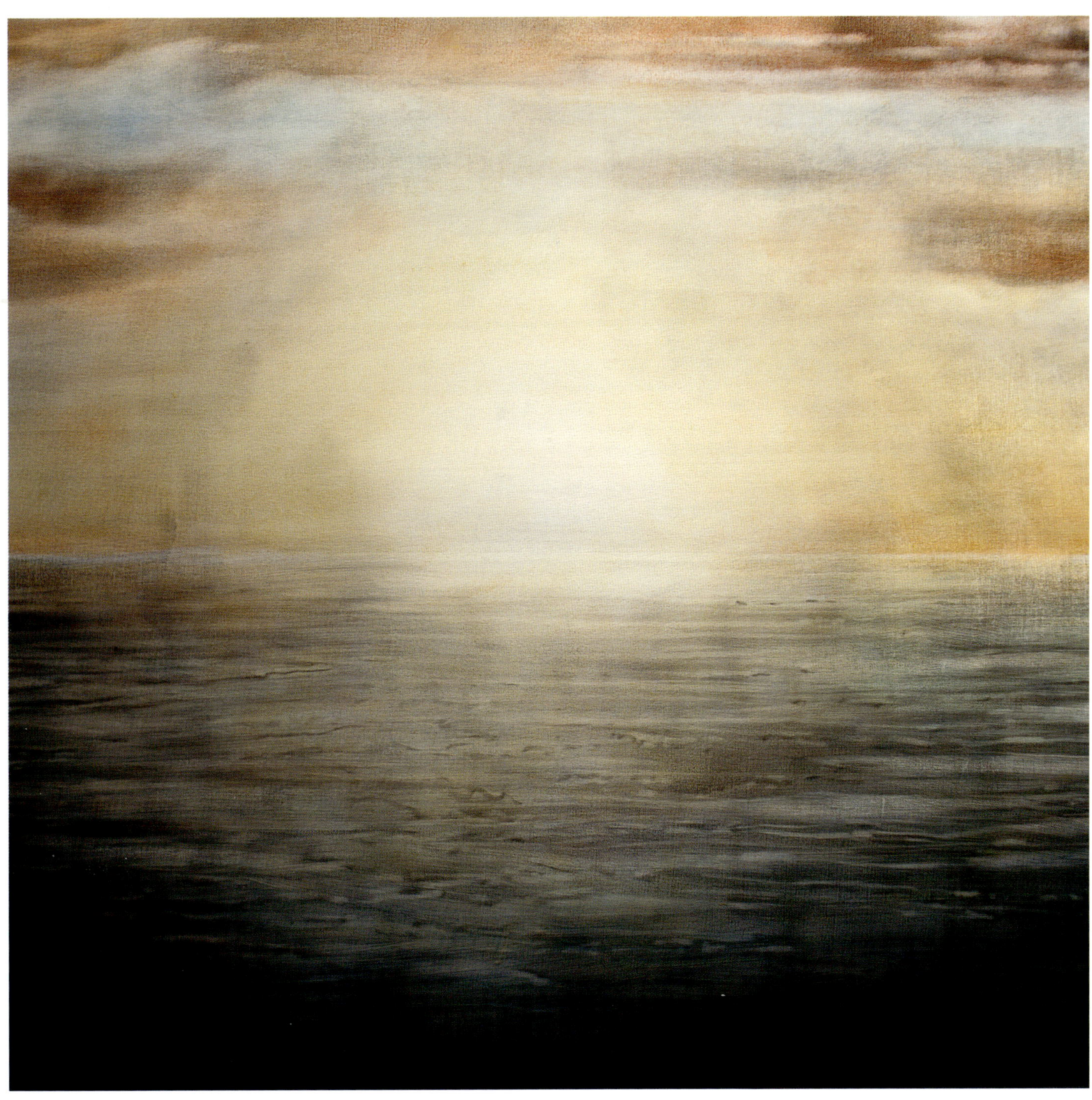

previous two spreads, above, and left:
Sky (details), 2010, oil and charcoal on canvas, 8' x 18'

Stephen Hutchings: Drawing Upon Memory
Mary Reid

I am writing this while at a cabin located in the very southeastern part of Manitoba. Here, I am surrounded by a landscape that is dotted by scrub brush and swamp, punctuated by tall, skinny poplar and pine trees. This is the transition zone between the open, surreal, prairies and the majestic, rocky Canadian Shield, both equally spectacular and awe-inspiring in their own way. Although this "in-between" landscape is quite unremarkable, it can be found anywhere. Perhaps because my day-to-day reality is an urban one, I find a sense of beauty in this overlooked geography.

It is this idea of the familiar coupled with the nonspecific, prosaic yet beautiful, that is imbedded in the large-scale drawings created by Stephen Hutchings. These are the concepts that have occupied him for more than a decade, encompassing his subject of inquiry and even directing his method of creating. Hutchings's most recent body of work, *Landscapes for the End of Time,* embodies this investigation with a depth of understanding that is a testament to his maturity as an artist.

Drawing

At the core of Hutchings's prodigious practice is drawing. Undoubtedly he is a highly skilled practitioner of this method of mark-making. When I first encountered his work in the late 1990s, he was creating hundreds of little four-inch-square improvised drawings of bushes, "spending hours, sometimes days, on a single image.... Each drawing [was] finished only when it reflected the way that he felt, a visual equivalent of his emotional state."[1] These bushes were a series of very private gestures for Hutchings, dealing with personal loss, championing the banal, and calling attention to the overlooked. In 1997, Hutchings wrote, "Drawing is the one constant in my life.... [It] is an act of personal discovery. It is extremely informal, relaxed and private."[2]

Hutchings's preferred medium for drawing is charcoal. This is significant because with charcoal it is difficult to be precise. Once a mistake is made it is there forever, and there is no going back. Although a mark may be erased, the charcoal trace will always be visible.

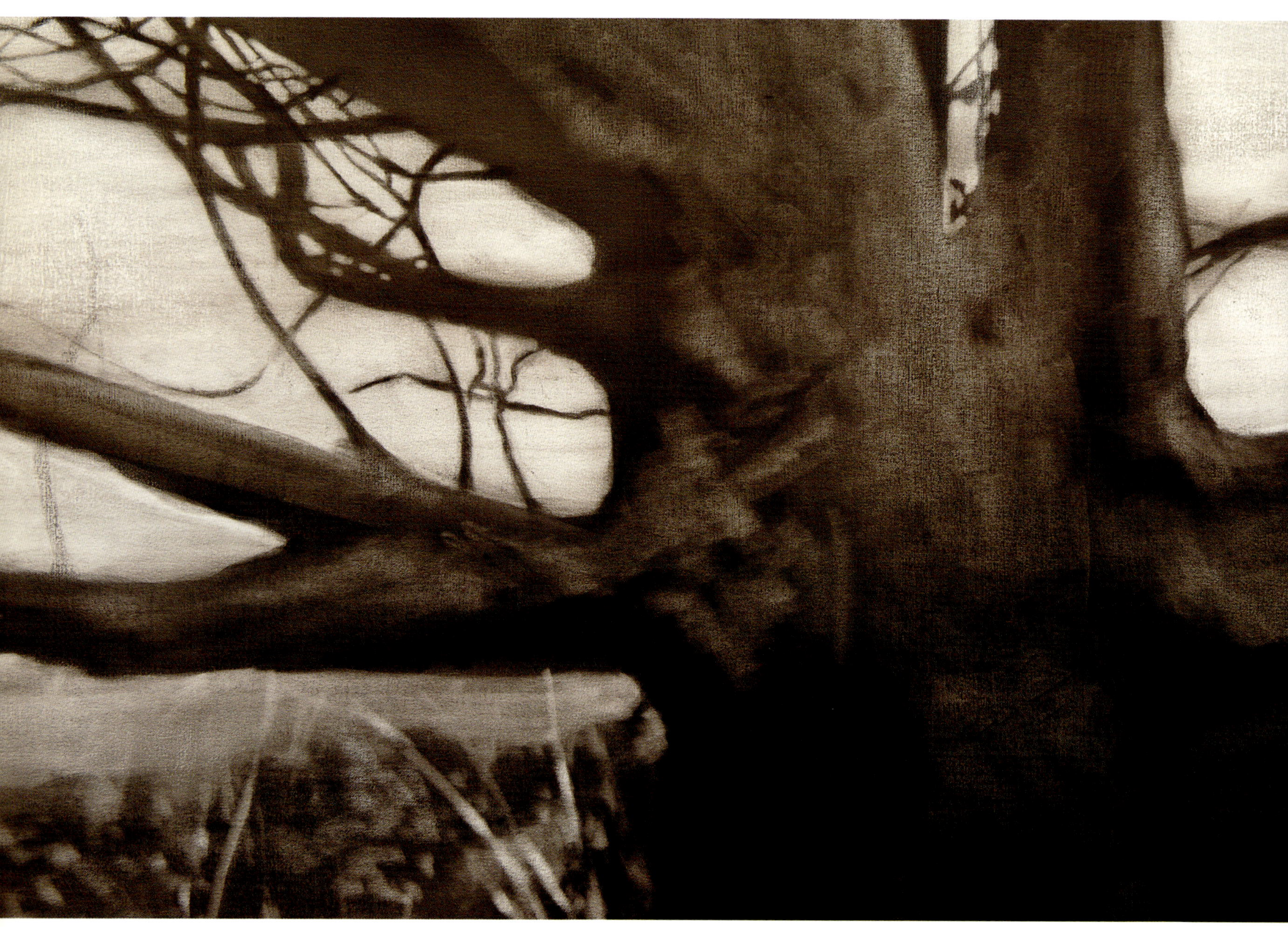

When he first draws an image, Hutchings takes the composition to a flat black and then draws into the charcoal with an eraser by removing and carving away the black to reveal the lightness of the ground. Once he is finished drawing with the erasers, he covers the surface of the canvas with a wash of coloured glazes and draws yet again using paper towels (his tool of choice) to take away some colour and add definition and texture. Hutchings

Tree (detail of charcoal drawing), 2010, charcoal on canvas, 8' x 18'

writes, "The drawing is essentially a resolution between the forces that push and those that pull…The black… pushed out; the eraser pulls back in. The process of establishing an equilibrium between these two forces is what the drawing is all about. Throughout this "push and pull," an edge is created and this edge defines the point of resolution."[3] Although referring to earlier work, this statement is quite appropriate in connection with his new work. The act of drawing took on a new dimension when the artist introduced another drawing tool: digital photography.

Photography

For Hutchings, drawing is a perceptual exercise of making choices. Acknowledging the great potential of the digital camera and computer photo manipulation software, he presently "sketches" using these technological devices. Digital photography allows him to engage with the world in a different and more spontaneous way than his earlier method of pure drawing. With direct pencil-to-paper sketching, the artist's eye is committed to one view for a certain length of time. The digital camera, however, provides for a greater fluidity of movement and speeds up the process of making "sketches." Once an image is captured in digital form there is almost no restriction in terms of creative play. All the note-taking and colouration can be

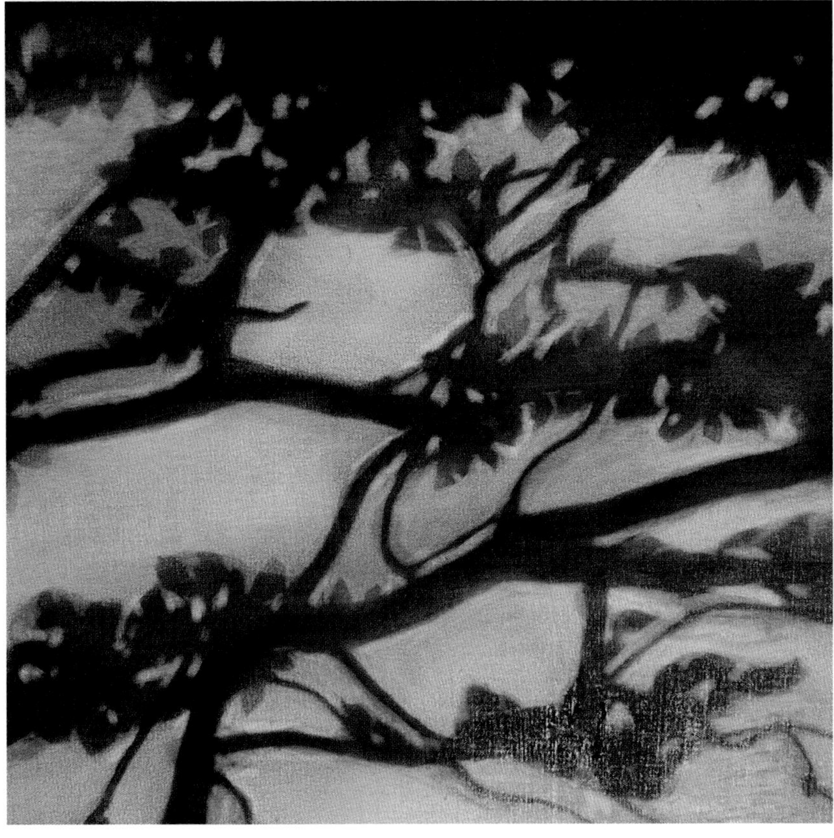

modified, adjusted, duplicated, and combined on the computer screen, eliminating hours of compositional problem solving. Once Hutchings has finished composing a digital sketch in the computer, he projects it onto a canvas and begins the labour-intensive process of drawing by hand. This introduction of the computer into the creative process has been like a gift to Hutchings, freeing up his time to work sketches up into immense drawings. The need to do hundreds of small detailed sketches is removed, allowing him the time and opportunity to go directly to the large-scale canvas.

The reference to photography, and in par-

Tree (detail of charcoal drawing), 2010, charcoal on canvas, 8' x 18'

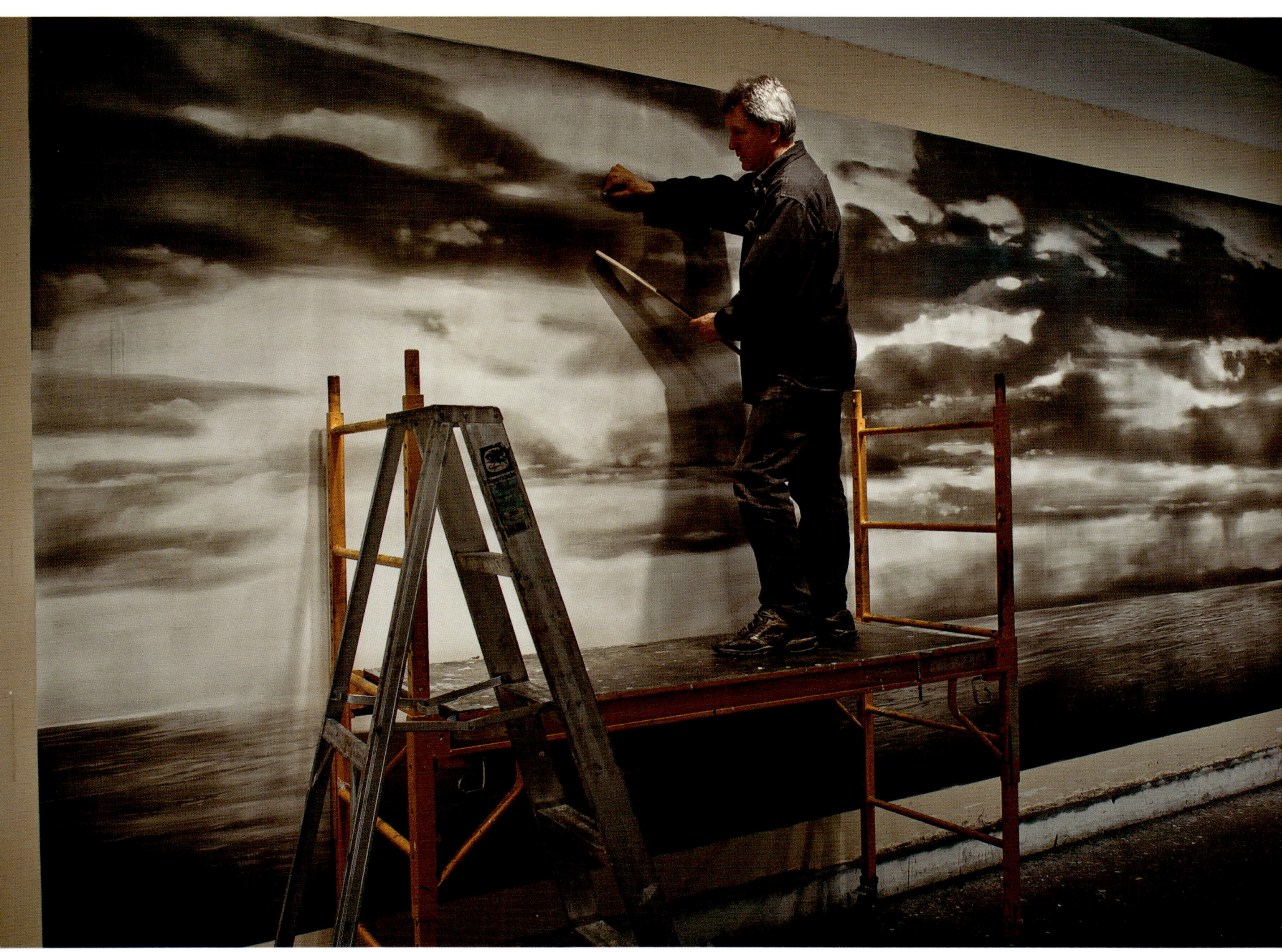

ticular to the early origins of wet photography, have been a longstanding component of Hutchings's work, and they are quite pronounced in this recent body of work. In the aforementioned small bush drawings from the late 1990s, his intensive working process incorporated smudges, erasures, and many corrections, and as a result the drawings tended to

Working on the charcoal drawing for *Sky* in the studio, 2010

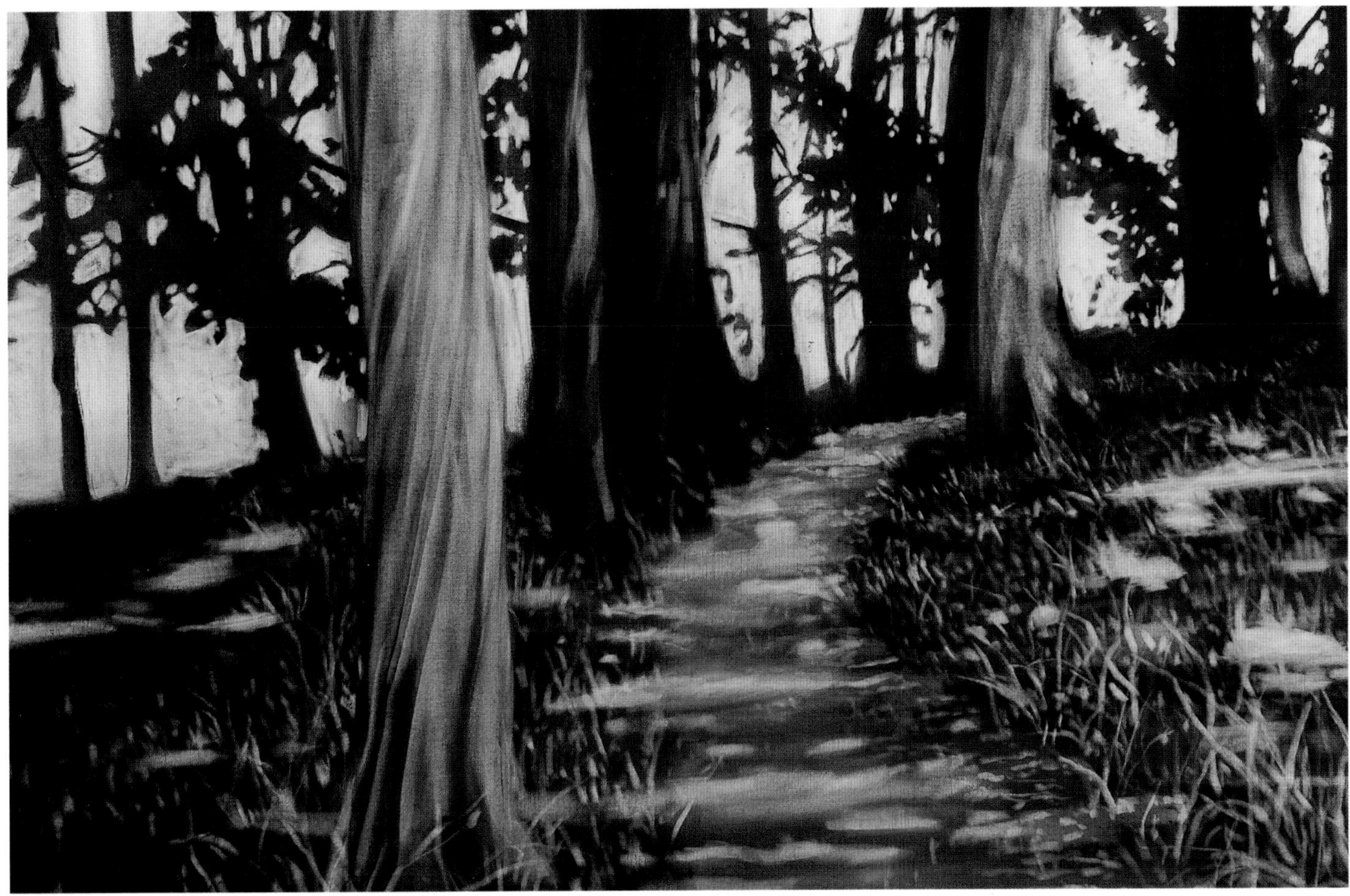

look like fuzzy snapshots. When interviewed regarding this past body of work, Hutchings stated that he wants his images to be reminiscent of photographs, both consciously and unconsciously.[4]

With *Landscapes for the End of Time,* the connection to photography is much more apparent, not only in the beginnings of creating the sketch but also in the working up of the image itself. While transferring the image from the digital form, the artist works in the shadows of the projected image, using charcoal to record the darkness, taking it to a flat black on the surface of the canvas, similar to the surface of a photograph. However, unlike the inherent flatness of digital photography, Hutchings's drawings underscore the gesture of the artist, almost reverting back to when developing marks in photographs were evident and commonplace, revealing the human element in the process of creation. With the addition of the coloured glazes, the end results are akin to hand-coloured, animated, humanistic photographs, and share the pictorial sensibility of old

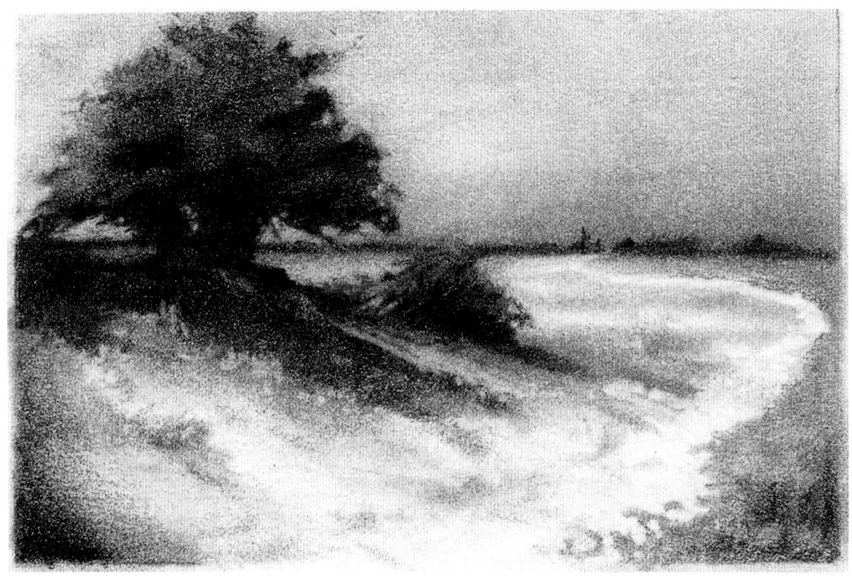

photos from the turn of the twentieth century, imbued with a sense of time and memory.

Memory

The acts of drawing and photography have strong associations with memory. The traditional form of sketching or even copying (from another work of art, a person, a still-life arrangement or nature) is a technique that has long been used in the teaching of art. Drawing can train one's memory to retain and to recreate, to embed images into one's mind. In many cases concentrated drawing can help one see things that had previously gone unnoticed. It can uncover and bring to light the overlooked or the discreet.

When vision starts to fade, memory starts to take over. Memory is a powerful component that plays a major role in understanding and reasoning. The body and brain also remember in different ways. While the brain recalls, the body retains. As a dancer is trained not to think about the moveme nt but to feel it, a visual artist who draws and paints responds in a similar fashion. The gesture of mark-making is second nature — not thought, but felt. A highly-trained artist can draw relying on memory alone, the memory gleaned from years of observing the world in an intense and concentrated fashion.[5] In other words, drawing creates memory, whereas photographs capture memories.

Photographs act as prompts for our memory. They can help us recall the past, and they are just as subjective and incomplete. They can be clear or fuzzy, forgotten and found. In memories, "the sign functions not so much as object to object, but beyond this relation, metonymically, as object to event/experience."[6] In conversation, Hutchings remarked that with memory comes "all of the other subjective parts of our lives: emotion, spiritual awareness, cognitive understanding, botanical knowledge, and so on."[7] In other words, memory is not accurate, but highly personal, morphing and changing through time, attitude, and perspective. Although the photograph as object remains unchanged, the memory associated with it is highly fugitive, subject to the additional information and highly individual meanings we bring to bear at different times in our lives.

above: ***Along the way,*** 2004, graphite on paper, 3" x 5"
right: ***Grove*** (detail of drawing), charcoal on canvas

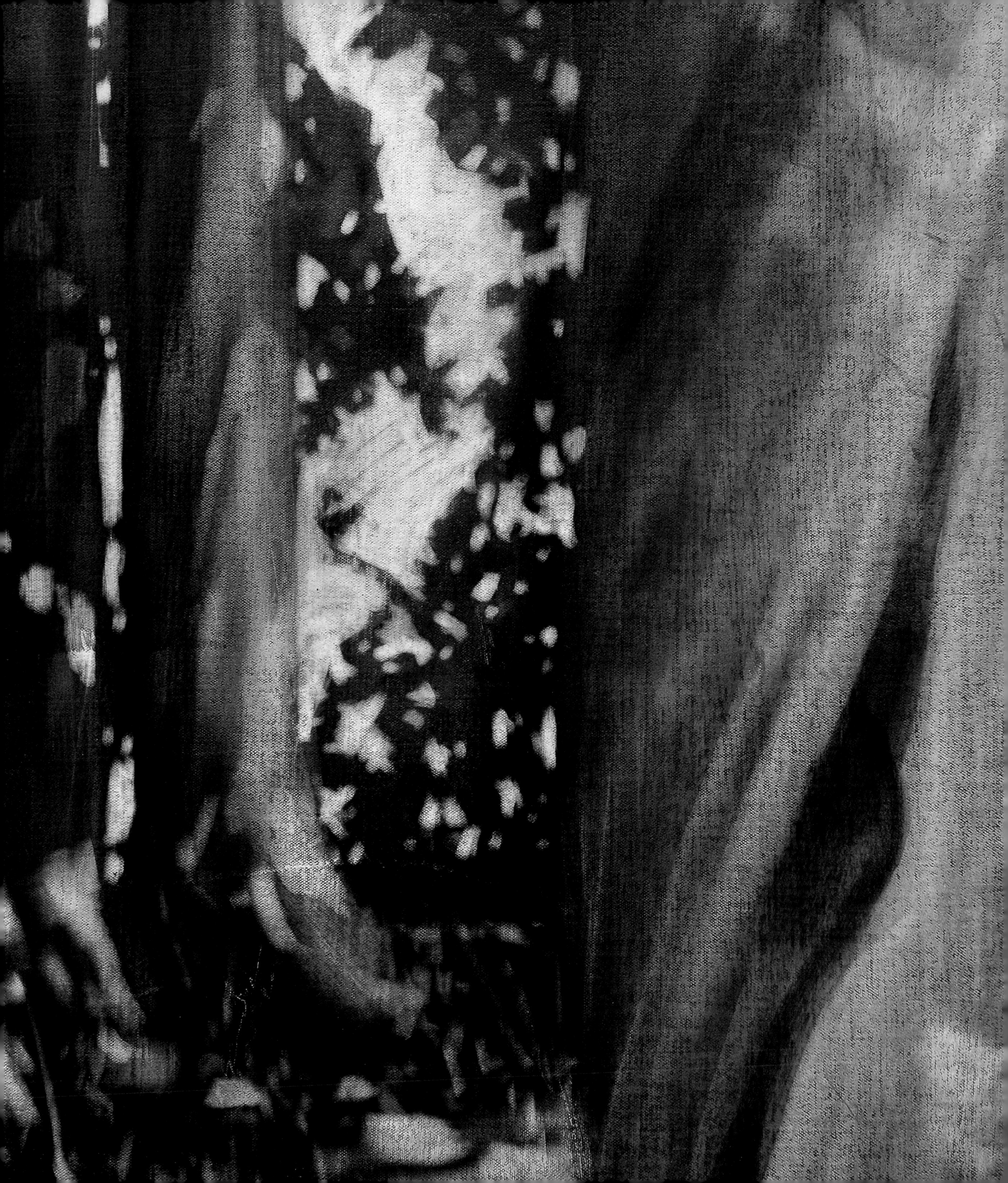

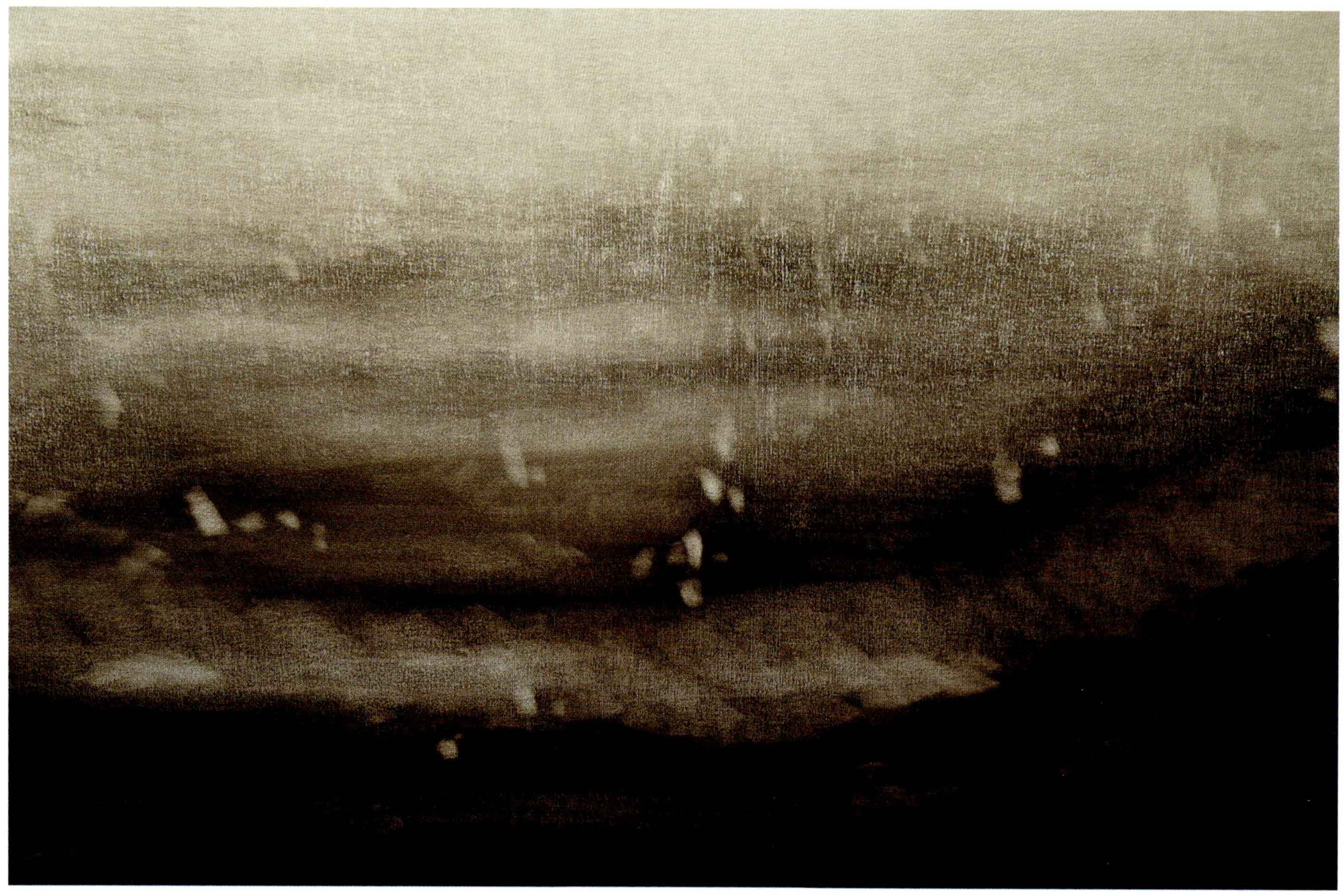

It is this subjective additional information of memory and time and life's experiences that Hutchings draws upon when he transfers a digital image into a compelling drawing. The projected shadows of the digital sketch that are part of Hutchings's process are akin to a form of memory, a trace of what the image once was in the process of forming into a new reality through the hand of the artist. According to the artist: "The 'glue' that binds the photo-derived image with the drawing, and with the interaction of memory, is time — the time required to work on the image, to shape it physically with the charcoal and the erasers, and to colour it with the glazes. The temporal aspect creates an extended environment within which the subjective can be brought into play. In other words, the crafting of the drawing and the painting allows for an amalgamation of the objectively-derived image with a subjective interpretation. And in that amalgam, in that synthesis, lies the strength and power of the final work."[8] Just as memory is idiosyncratic and indeterminate, so is the subject of Hutchings's work — the natural landscape and time.

Sky (detail of drawing), 2010, charcoal on canvas

The Landscape

The genre of landscape holds an "in-between" sort of place in the history of art. In terms of the canon of art, the natural landscape was generally the backdrop to grand allegorical or historical paintings, yet was considered of more importance as a subject than still-life scenes. During the dawn of the modern era, landscape painting was elevated to a new and higher status. As cities grew and became dominated by industry, the representation of the natural landscape became a window or stand-in for the loss or disconnect with nature. As European colonization spread to North America, landscape paintings became represen tations of potential wealth in terms of mining, deforesting and areas of future settlement. Soon thereafter the landscape painting became a souvenir, establishing the "I was here" of the traveller for family and friends at home.

It was earlier, during the eighteenth century, that the landscape as subject matter made an important shift in representation under the guise of the "picturesque." This manner of depicting the landscape finds its roots in the style that was championed by seventeenth-century French painter Claude Lorrain (1600-1682) and his followers. However, it was British artist and author the Reverend William Gilpin (1724-1804) who in 1770 first defined the picturesque approach as typified by a dark coulisse on one or both sides of a painting in the forms

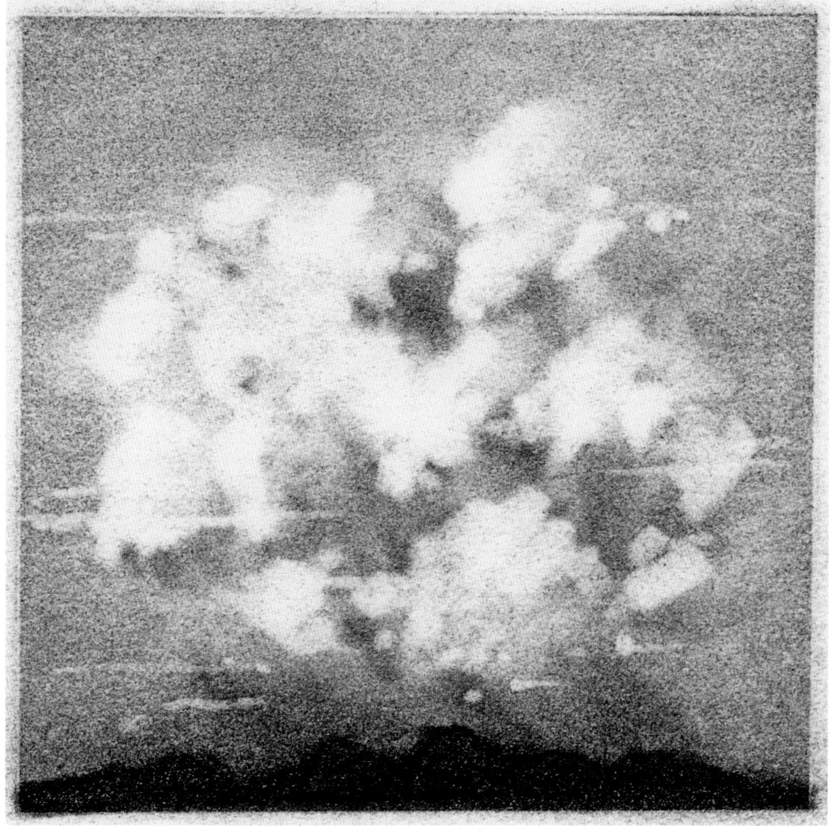

of trees or rocks, a shadowed foreground, a well-lit middle ground where the main emphasis of the picture lay, and a deep background whose misty distance merged into the sky.[9]

Several works from *Landscapes for the End of Time*, particularly *Roads, Tree, Hill* and *Branch* (all 2010) incorporate aspects of the eighteenth-century concept of picturesque framing where the edges or borders are filled with imposing vegetation leading the eye to the centre of the canvas, in many ways picking up on the Renaissance notion of the "window onto the world." These compositional choices are certainly purposeful on the part of Hutchings, who has an in-depth knowledge of the history

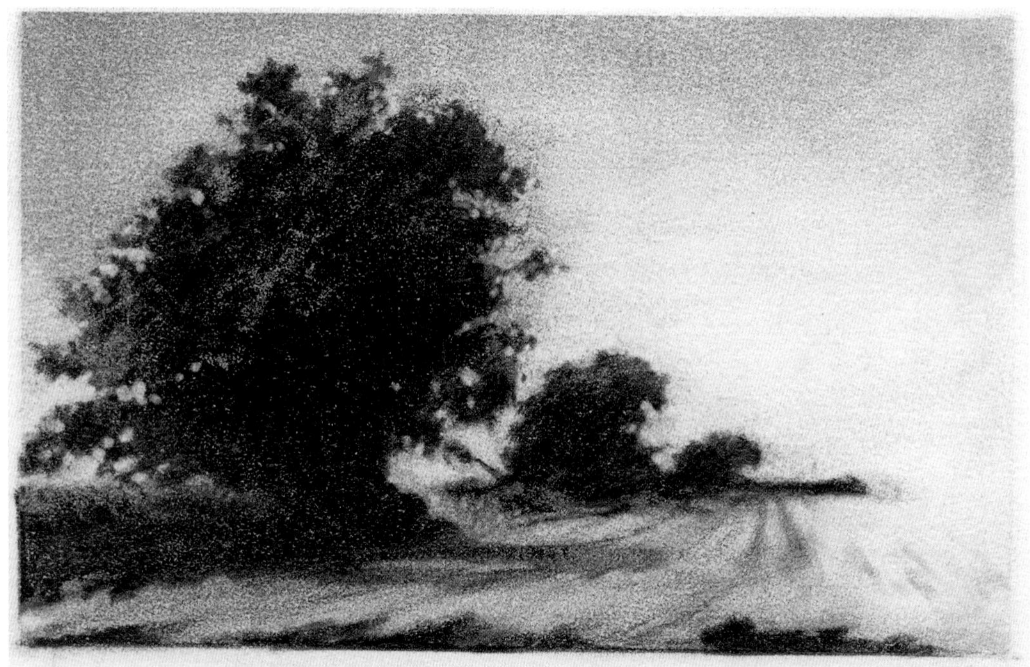

Landscape as Memory

The concept of the natural wilderness resides in our memory. For those of us who were raised and now live in urban environments, being in nature evokes the memory of summer holidays, of periods of rest and reprieve from the business of city life. It is the quest to slow things down, to recharge our batteries, to get back to the core — to the truer, simpler, and more essential things of life. But our connection to nature is mediated by our contemporary reality, which is dominated by technology. Hutchings's landscapes of indeterminate places and time broach this barrier.

By taking the photographic objective of capturing or recording the landscape and transferring it into the subjective act of memory and associations related to experiencing being in nature, Hutchings's large-scale drawings strive to reference complex ideas and philosophical concepts about our place in the world and the ability of our spirit to transcend the physical.

The near-life-sized aspect of Hutchings's work gives a viewer the feeling of almost stepping into another world. One almost feels it would be possible to step into these images and walk into nature, or, to be more precise, walk into a memory of nature, be it your own or someone else's, reminded of a place you have

of landscape painting. He acknowledges that the "picturesque" is considered the soft underbelly of the arts[10] and he exploits this association to the fullest extent. In doing so, he creates a foundation of understanding, a starting point, upon which to build and in many cases subvert. By flipping back and forth between objective and subjective meanings, employing historical references and traditions in terms of painting and photography, Hutchings uses this shared visual language as a means to lead the viewer in and to consider larger contemporary issues. As a result he composes incredibly beautiful drawings which hold so much more in terms of information and exchange. *Landscapes for the End of Time* communicate very directly, unmediatedly, and universally.

Trees and field, 2005, graphite on paper, 3" x 5"

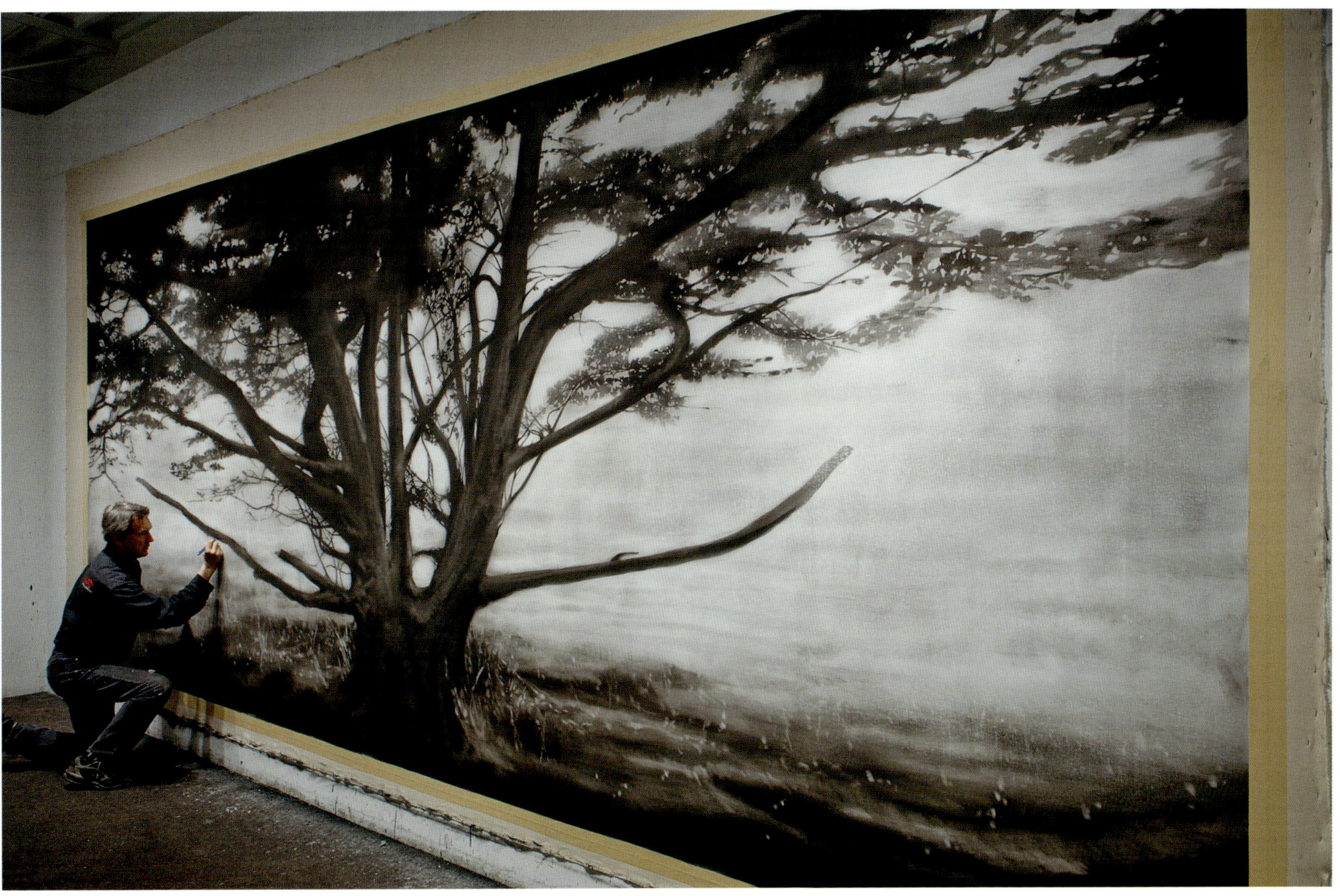

been or think you have been.

It is these traces of former meanings and memories coupled with the concept of time that each of Hutchings's paintings expresses with their own individual character. In both *Roads* and *Hill,* the bushes in the background act as witnesses that hold memories standing along paths that appears to lead into clearings of light, clarity and even truth. With *Tree* and *Branch'* the foreground of the work is dominated by a screen of leaves and branches that the viewer must visually probe to access the light coming from behind. This experience of looking acts as a visual metaphor of sorts, moving into the deep recesses of one's mind and memory. The way in which these drawings move from darkness to the light offers a sense of spirituality that we may all respond to — perhaps the presence of hope, or the search for truth.

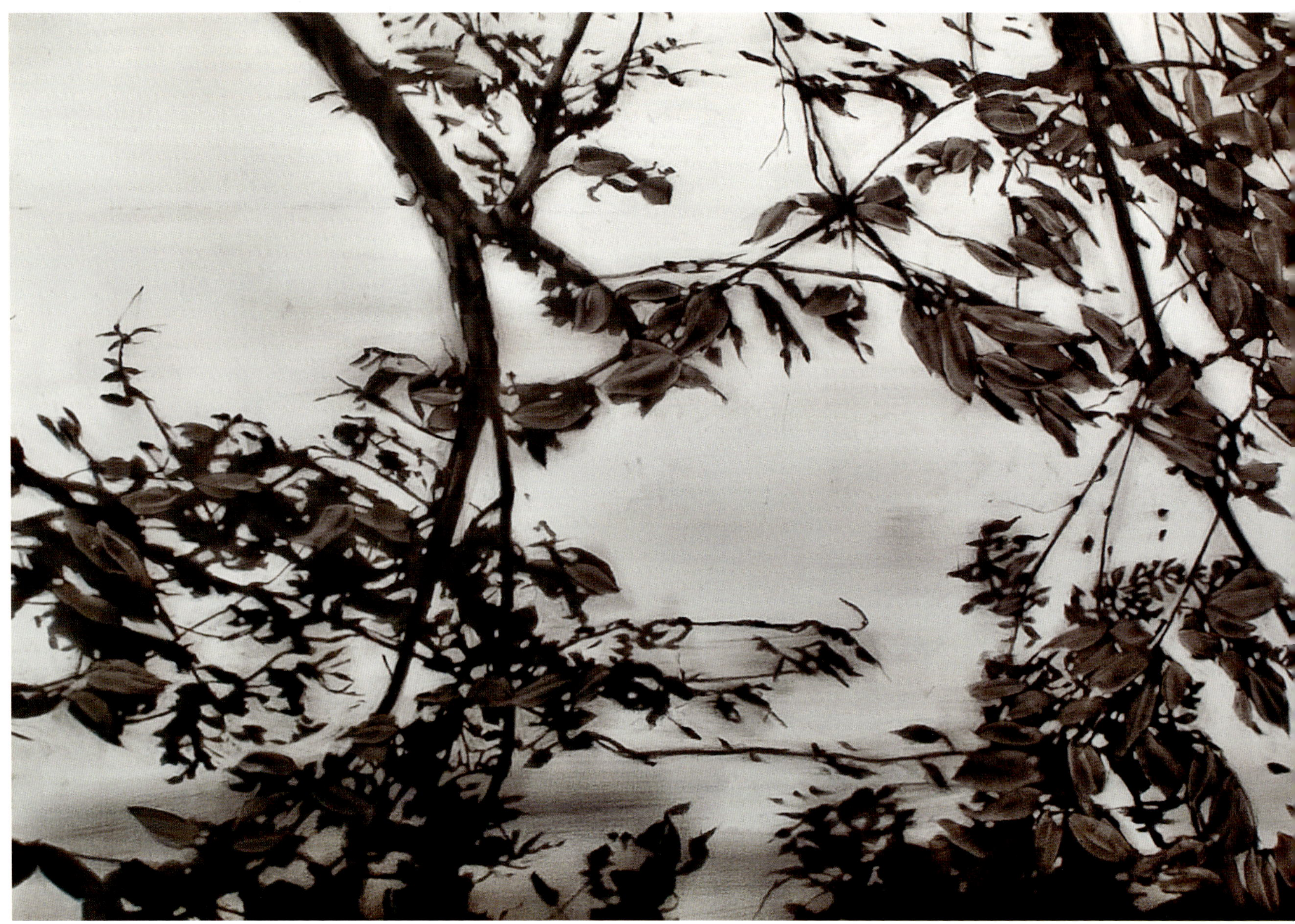

Landscape – The Universal Experience

In 1997 Hutchings stated that the purpose of drawing hundreds of tiny little portraits of bushes was "to establish some sort of link between the external and the internal world." The internal world can be interpreted as a more spiritual or moral relationship that one holds within one's own consciousness and understanding of who one is, while the external represents the outward facade that we wear to manage in our surrounding environment. For Hutchings, the act of drawing provides a tangible and physical link between these two realities of existence — self and place. Well over ten years later, he

Branch (detail of drawing), 2010, charcoal on canvas

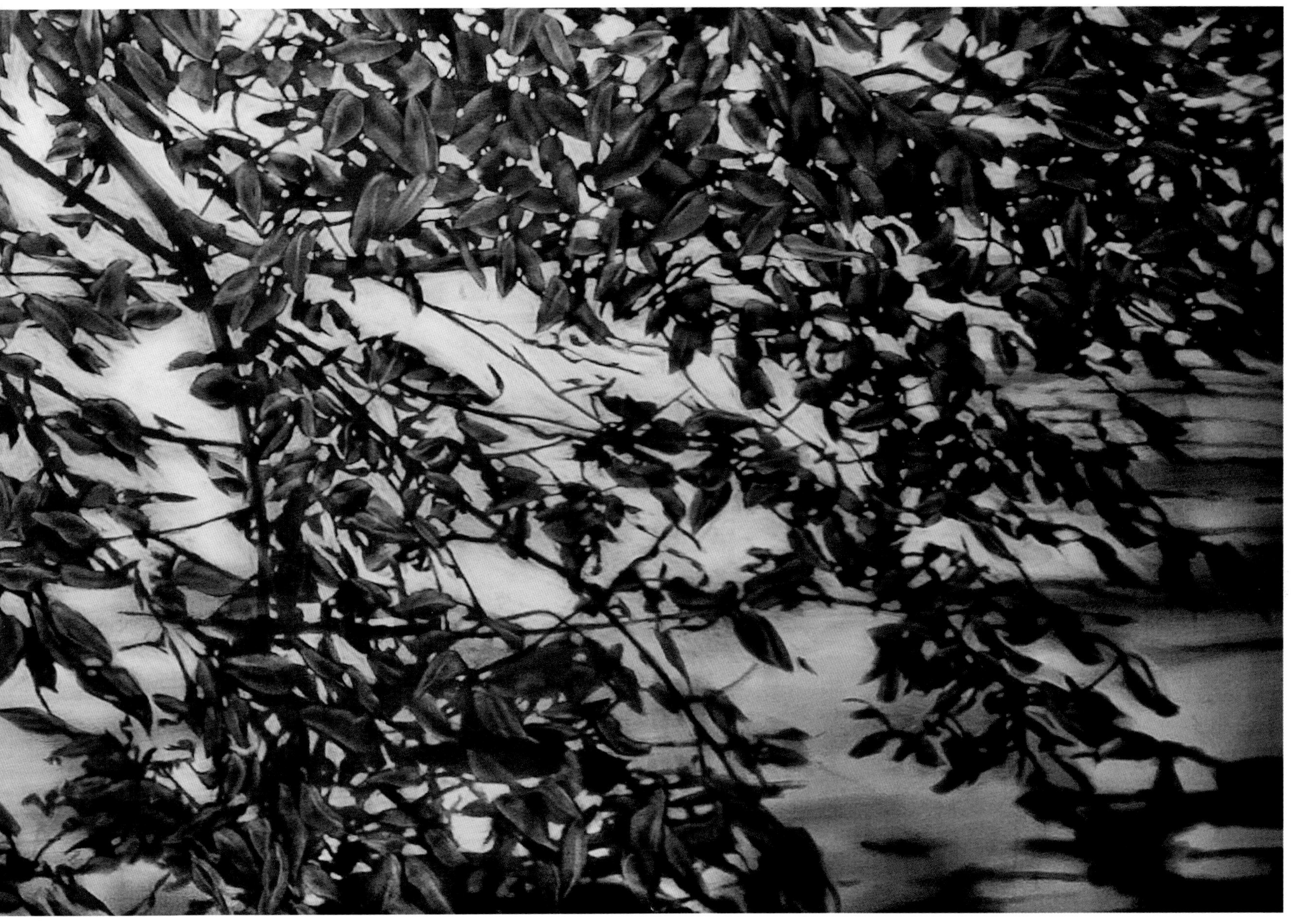

has moved from a manifestation of something that existed inside his own mind to an external expression of much larger, more broadly shared human questions.

The landscape, or in other words, our connection to nature, is a shared, universal experience. It holds a fundamental connection to the human condition. The complex patterns of life are imbedded in this relationship, no matter how estranged or separated we are from it. What it means to be human, what happens when we cease to exist, what we understand to be our own personal reality are tied to the construct (both real and imagined) of nature.

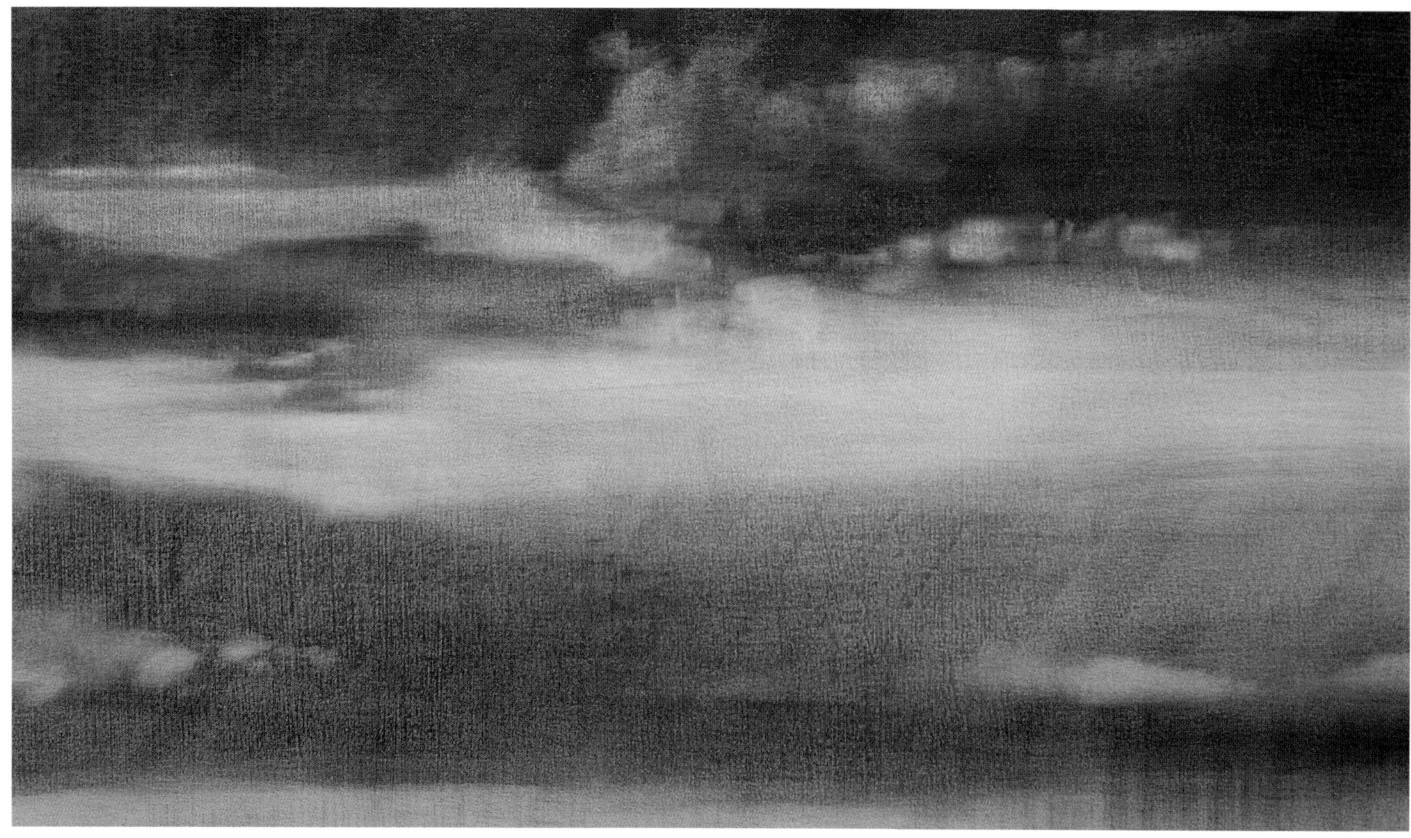

What we do know for certain is that the landscape is all around us. However, we operate in a world larger than our imagination, our personal understanding of place, of belonging. It is the larger spiritual questioning of who we fundamentally are, which can at times be completely inspiring or absolutely anxiety-inducing, that Hutchings addresses through the *Landscapes for the End of Time.*

• • •

The subtle colour that comes through Hutchings's drawings references the nature and mystery of life. The shadowy images cast by the digital projector or drawn by the artist himself are traces of memories, as memory operates in the shadows of our minds. It is the ground of the drawing that reveals the "truth" of Hutchings's process, making evident the time and energy that went into creating each mark that results in a powerful representation of nature. Purposeful and accidental mark-making is a highly individualistic human act. Unrepeatable, mark-making captures time in a moment, and the presence of the individual.

To extend this further, while viewing the mark (in other words, an aspect of drawing), I

Sky (detail of drawing), 2010, charcoal on canvas

consider that someone other than myself has made that mark. In consequence, a connection is made on a personal, intimate level, through space and time, and I am reminded that I am not alone in this world, but am connected to the past and rooted in the present, and all of this will continue into the future.

Hutchings's *Landscape for the End of Time* create all these connections and more. They represent the journey of memories, the passage of time, and the bigger questions of humanity, yet provide no real answers, since all that exists is a series of possible interpretations. They are testament to Hutchings's highly skilful ability to draw upon memory and the human psyche to create an open-ended reflection on our highly disconnected and fragmented place in contemporary existence.

Mary Reid would like to acknowledge Garth Hilderman, and Denis Longchamps for their helpful comments on initial drafts of this essay.

Notes

1 Lelde Muehlenbachs, "Experiencing the Bush," *Bush: Stephen Hutchings,* (Lethbridge: Southern Alberta Art Gallery, 1991), 18.

2 Stephen Hutchings, *The Bush Series* (Banff and Toronto: Altitude Publishing and Mira Godard Gallery, 1997), 7.

3 Ibid, 9.

4 Muehlenbachs, 18.

5 Stephen Hutchings, e-mail correspondence, July 24, 2010.

6 Susan Stewart, *On Longing : Narratives of the Miniature, the Gigantic, the Souvenir, the Collection* (Durham and London: Duke University Press, 1993), 136.

7 Stephen Hutchings, e-mail correspondence, July 24, 2010.

8 Ibid.

9 Sutherland Lyall, "Introduction" in William Gilpin, *Observations on the River Wye and several parts of South Wales, &c. relative chiefly to picturesque beauty; made in the summer of the year 1770* (London, 1782; Surrey, England: Richmond Publishing Co., 1973), v.

10 Stephen Hutchings, interview with author, May 20, 2010.

11 Hutchings, *The Bush Series,* 7.

The Painting Process

Hutchings's painting method incorporates a number of different techniques and strategies, as illustrated here in the creation of the painting, "Hill." Starting with a digital photograph and referencing the work of the Pictorialist photographers from the late 1800s, he removes the colour and re-works the image on the computer, manipulating the composition, the focus, and the tonal balance. The resultant image, or "digital sketch," is then transferred to the canvas and translated into a fully-realised charcoal drawing. On top of the finished drawing, Hutchings applies layers of coloured glazes to arrive at the final painting. Although both the glaze formula and technique were derived from eighteenth-century models, Hutchings developed the process out of his familiarity with CMYK offset lithography, the most commonly used printing process in the contemporary graphics industry.

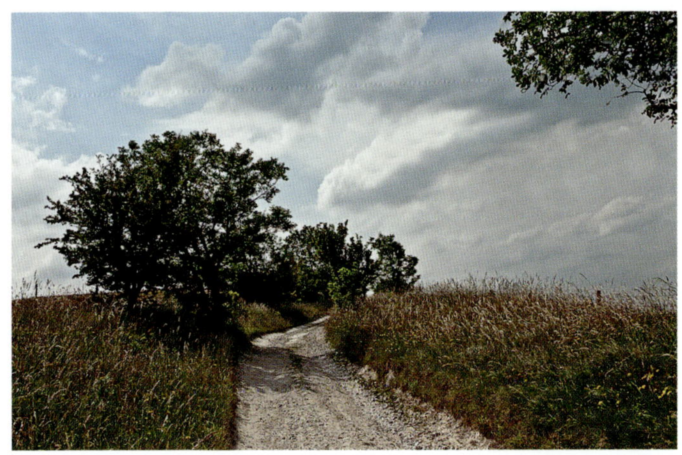

1

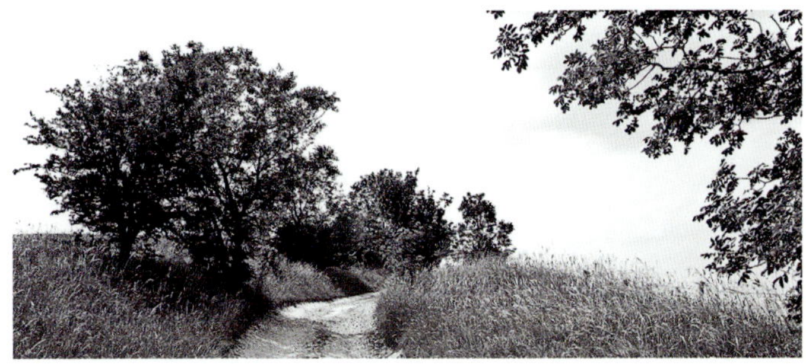

2

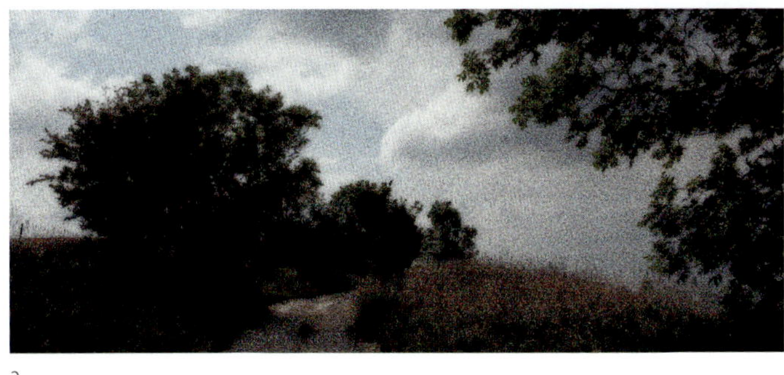

3

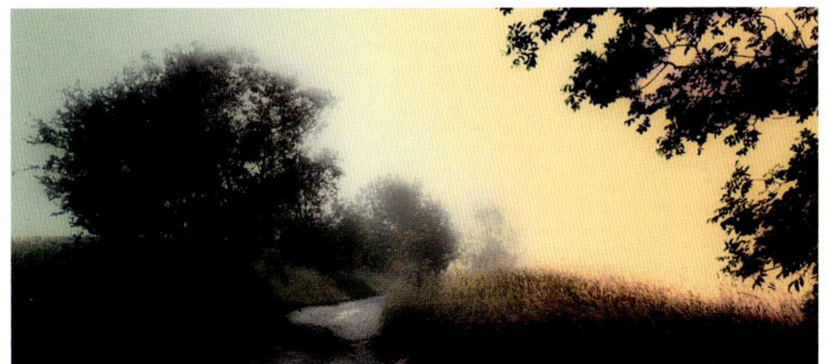

1 The original source photograph for the painting, "Hill."

2 A digital sketch is made based on the original photograph. Major adjustments have been made to the direction of the road and to the leaves and branches on the right hand side. The digital sketch is cropped into the correct proportions.

3 The digital sketch with adjustments to the grain, the exposure and the tone of the image.

4 Final digital sketch with colour added and tree branches highlighted, ready for transferring to the canvas.

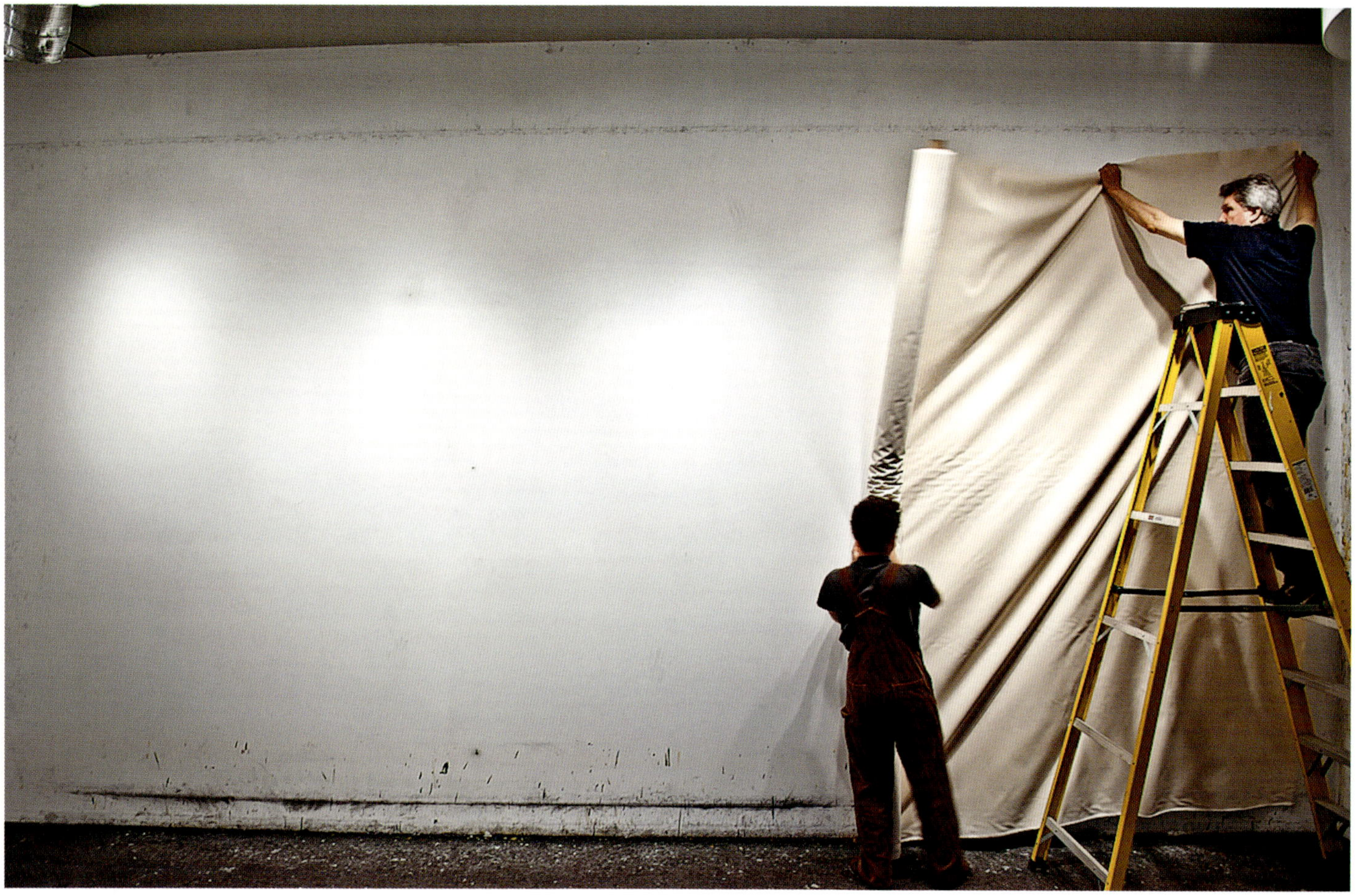

5. Unrolling the canvas.

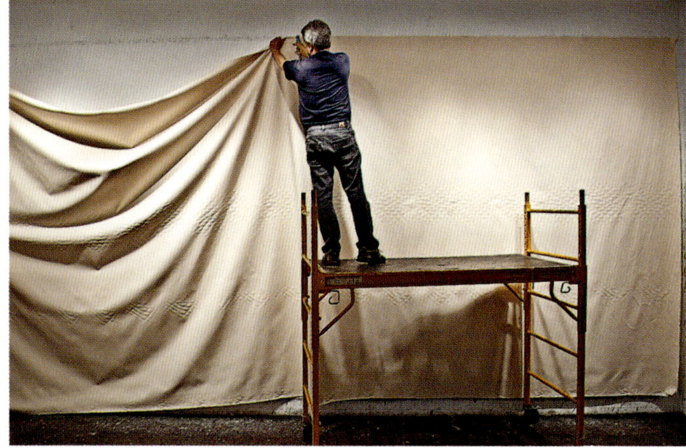

6. Attaching the canvas to the studio wall.

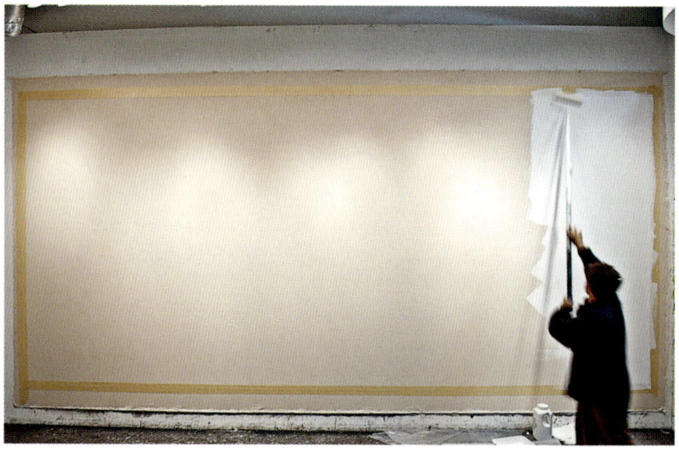

7. Applying the first coat of gesso.

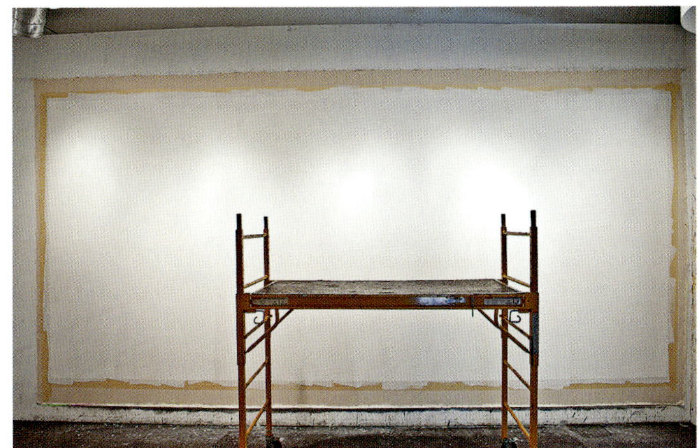

8. The gessoed canvas, sanded and ready for the charcoal.

9. A grid is created to help transfer the composition from the small digital sketch to the full size canvas.

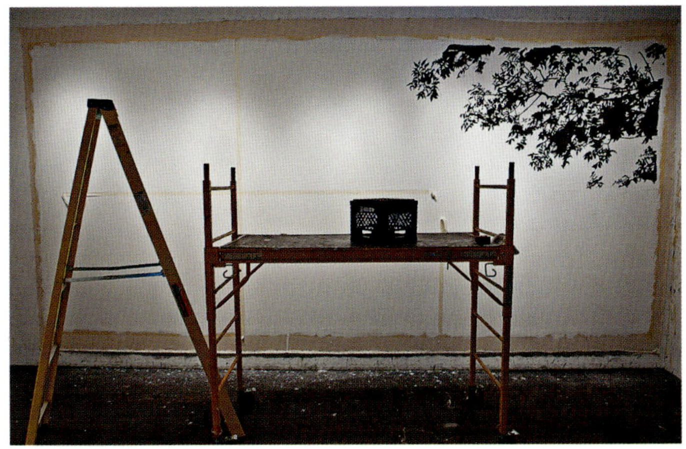

10. The initial application of charcoal defines the composition in the first grid section.

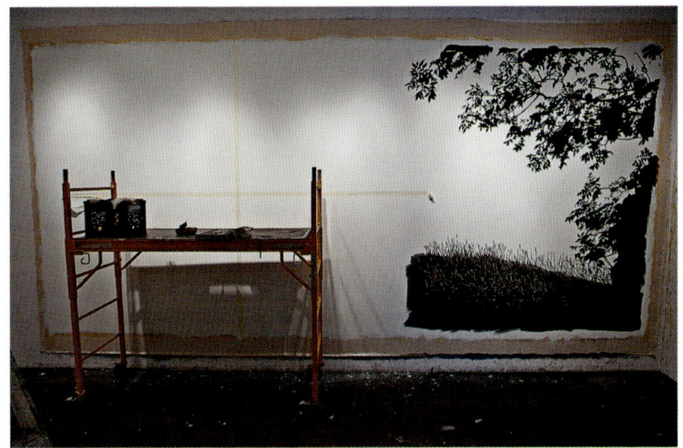

11. The branch section and lower foreground grass area is now blocked in with charcoal.

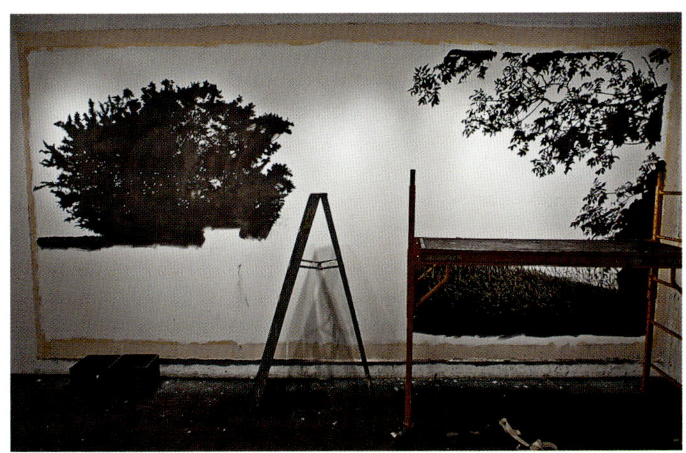

12. The charcoal application is continued across the entire canvas

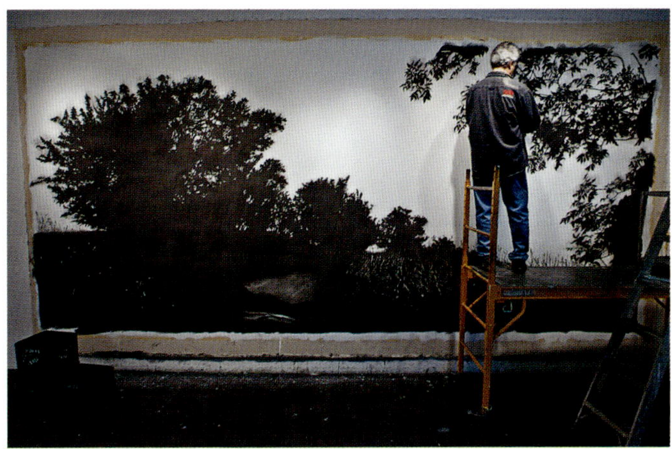

13. With all of the charcoal applied, the drawing is shaped and refined with erasers.

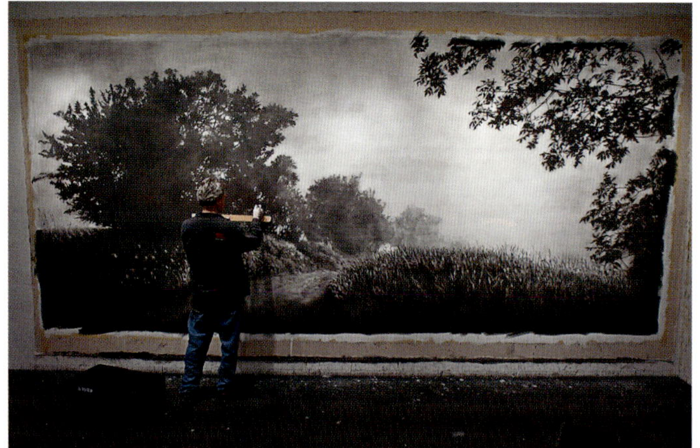

14. The last touches are put on the drawing layer.

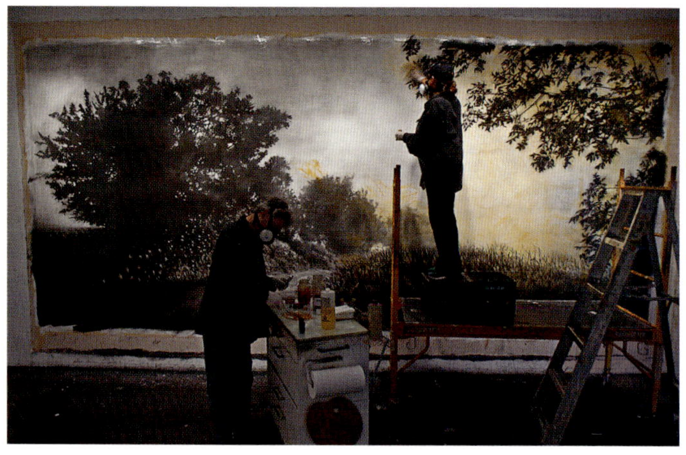

15. The first coat of coloured glaze is applied.

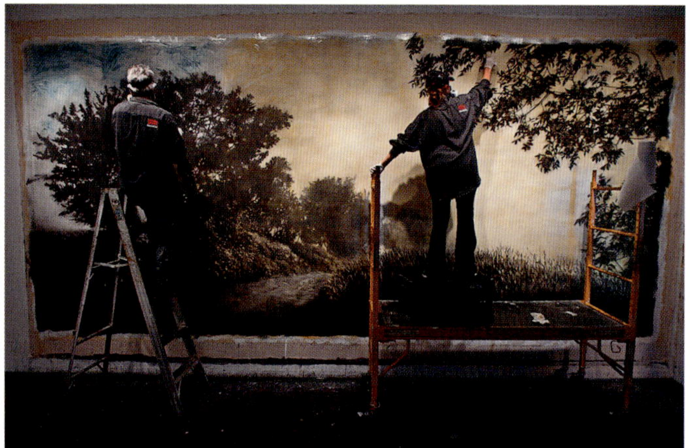

16. The second coat of glaze is applied

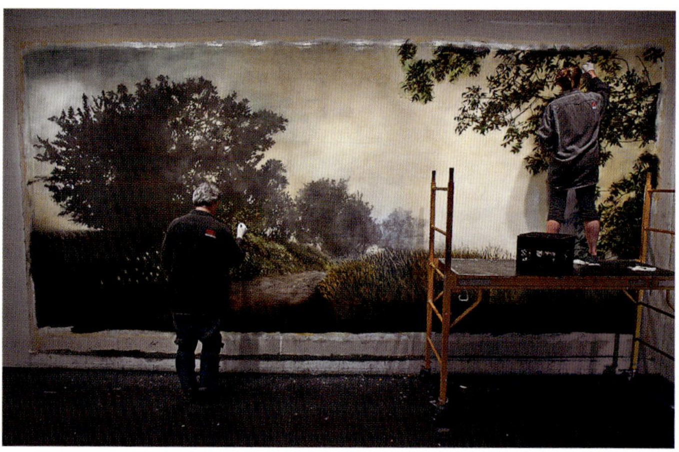

17. Local colour glazing is applied to the details.

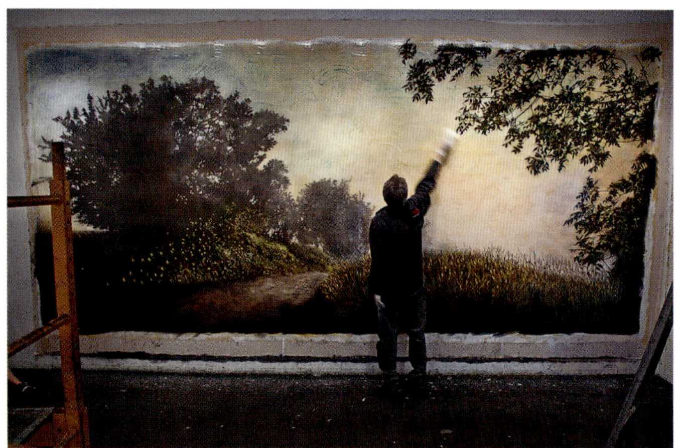

18. A third coat of glaze is applied over the entire surface.

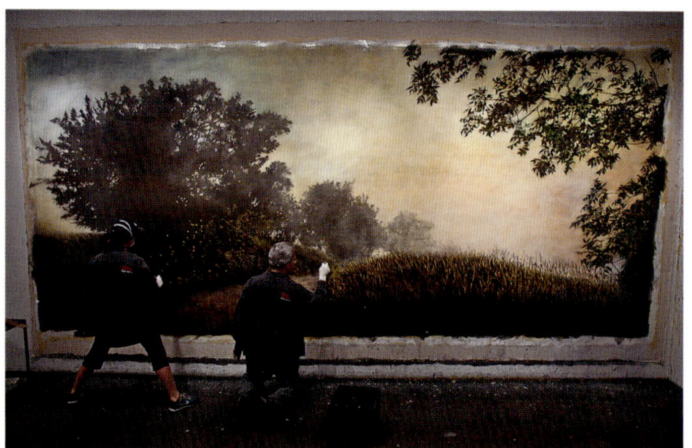

19. Spot glazing is added to the foreground grass areas.

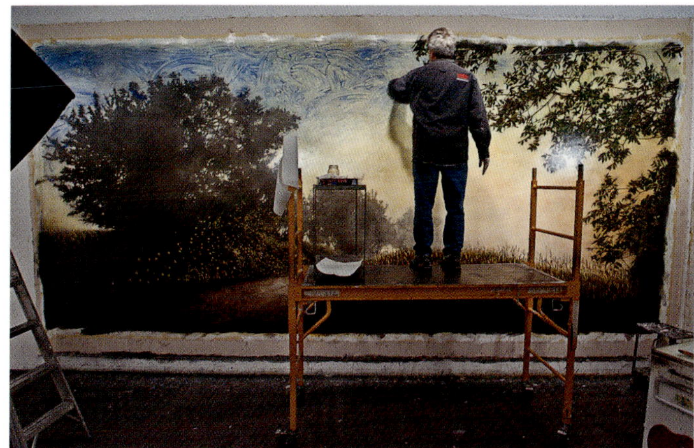

20. The fourth coat of glaze includes a major colour boost to the sky are..

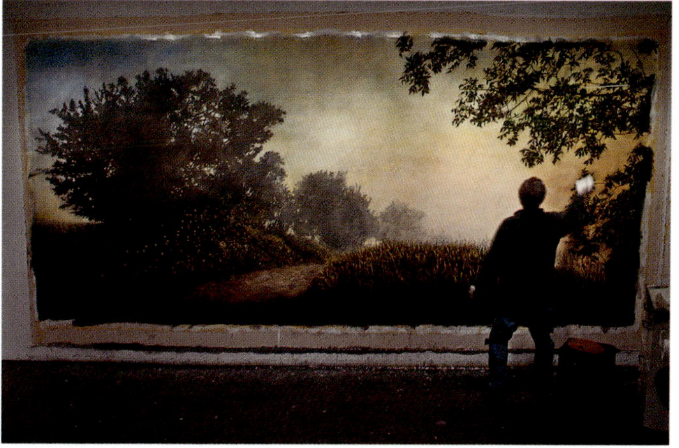

21. A fifth glaze brings back the warm tones.

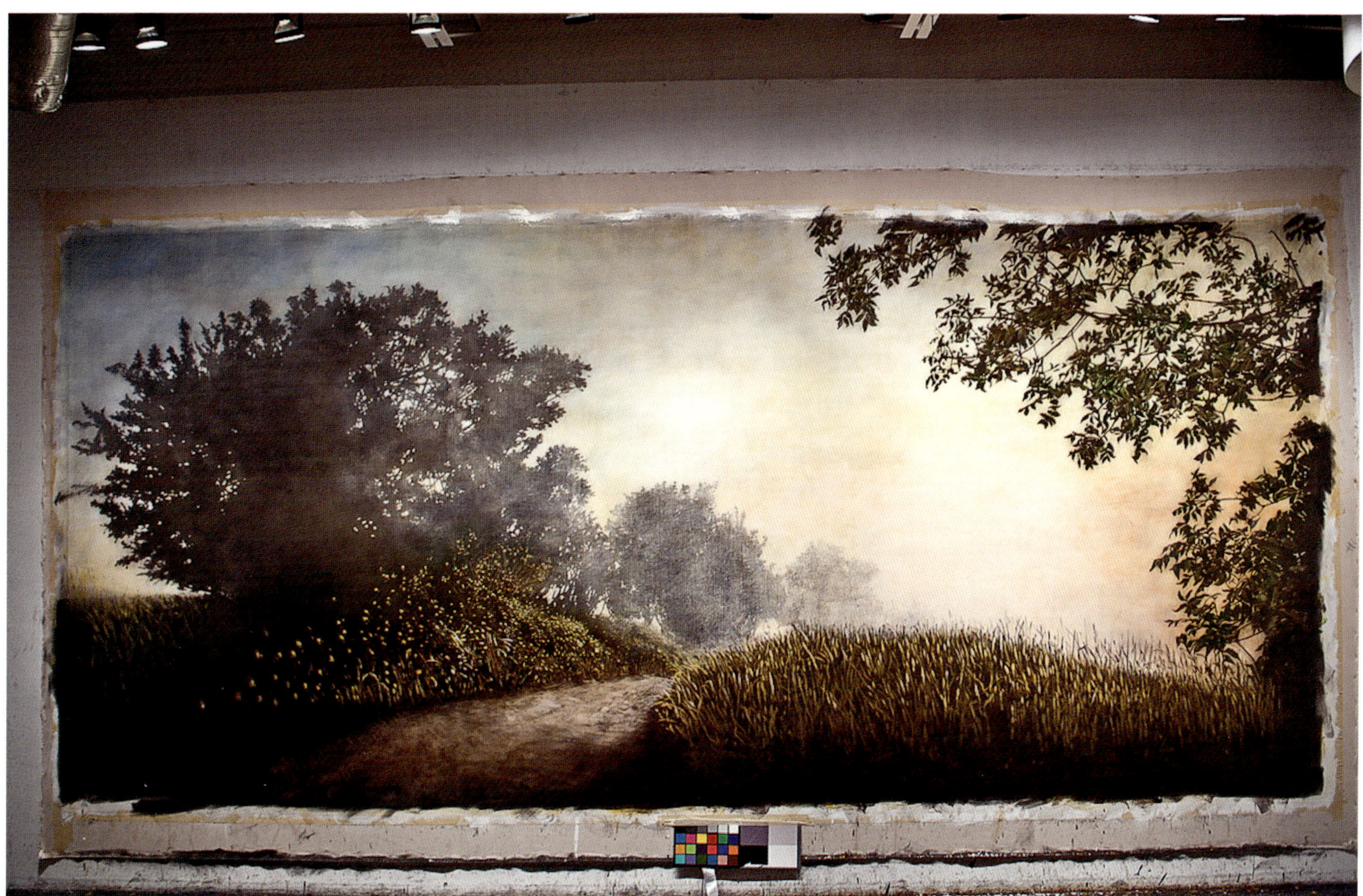

22. The painting is finished, ready to be photographed.

nostalgia because they aren't real themselves, merely flat images, and in experiencing them, we feel a "nostalgia" for the reality that they allude to, that they evoke. It's kind of like being nostalgic for the "present," in that we don't live in the moment directly without some sort of mediation, perhaps through technology or some social construct.

The work is also about the fundamental aspect of being alive: physically trapped in our bodies, in our world, on our planet, and yet having internal, subjective states of minds, full of memories and feelings that are clearly not part of a simple physical existence.

I am interested in why our human world is so full of despair, of tragedy, of hurt and loss, and yet how we still have such hope and expectation and such yearning for wholeness and completion. For me the work is about the gap that exists between us as unique individuals caught up in our own quotidian lives, and those overwhelming ideas such as "eternity" or "the end of time." How do we get from one to the other? From the everyday to the universal? My intention is to capture a moment that is unique yet eternal. For example, the light in the paintings is a light that casts shadows, and as such, it is a light "of the moment." It is also, however, the light of all time because essentially, it is an internal, subjective light and only bears slight resemblance to the light of the the natural world.

I think it is possible for the viewer to "get" these concepts, to understand and consider them, because the images are based on the common currency of photography — a currency that we, as a society, all use and share in our daily lives.

VV: So it's a vernacular language?

SH: Yes, absolutely. The work is not meant to be at all esoteric; it's not specialized or difficult to appreciate; it uses the everyday visual language of photography to make the work easily accessible. My strategy is to take the digital photographic image, re-work it in the computer — perhaps changing the composition, perhaps the shapes, the focus, the colour — and then to transfer the image as a pencil outline onto the canvas. The aspects and details that made that photograph specific to a particular time and place are now changed. At this point, when I make a fully realized charcoal drawing on the canvas, the image is generalized even more, so that instead of the image in *Tree* being a specific tree in a specific forest in a particular part of Dorset, England, for example, it could be a tree in any number of places throughout the world, and it could have existed in the past, or even exist as a potential tree in the future.

The conversation in and around the work, then, goes from a very specific, relational conversation based on a particular photograph to a very general conversation about the nature of, in this case, Tree.

VV: *So, an archetype.*

SH: Yes, in a way, an archetype.

VV: *We think of artists before the twentieth century as dealing with grand themes, big ideas — things that had a sense of gravitas and consequence. With respect to these large paintings, what in your estimation are the big ideas or the themes that are of importance within our contemporary culture? Is it possible in contemporary society to address big ideas now?*

SH: In the past, and as you suggested, before the twentieth century, big ideas most always implied big scale. I'm thinking of the religious themes of the Renaissance and the Baroque, and narrative art or history painting like that of David and Géricault in the eighteenth and nineteenth centuries. There seems to have been an equation between scale and importance.

With the scale of the paintings of *Landscapes for the End of Time,* I am thinking about the idea of the heroic, the monumental, not just for religious or political or social issues, but also for the notion of the "heroic landscape," if I can use that phrase. Church, Cole, and Bierstadt are nineteenth-century American artists who used enormous large-scale paintings to help express the vastness of the American west. Although I certainly don't share their interest in the sacredness of the wilderness or the essential transcendental aspect of our relationship with the natural world, I do share their predilection for equating scale and impact, of equating scale and import.

Messiaen, in his *Quartet for the End of Time,* raised the issue of the nature of time, of temporality, of eternity. In *Landscapes for the End of Time* I want to apply the same questioning to the visual ideas about the gap between specificity and generality, between a static scene and an enduring image, between a unique moment and an enduring reality and, most of all, between the time frame of an individual life and the idea of eternity.

As far as the heroic and monumental are concerned, I think that to raise questions about the nature of life itself, in our day and age, is in itself a heroic act. Well, perhaps "heroic" is overstating it, but at least raising fundamental questions about the nature of our world and our apprehension of it is an act of supreme importance. I want the large scale of the work to suggest that the questions the paintings raise are large issues, fundamental issues. If there is heroism here, or if there is anything heroic in these paintings, it is in the act of asking of the question, "What is the mystery that is life? What is the mystery that is beyond life?"

VV: *Are you suggesting that the conflation of a photo-based image with a painterly execution is a way of defining the tension that we feel as a society around some of the larger concepts, such as "How does one relate to the world we live in?" and "How do we reconcile humanity and nature, or that tension that always exists between technology and nature?" That's more of an observation than a question, but it seems that the work you've presented here is evocative of a variety of key elements of our contemporary culture. I mean, if Twitter and Facebook are, as McLuhan's theory would suggest, the medium for our current era and it's all about ego and it's all about promoting the self, then these paintings are in complete contrast to that because they ask the individual "How do you relate to the larger world?"*

SH: You know, Vince, in terms of my own work, I hadn't really considered the issue before of the relationship between technology and nature, but you are correct in pointing out that the use of a digital camera and a computer as mediating tools between my experience of nature and my expression, or my ideation of it, is certainly a way of distancing me from the natural world, much the same way that technology such as Twitter or Facebook is a way for others to relate through a technological filter. The difference, however, is quite vast in that Twitter and Facebook are tools at the service of social interac-

tion, while the camera and the computer have different interactive aspects, including personal as well as a social and cultural ones.

There was a time when my art practice began with pencil sketches, either directly from nature or from my own imaginings, and these were then turned into paintings. So I am quite aware that my current use of technology is a direct intervention into what was, at one time, a more direct connection with the source of the image. But over time, there have been a lot technological additions to my procedure. The digital camera provides me with raw material that I can adjust in almost any way I wish — from changing the exposure, to the colour balance, the hue, saturation, and on and on. Then there is the computer and the photo software that allow me to change the composition, sometimes quite radically, sometimes adding or subtracting elements, or changing the focus, or removing the colour and adding my own tints, and so on.

At that point, when I have something that I think will make a strong painting, I project the image onto the canvas, outline the shapes with a pencil and make a completed charcoal drawing without much further reference to the photo-based image. The colour is achieved through a series of colour glazes that are applied sequentially. The glazes, though, have more to do with my long experience with the graphic arts and four-colour offset lithography than they have to do with nineteenth-century oil glazing techniques. So, really, other than the charcoal drawing itself, most of my process owes a lot to contemporary technology.

VV: *Stephen, what compelled you to take on subject matter that is so philosophically expansive and to a certain degree unpopular within contemporary art practice?*

SH: You're right, Vince, in identifying landscape painting as unpopular. There does seem to be a big, collective sense of ennui around the whole genre — a sense that everything that could be said about landscape has already been said before. Of course for me that comment is off the mark in terms of what I am dealing with, because with this body of work there is a direct link between ideas that deal with the mystery of life, the nature of time and so on, and the use of landscape images as a context within which these ideas can be worked out.

If one takes the work at face value and describes what one sees in the paintings, I think one would find a number of elements that characterize all of them. For instance, there are no people in the landscapes, nor are there any particular items or views that could situate the painting as being a view of a specific locale or place. The roads all disappear without resolution, around a bend or over a hill. The light that imbues the scene is hard to define. What time of day is it? What season? So, with few clues as to locale, we are led into describing the elements in the painting in more general terms. They can all be described as representing a type of place, although it is more difficult to describe them as representing a particular place since the specific referents have been replaced by more generalised forms. So what we have, then, in these landscapes are images that are difficult to talk about without resorting to a language that includes concepts and ideas outside of a casual discussion.

To use the same example again, if one tries to describe *Tree,* one has to talk about its nature and about its form, since it is not at all clear what type or species of tree it is. I think it soon becomes clear that the tree in this painting can be more easily talked about in terms of the tree as a reference to other trees, perhaps as a symbol of trees in general, not as a particular species in a particular geographic place at a specific time of day.

The paintings themselves tend to lead into a discussion about the nature of our perception, into thoughts about the nature of our apprehension of the world around us, and towards a discussion of how we represent and understand our world.

Another way to answer that question would be to suggest that I am more interested in "why" questions than in "how" or "where" questions. Certainly in terms of my art practice, the most compelling conversation I can have through my work is dealing with what lies beneath, or behind, or within the objective aspect of the world. It is a fundamental question. Perhaps what compounds the problem is that the images I have chosen for this conversation are landscape images, so there is a double jeopardy at play in that not only are they not part of contemporary art parlance, but they fall into the no-man's-land of a genre that has been dismissed for its lack of relevance in our contemporary world. My sense is that landscape painting is perceived as a backward art form, a rearguard activity at best.

Of course, that is not my view of things. Landscape imagery is a perfect vehicle for considerations of eternity, of timelessness, of, if you like, seeing time as a continuity, not as a tripartite division into past, present and future. The myth of eternity is as old as conceptual thought itself, and a recent iteration — recent, at least, in terms of historical thought — is the idea of Arcadia, an idyllic place where humans and nature coexist in equal balance. Arcadia, as painted by Poussin in *Les Bergers d'Arcadie* (1647) is an example of this type of idealised landscape. And yet, in that painting, the shepherds are looking at a tombstone on which is inscribed the Latin phrase "Et in Arcadia ego" ("I, too, exist in Arcadia"). In spite of the idealized life in Arcadia where peace and joy reign supreme, even this will come to an end, will

end in death. There is no escaping the transitory nature of life.

Landscapes for the End of Time is a reconsideration of this notion, but brought up to date with current thinking about time, about parallel universes, about time travel, alternate realities and so on. When Messiaen wrote his *Quartet for the End of Time,* he was thinking about the Revelation of St. John and the Apocalypse. When I think about *Landscapes for the End of Time,* I think about the continuity of life as expressed in landscapes and landscape elements, all of which preceded the advent of humans, and undoubtedly will continue, in one form or another, after humans.

VV: *The term "memento mori" comes to mind. Do you see these paintings as documents at the end of time, or are they a punctuation?*

SH: A memento mori is a reminder or contemplation of death. This is not a contemplation of death but a contemplation of continuity. So in, a sense, they are the opposite of death, or at least the opposite of physical death. Eternity is not the end; it's a continuation.

VV: *The calm before the storm?*

SH: I think the phrase "The End of Time" assumes "The Beginning of Time," which suggests that since time is a construct, there can be something that is outside of this construct and therefore outside of time itself. To be outside of time is different than having time end.

VV: *Time as we know it.*

SH: Time as our ego knows it because without the ego there is no identity, without identity there is no self, without self there is no individuation, and without individuation, there's only eternity.

VV: *The abyss?*

SH: The abyss. Eternity.

VV: *When you are making the paintings and the videos, it's partly about process, partly about concept. How do you come up with a cohesive image or a series of images that somehow relate?*

SH: Perhaps I am looking for an understanding that resides just outside of our ken. The ineffable. The interstitial area between knowledge and belief, between hope and despair, and in my paintings, between the light of the thin ochre glazes and the flat black of the charcoal. For me it's a question of bringing many things together at one time: an approachable image, an abstracted presentation, memory, emotion, and perceptual intelligence. The goal would be to create a spiritual ambiance within which dis-parate parts of the way we apprehend, understand, and remember the world can coalesce into something more than the sum of its parts.

VV: *So, after viewing these works — the videos and the huge paintings — what does one does come away with?*

SH: Well, perhaps one might come away with an acceptance that life is a mystery, and that within that mystery we are just a part, a small part, of the unknown.

VV: *But an aware part?*

SH: An aware part. Absolutely!

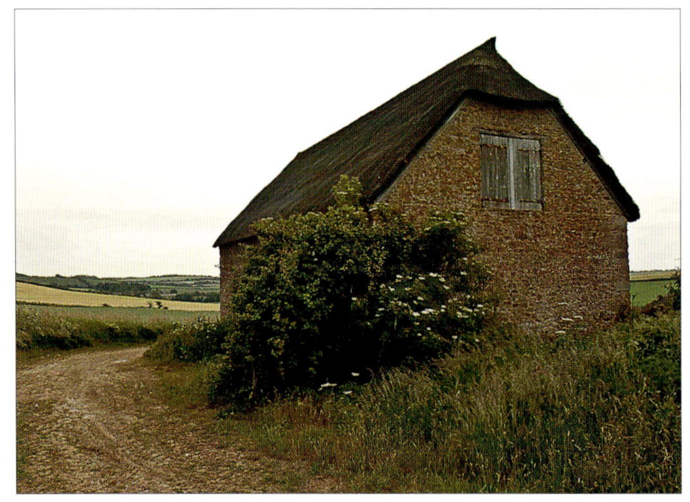

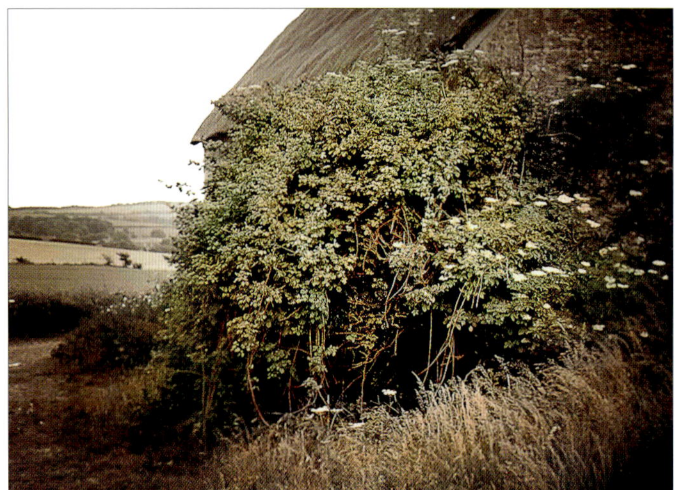

Landscapes for the End of Time video

The Bush

7 minutes, 50 seconds
Music composed by
Sebastian Hutchings

The two videos in the *Landscapes for the End of Time* exhibition address the issue of transformation, both literally and figuratively. Together with the paintings, they share the common theme that conflates the limited life span that we experience as individuals with our understanding of eternity. In both the paintings and the videos, the link between these two temporal "states" is through an allegorical reading of the natural world.

The Bush starts by gradually revealing a mediaeval barn emerging out of a pure white screen. We soon focus on the bush in front of the barn as it slowly fills the screen. In a series of soft and quiet changes, the bush assumes the colours and styles of a series of old photographs until we slowly zoom towards, and then into, the bush itself, the leaves and branches giving way to a single flower. The zoom explodes the flower into a puzzling, Mondrian-like pixelated mosaic that then dissolves into the pure white of the screen.

stills from the video, *The Bush,* 2011,

Landscapes for the End of Time video

The Boat

8 minutes, 30 seconds
Music composed and performed by
Sebastian Hutchings

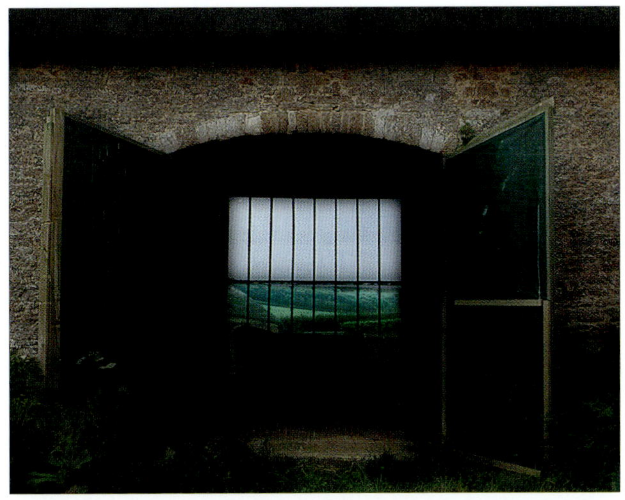

The Boat is a narrative journey that takes place in a barn where we discover an old boat lying on the straw-strewn floor; a rural landscape stretches beyond. The video takes the viewer around the boat as it "floats" in and out of mists, shadows, and pools of light. Our journey moves us through a stained glass window, through night and day, and eventually settles back to the the boat, a vessel alone, timeless and still.

The accompanying music for both videos was composed by Sebastian Hutchings. The musical score for *The Bush* utilises the same instruments that Messiaen used in his *Quartet for the End of Time* (piano trio plus clarinet); *The Boat* soundtrack features Sebastian performing his composition on solo piano.

Both pieces of music address the sound space that can exist between finite, physical objects and the unlimited dimensions inherent in a subjective interpretation of those objects, expressed musically through an ambient soundscape.

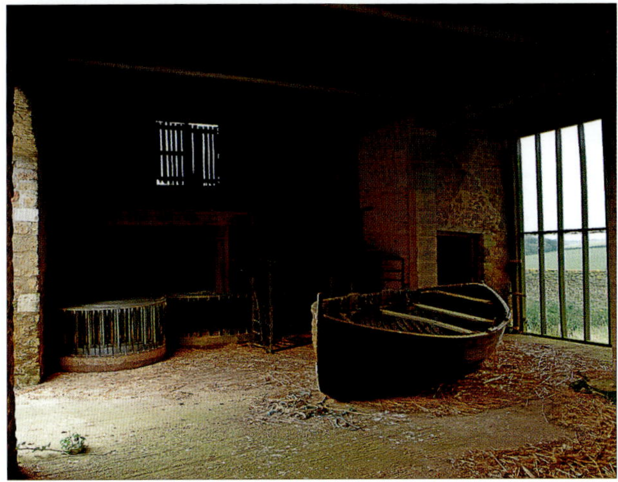

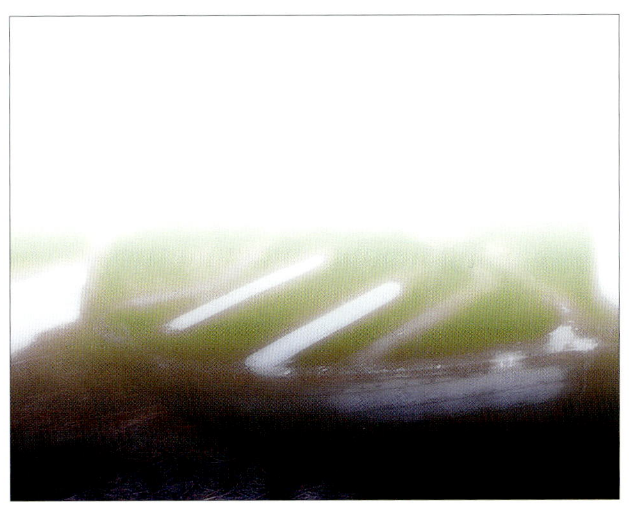

Gryphon Trio
Collaborative performances

During the summer of 2010, the Gryphon Trio, together with clarinetist James Campbell, performed Olivier Messiaen's *Quartet for the End of Time* while images of *Landscapes for the End of Time* were projected behind them.

The eight paintings were matched with the eight movements of the music by the Gryphon Trio during a visit to Hutchings's studio. It was decided to name the painting *Abyss* specifically for the difficult clarinet solo that comprises the third movement. Messaien's Quartet is in eight parts, correlating to the seven stages during which God is said to have created the earth. The eighth movement represented eternity. Here is the order of the movements in *Quatuor pour la fin du temps* (corresponding painting titles are in brackets):

I.   Liturgie de cristal *(Approach)*
II. Vocalise, pour l'Ange qui annonce la fin du temps *(Roads)*
III Abîme des oiseaux *(Abyss)*
IV. Intermède *(Branch)*
V.   Louange à l'Eternité de Jésus *(Hill)*
VI. Danse de la fureur, pour les sept trompettes   *(Tree)*
VII. Fouillis d'arcs-en-ciel, pour l'Ange qui annonce la fin du temps *(Grove)*
VIII. Louange à l'Immortalité de Jésus *(Sky)*

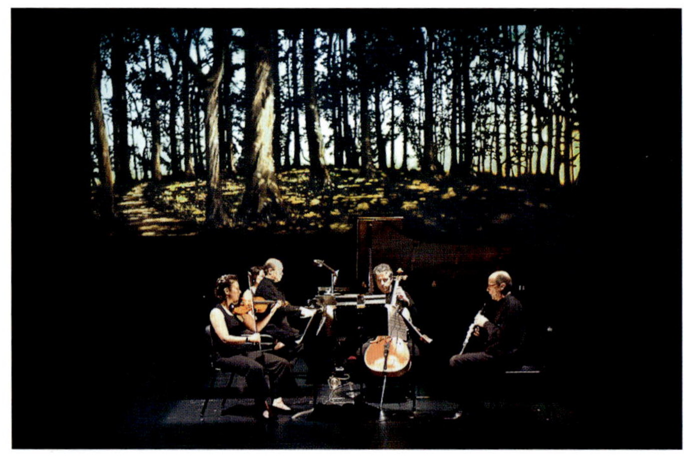

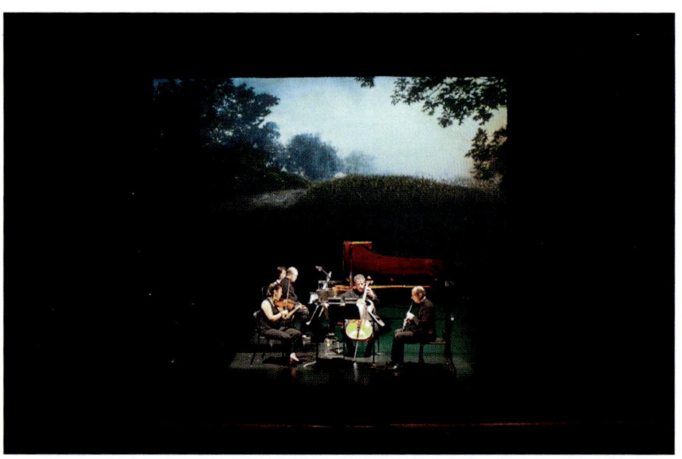

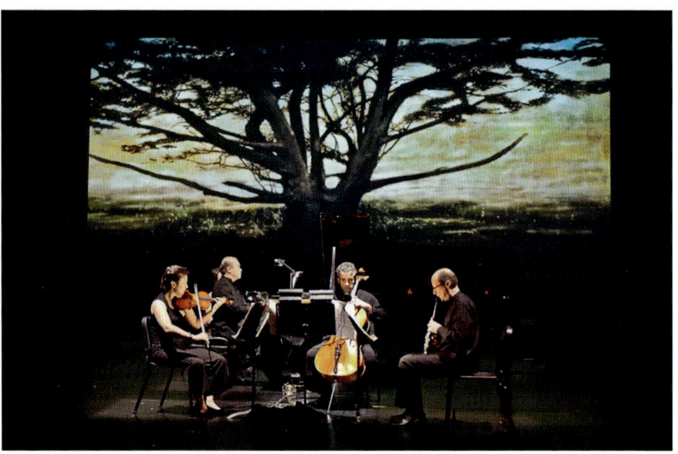

The Gryphon Trio (Annalee Patipatanakoon, violin; Roman Borys, cello; Jamie Parker, piano) and James Campbell, clarinet, performing *Quartet for the End of Time* at the Toronto Summer Music Festival, while images of the *Landscapes for the End of Time* paintings are projected on the wall behind them. August 2010

Playlist

Contemporary classical music is a significant factor in my work, not only because it creates a quasi soundtrack or auditory context, but also because I find that the themes, issues, structures and allusions of contemporary music substantially overlap with many of the iconographic, compositional and procedural issues that I incorporate into the production of my paintings and videos. Below are some of the pieces that have made a large contribution in this way.

— Stephen Hutchings

Composer	**Title (composition or album)**
John Adams	*Violin Concerto, Shaker Loops* (album)
Samuel Barber	*Knoxville, summer of 1915,* with Dawn Upshaw
	Complete Songs (Thomas Hampson and Cheryl Studer) (album)
Gavin Bryars	*South Downs*
	On Photography (album)
Martin Feldman	*Rothko Chapel* (album)
Osvaldo Golijov	*Ainadamar* (album)
Henryk Górecki	*Symphony no.3* (Symphony of Sorrowful Songs) (album)
Rachel Grimes	*Music for Egon Schiele* (album)
	Book of Leaves (album)
Christos Hatzis	*Constantinople,* with the Gryphon Trio (album)
Earl Kim	*Exercises en Route* (album)
David Lang	*The Little Matchstick Girl Passion* (album)
Gyorgy Ligeti	*Chamber Concerto for 13 Instrumentalists*
Ingram Marshall	*Kingdom Come* (includes *Fog Tropes II*)
Olivier Messiaen	*Quartet for the End of Time* (album) Myung-Whun Chung, piano
	Vingt Regards sur L'enfant Jesus (album) Pierre-Laurent Aimard, piano
Nico Muhly	*The Only Tune*
	A Good Understanding (album)
Arvo Pärt	*Alina*
Max Richter	*The Blue Notebook* (album)
	24 Postcards in Full Colour (album)
Ann Southam	*Pond Life* (album)
Valentin Silvestrov	*Silent Song* (album) Alexei Martinov and Alexei Lubimov, piano
	Leggiero, pesante (album)
	Requiem for Larissa (album)
	Der Bote (The Messenger) Jenny Lin, piano
Nadia Sirota (viola)	*First Things First* (album)
John Tavener	*The Protecting Veil*

PORTFOLIO OF PAINTINGS

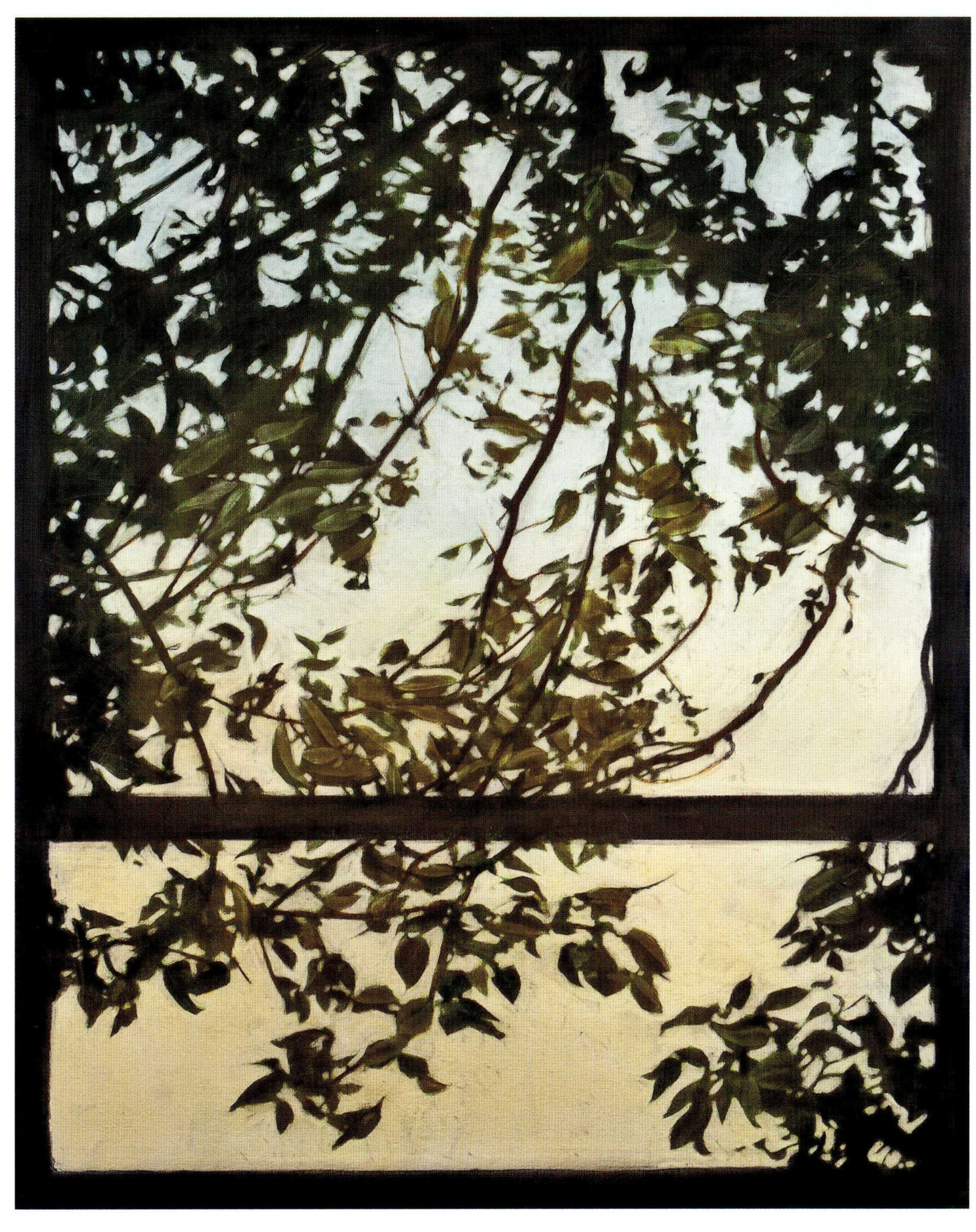

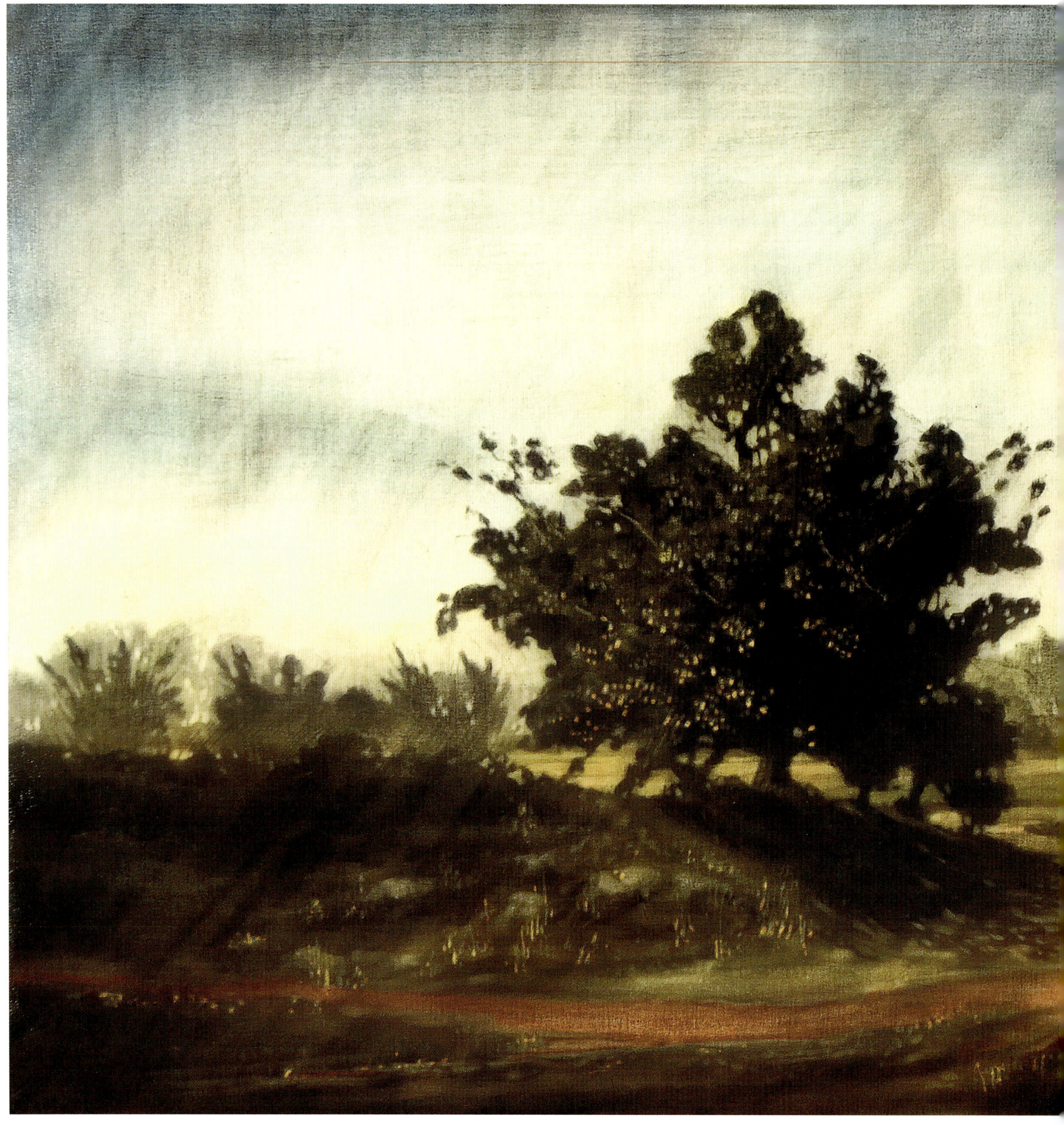

 Trees and path (after Corot), 2007, oil and charcoal on canvas, 36" x 72"

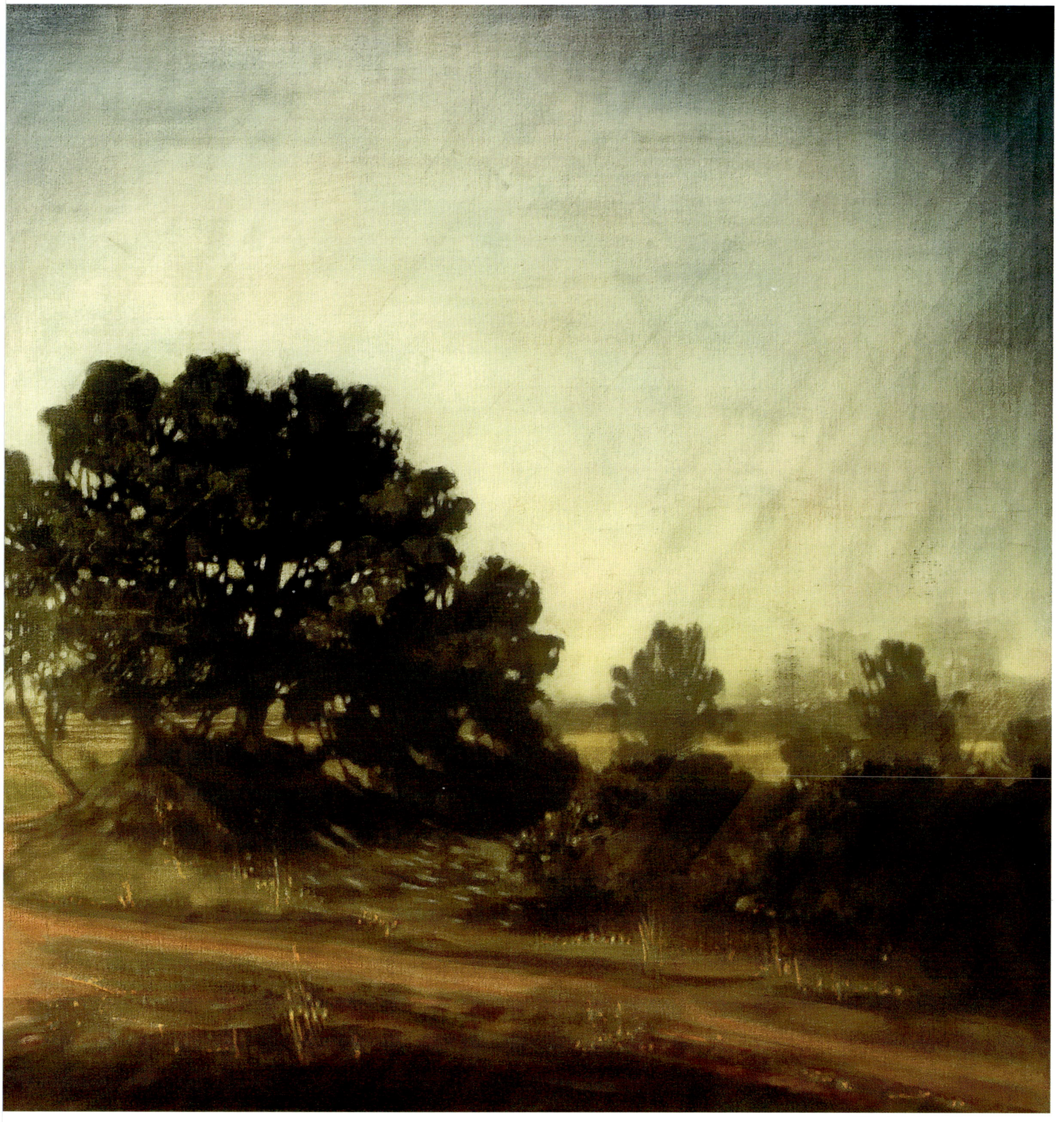

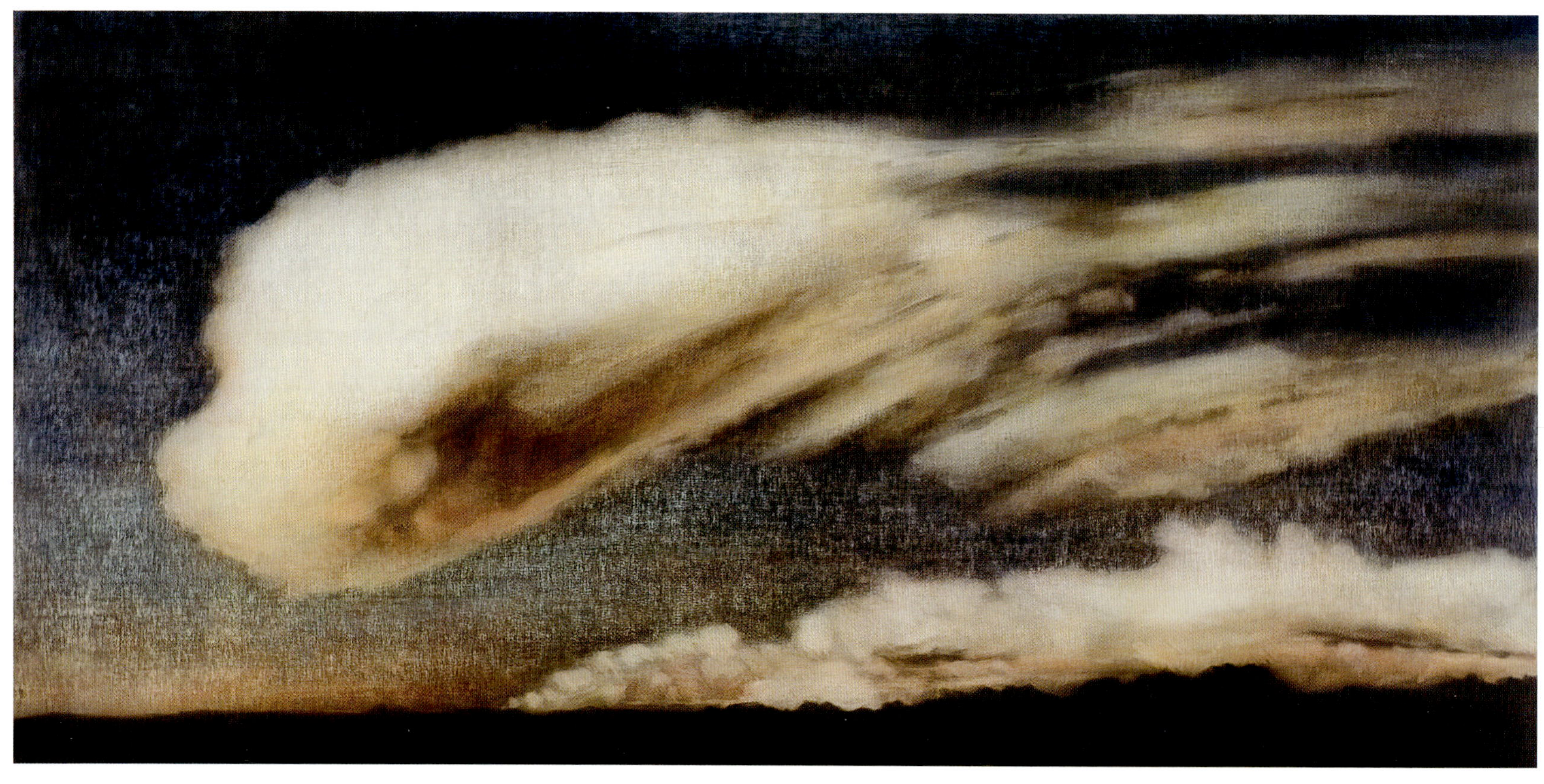

Falling Cloud, 2008, oil and charcoal on canvas, 36" x 72"

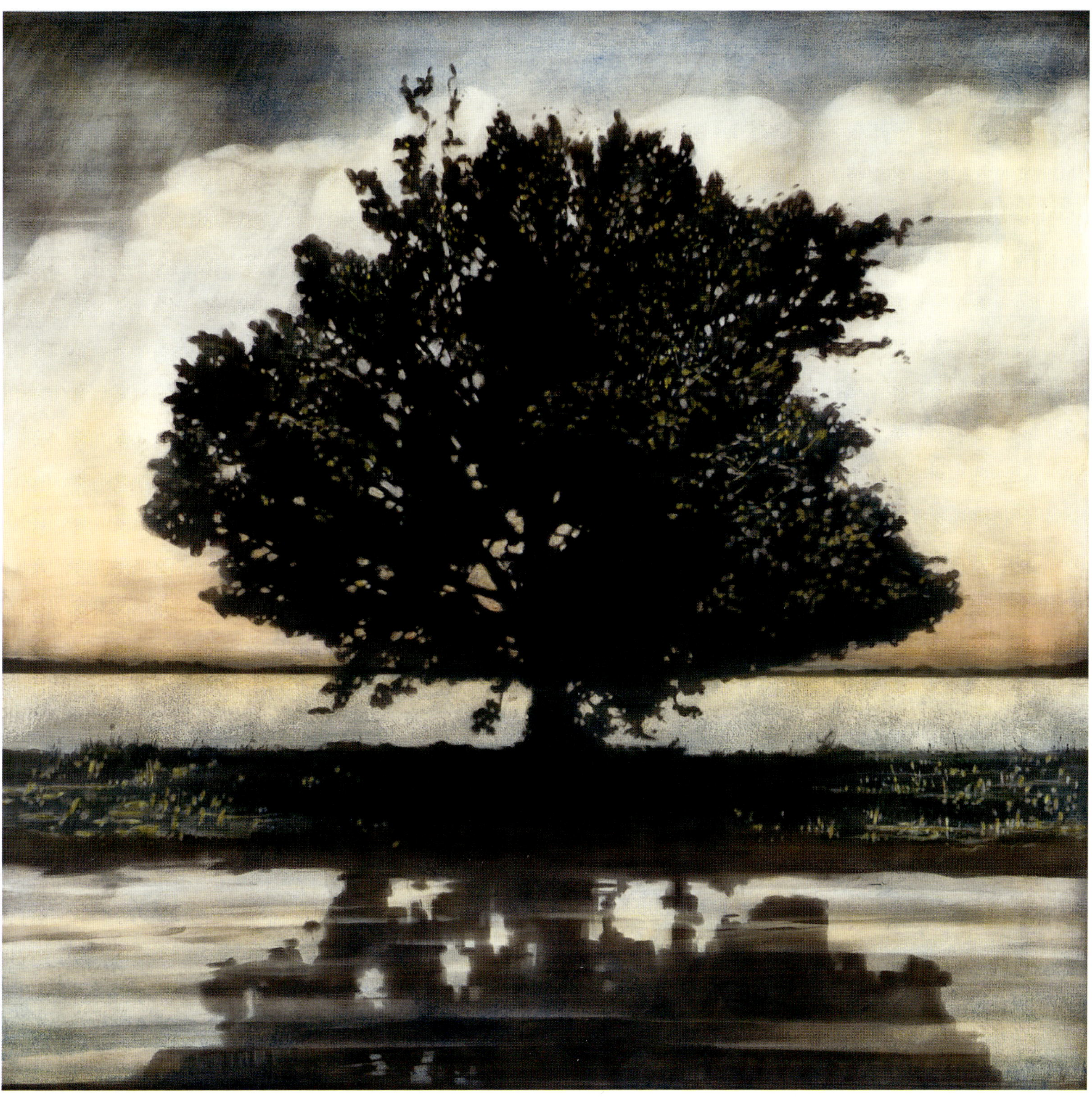

Tree with far shore and reflection, 2008, oil and charcoal on canvas, 72" x 72"

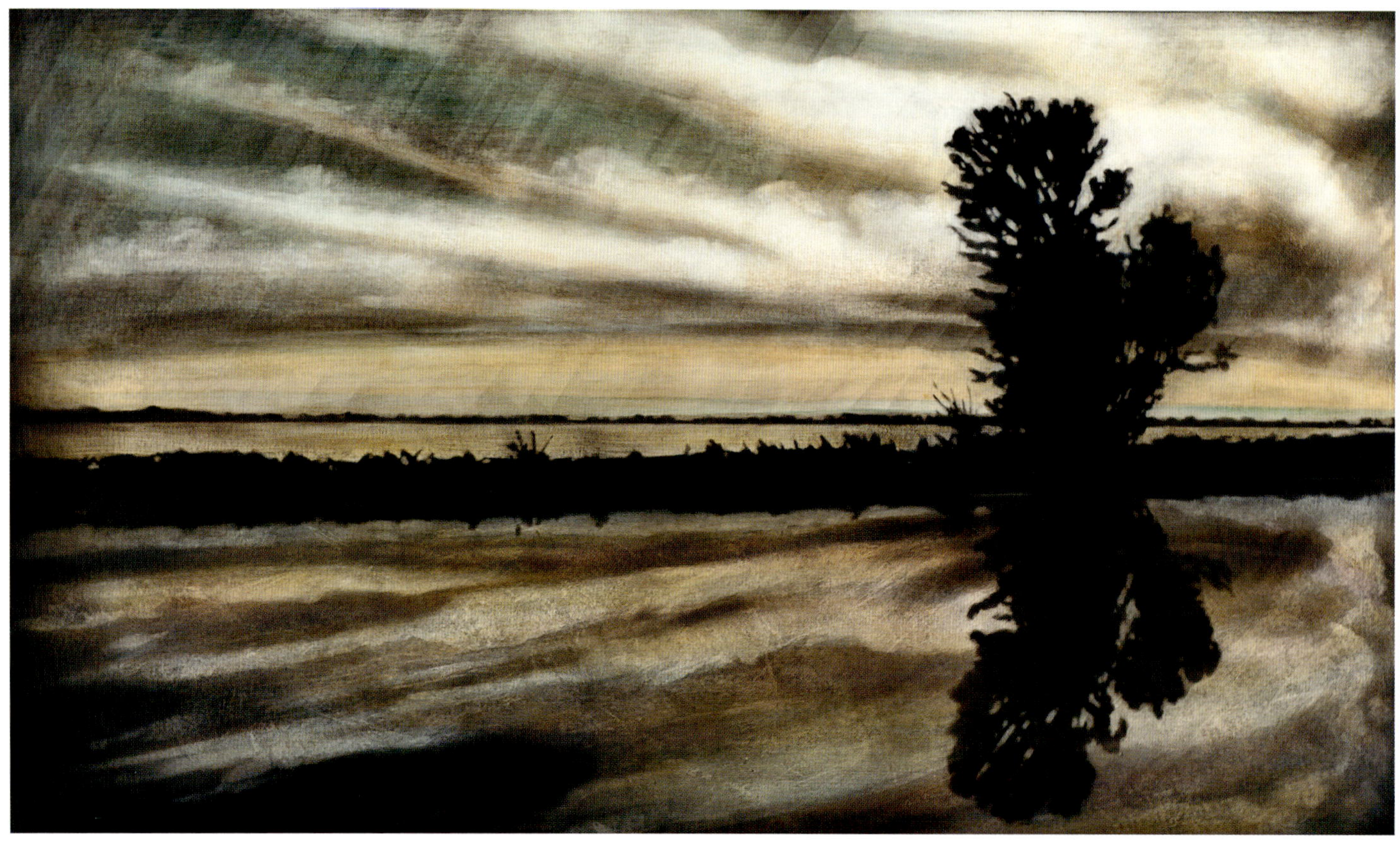

Landscape with tree and reflection 2008, oil and charcoal on canvas, 36" x 60"

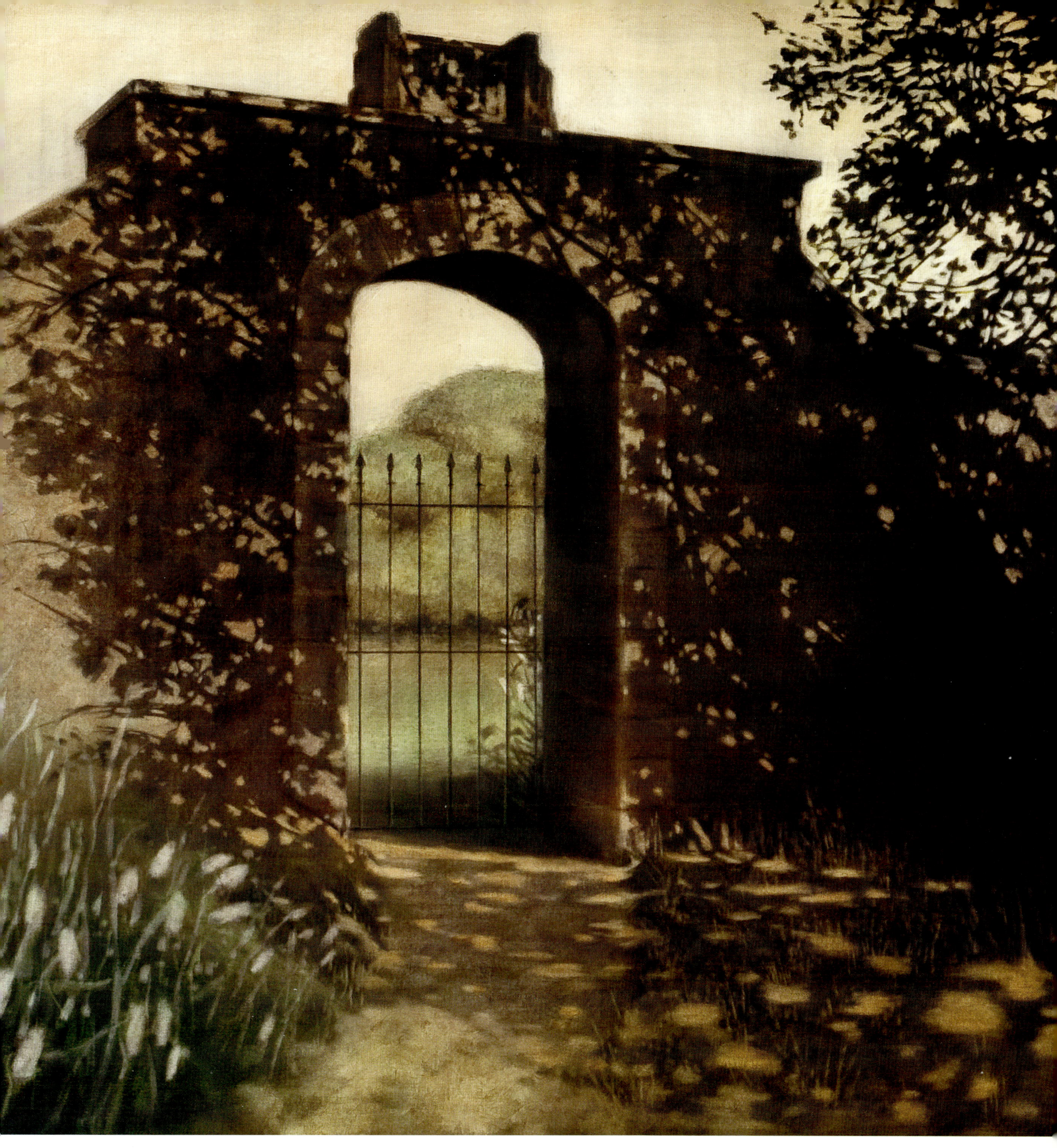

Landscape with gate 2009, oil and charcoal on canvas, 48" x 48"

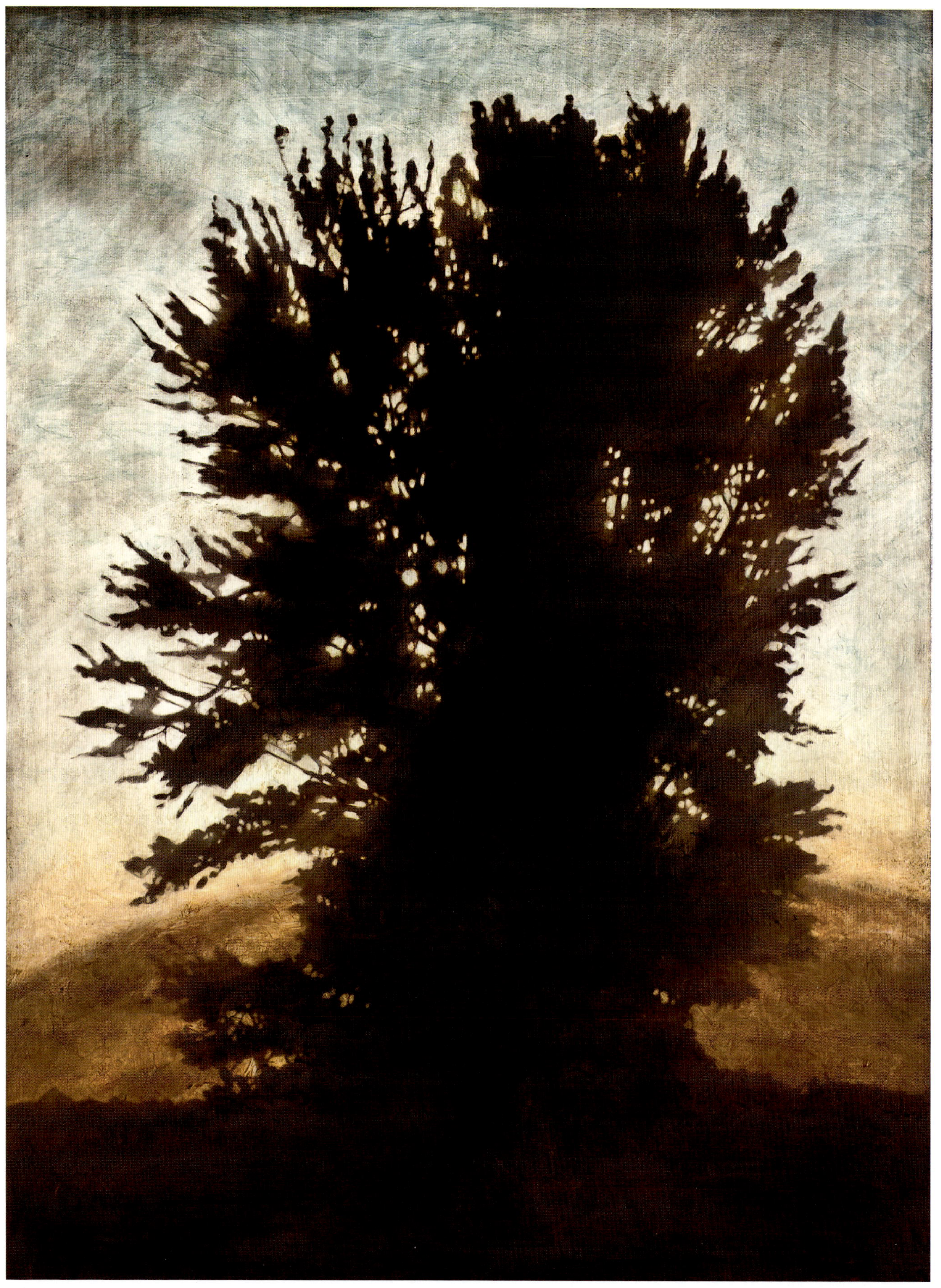

Tall tree, 2007, oil and charcoal on canvas, 84" x 64"

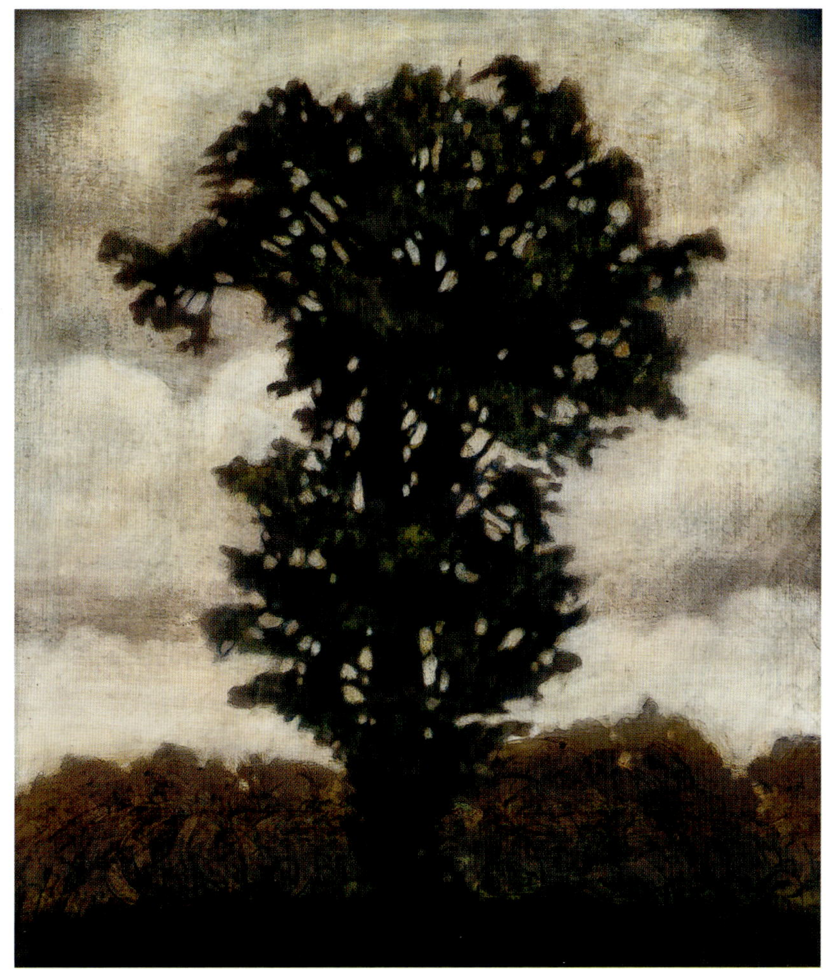

Tree with clouds, 2009, oil and charcoal on canvas, 24" x 20"

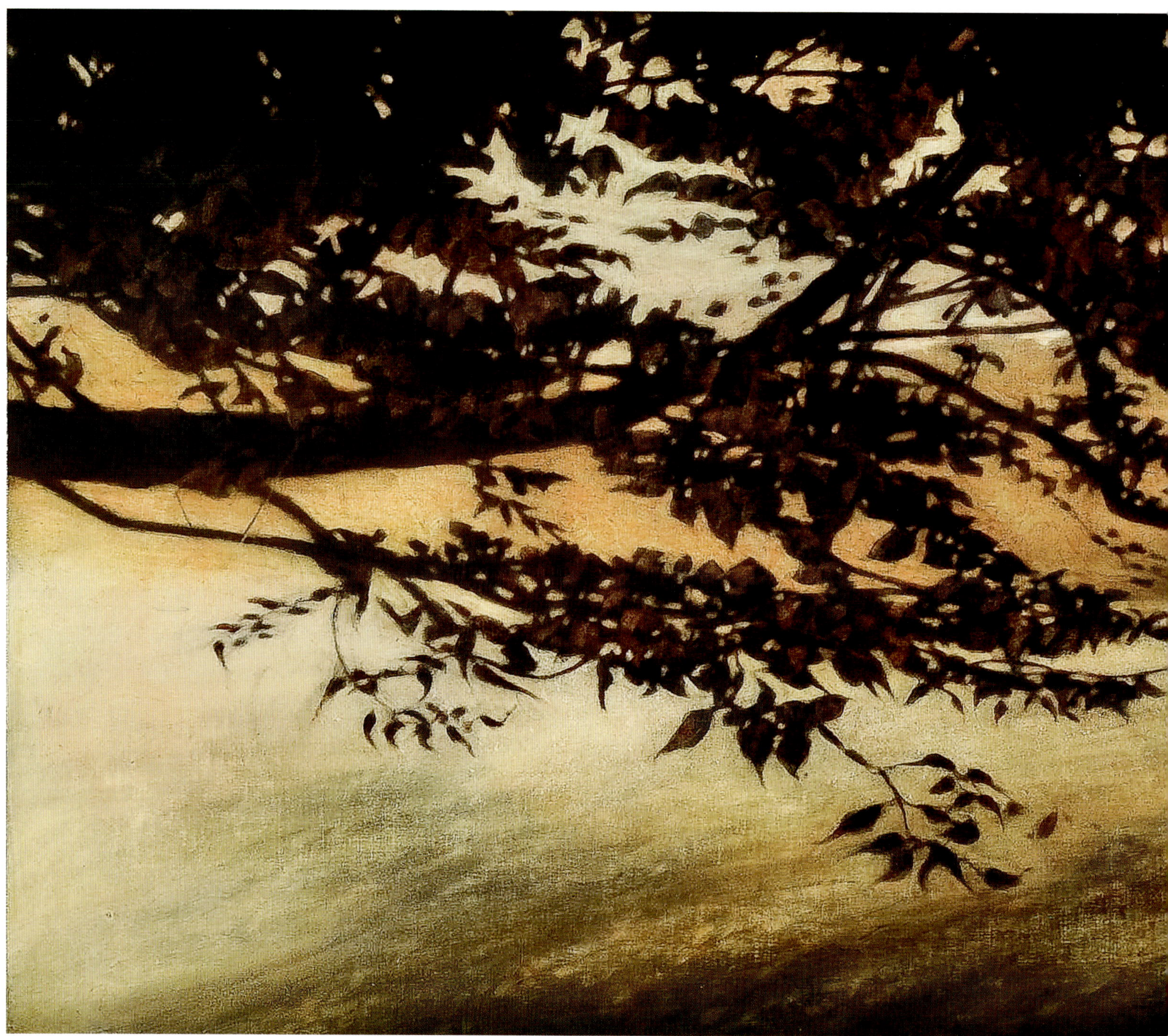

Branch extended over water, 2009, oil and charcoal on canvas, 30" x 72"

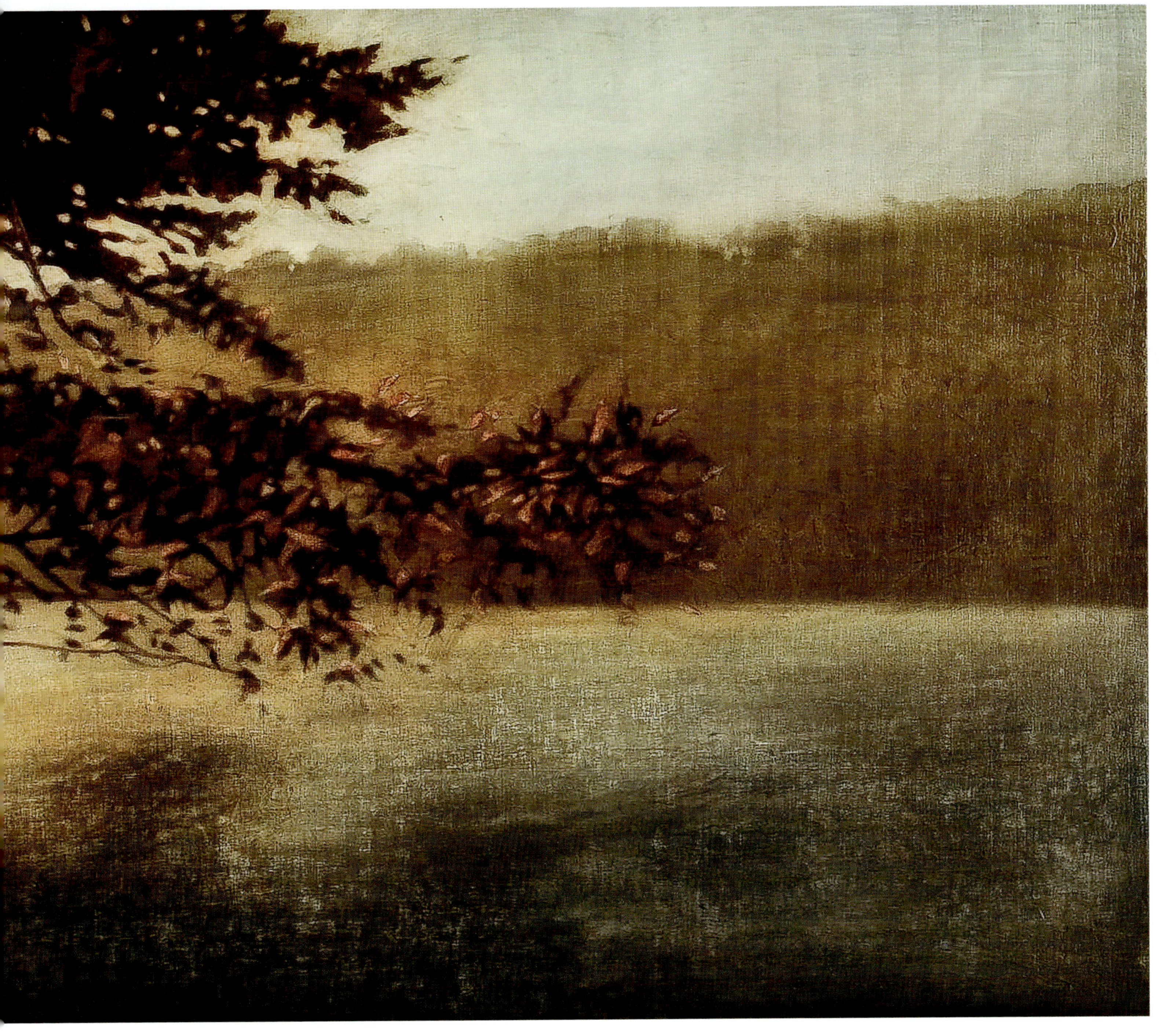

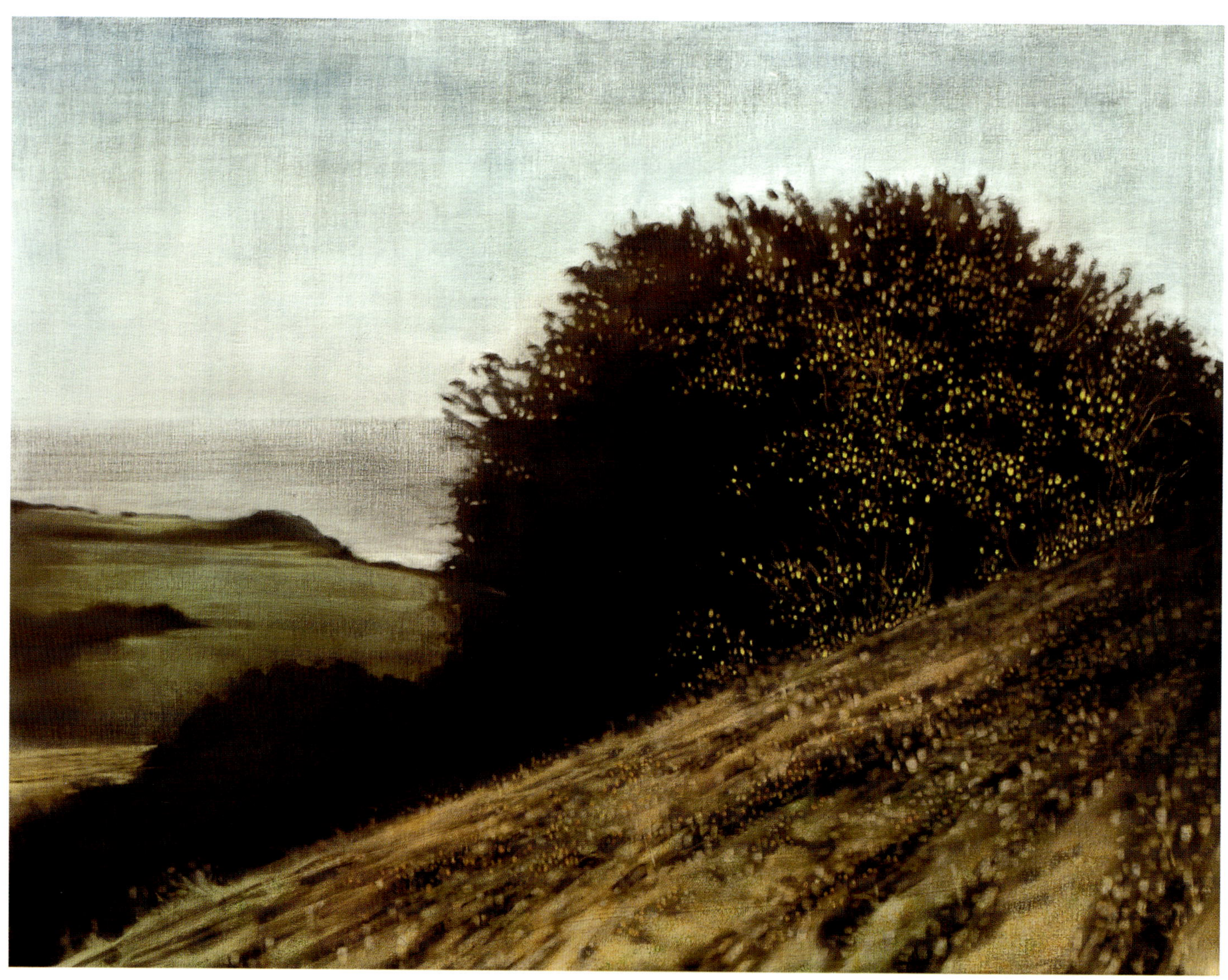

Landscape with bush, hill and ocean, 2010, oil and charcoal on canvas, 34" x 48"

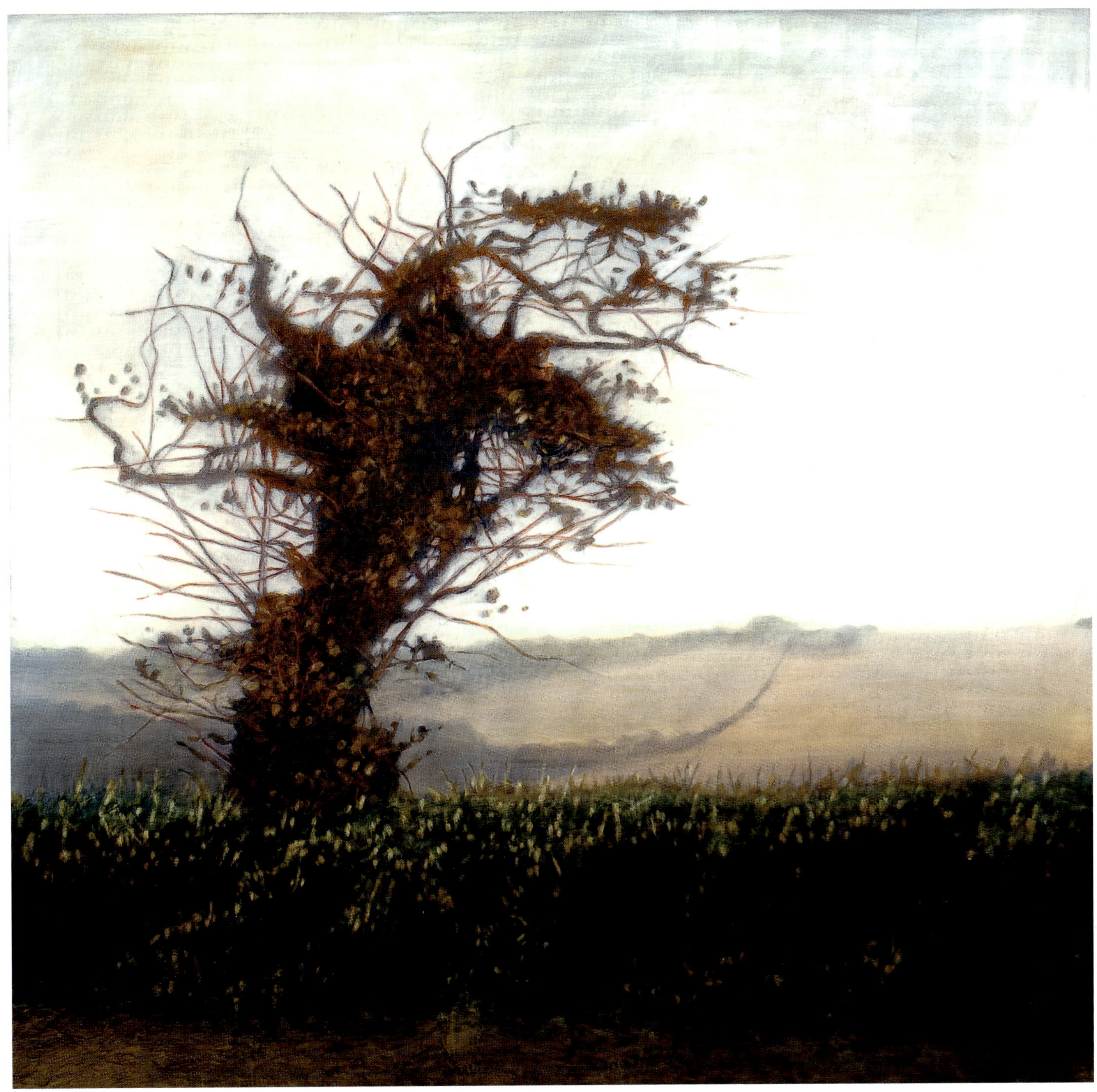

Misty landscape with single tree, 2009, oil and charcoal on canvas, 36" x 36"

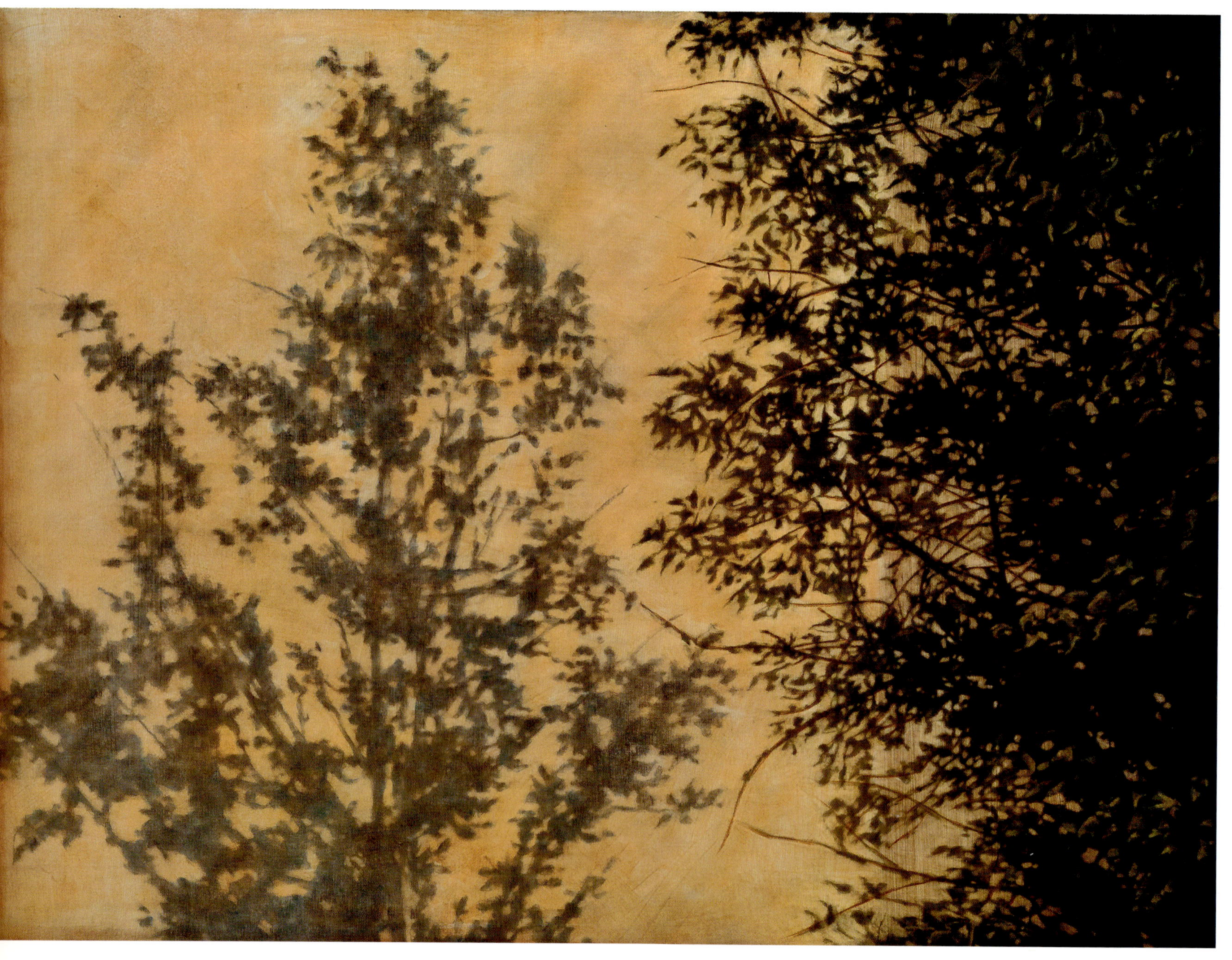

Tree with wall shadow #1, 2009 , oil and charcoal on canvas, 48" x 72"

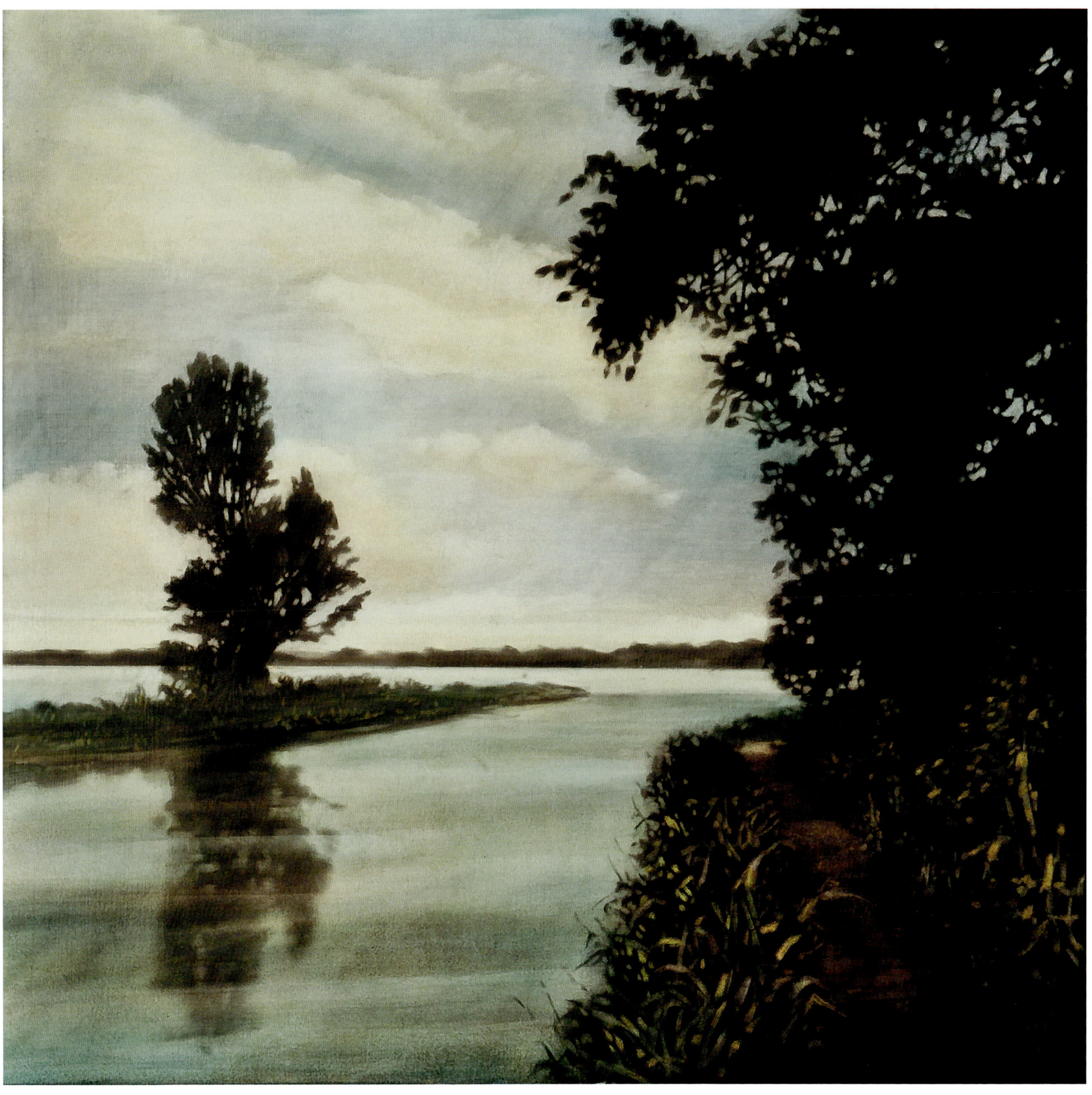

Landscape with far shore, 2009, oil and charcoal on canvas, 48" x 48"

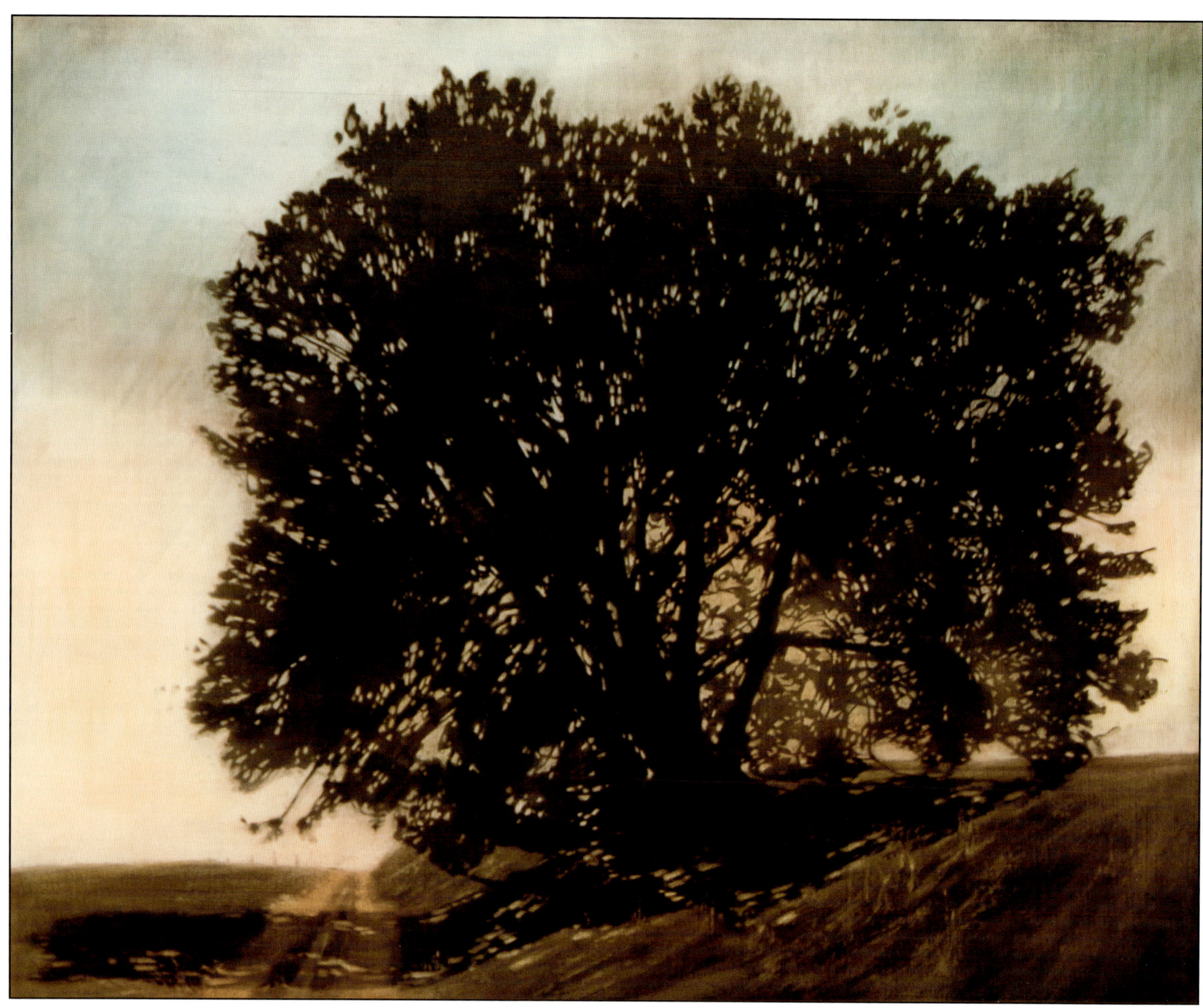

Towards Shadowland, 2007, oil and charcoal on canvas, 60" x 66"

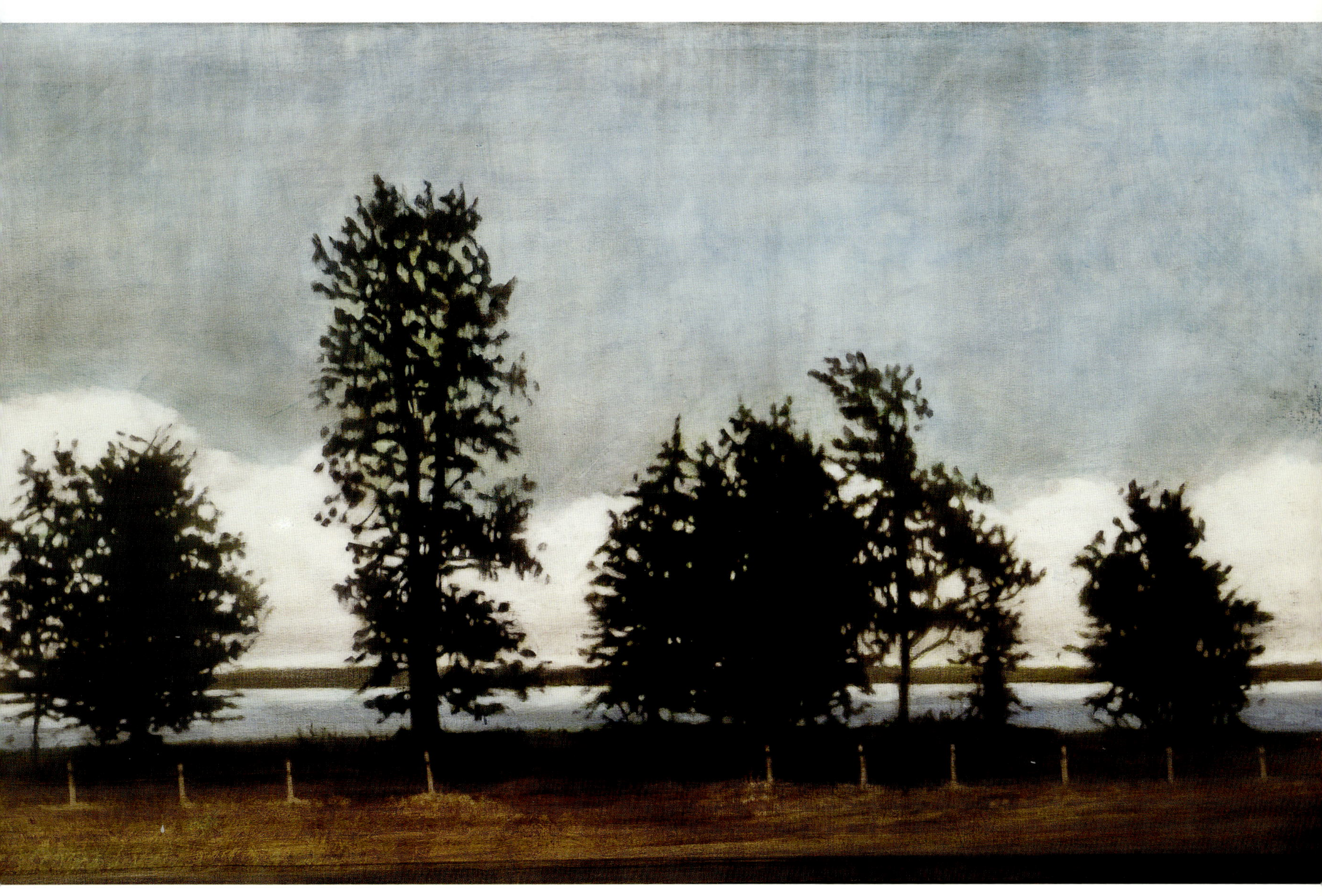

Lineup of trees and clouds , 2010, oil and charcoal on canvas, 32" x 48"

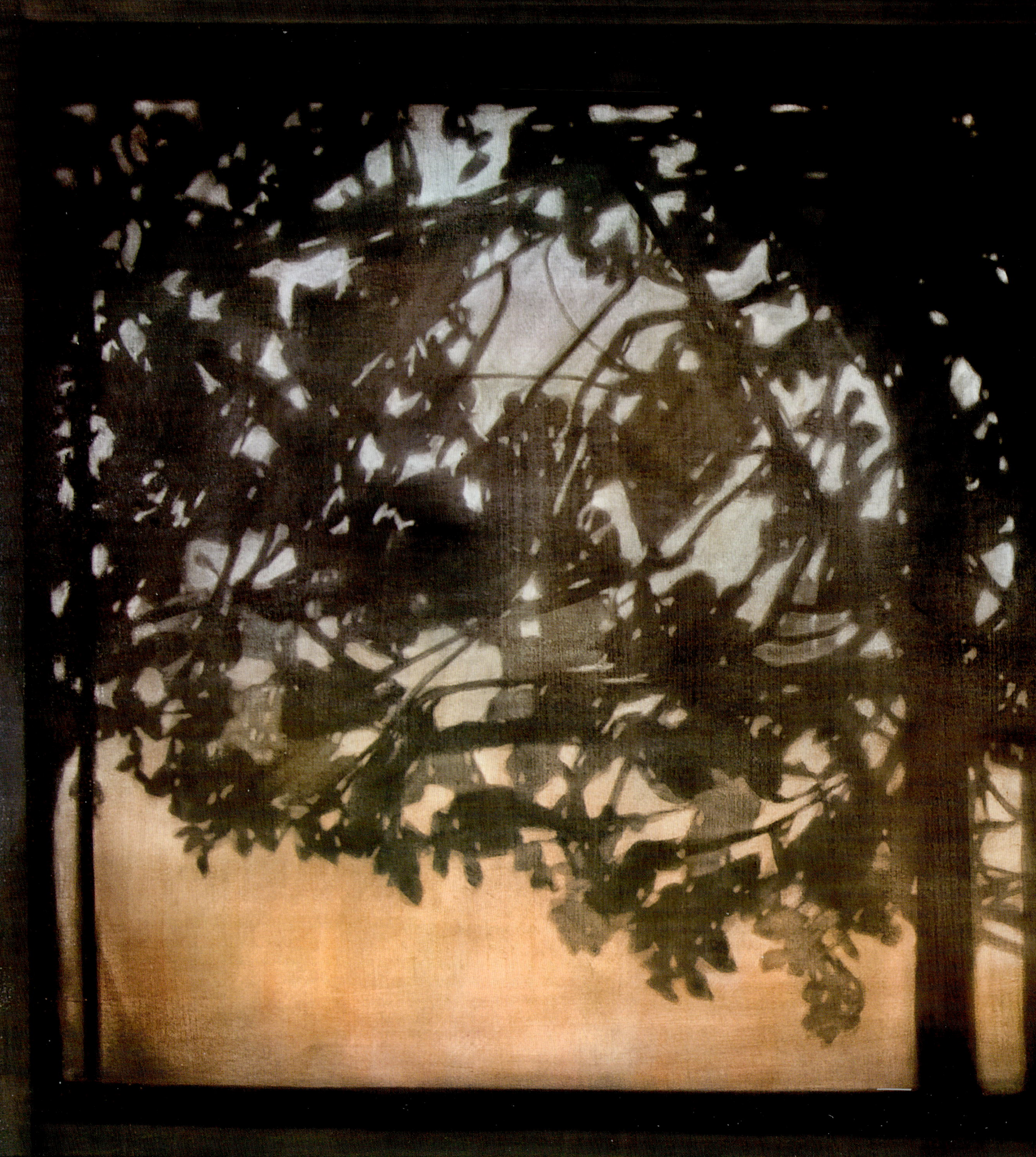

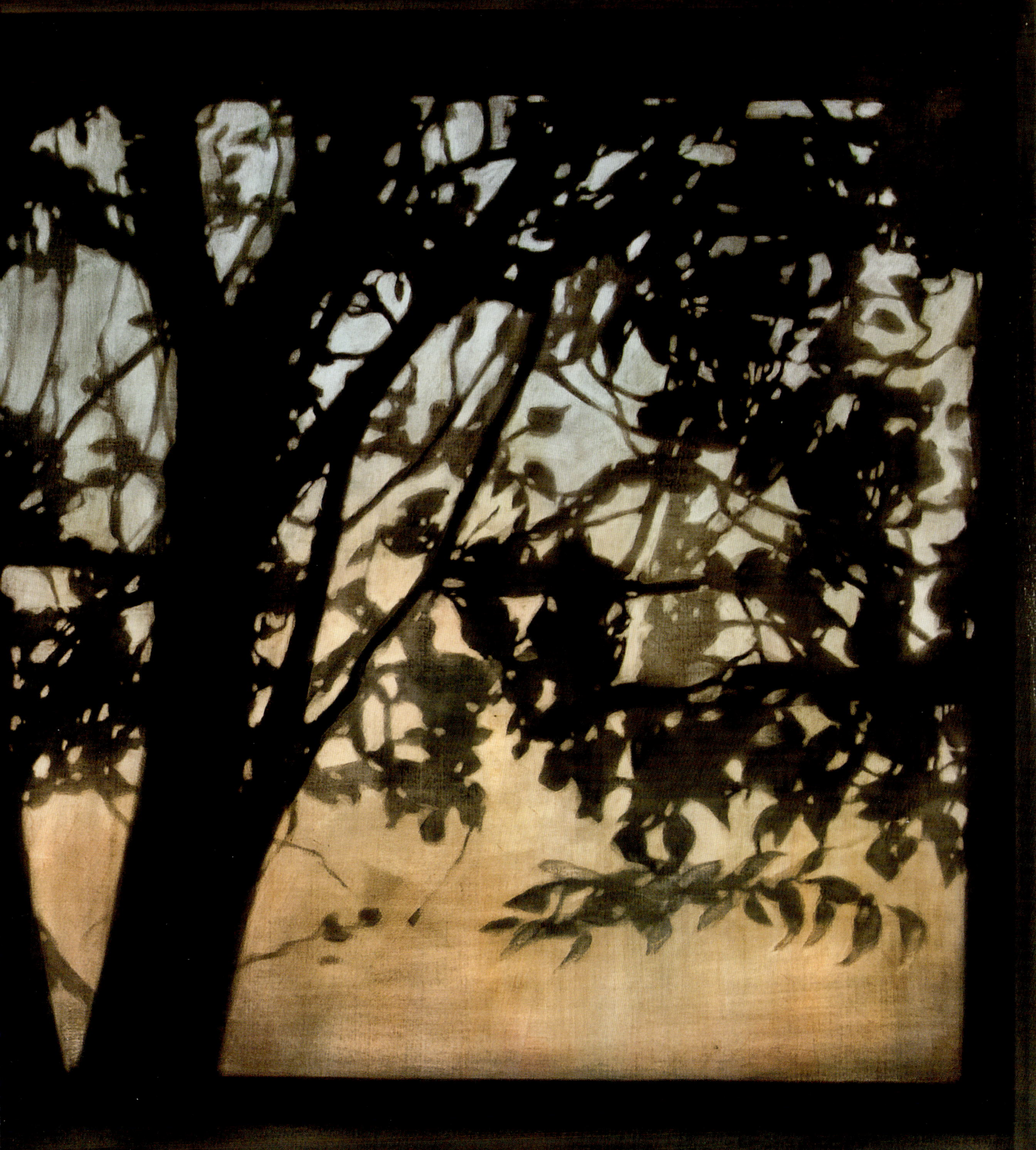

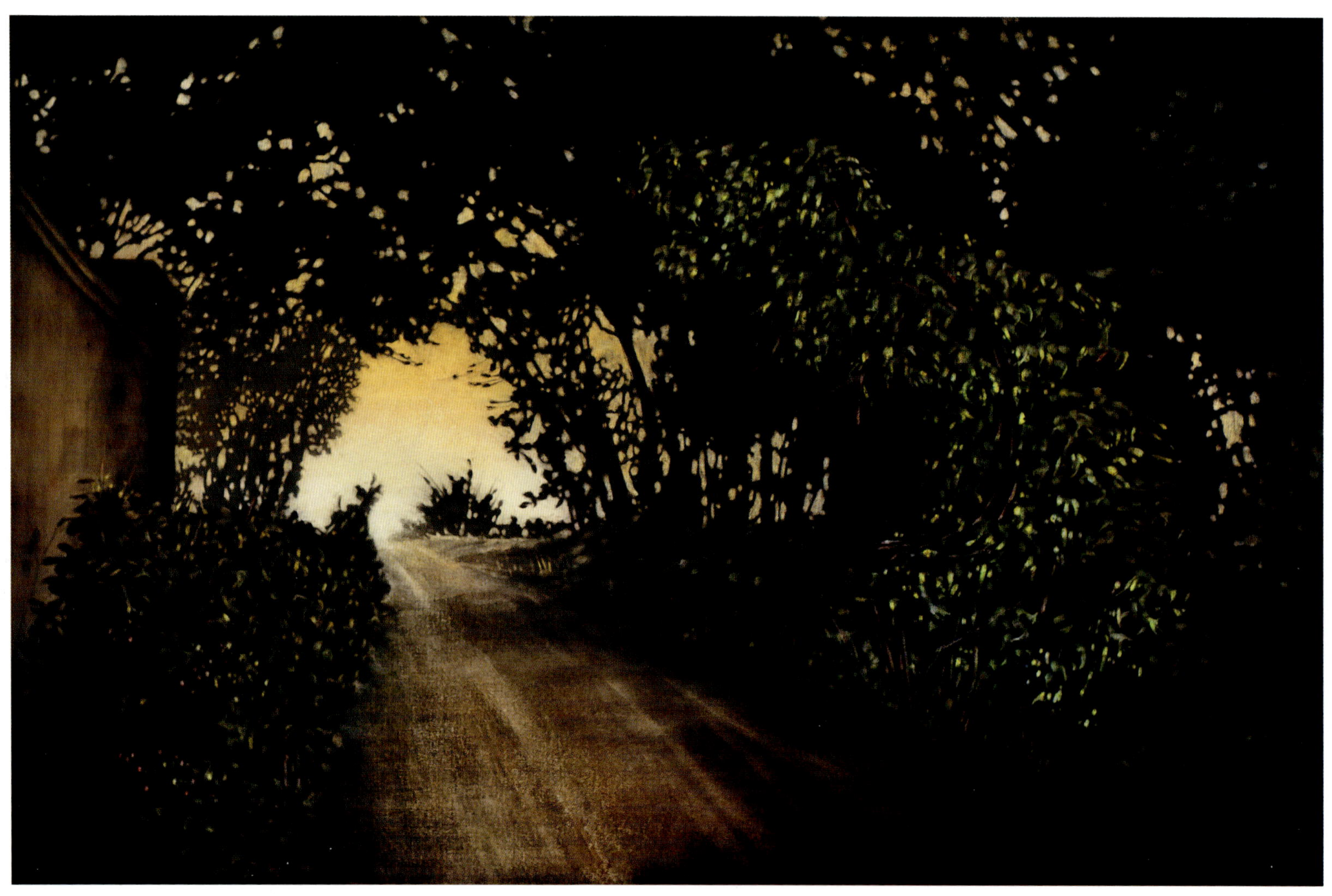

previous: ***Window on a world of shadows,*** 2006, oil and charcoal on canvas, 42" x 84"

above: ***Canopy,*** 2007, oil and charcoal on canvas, 32" x 48"

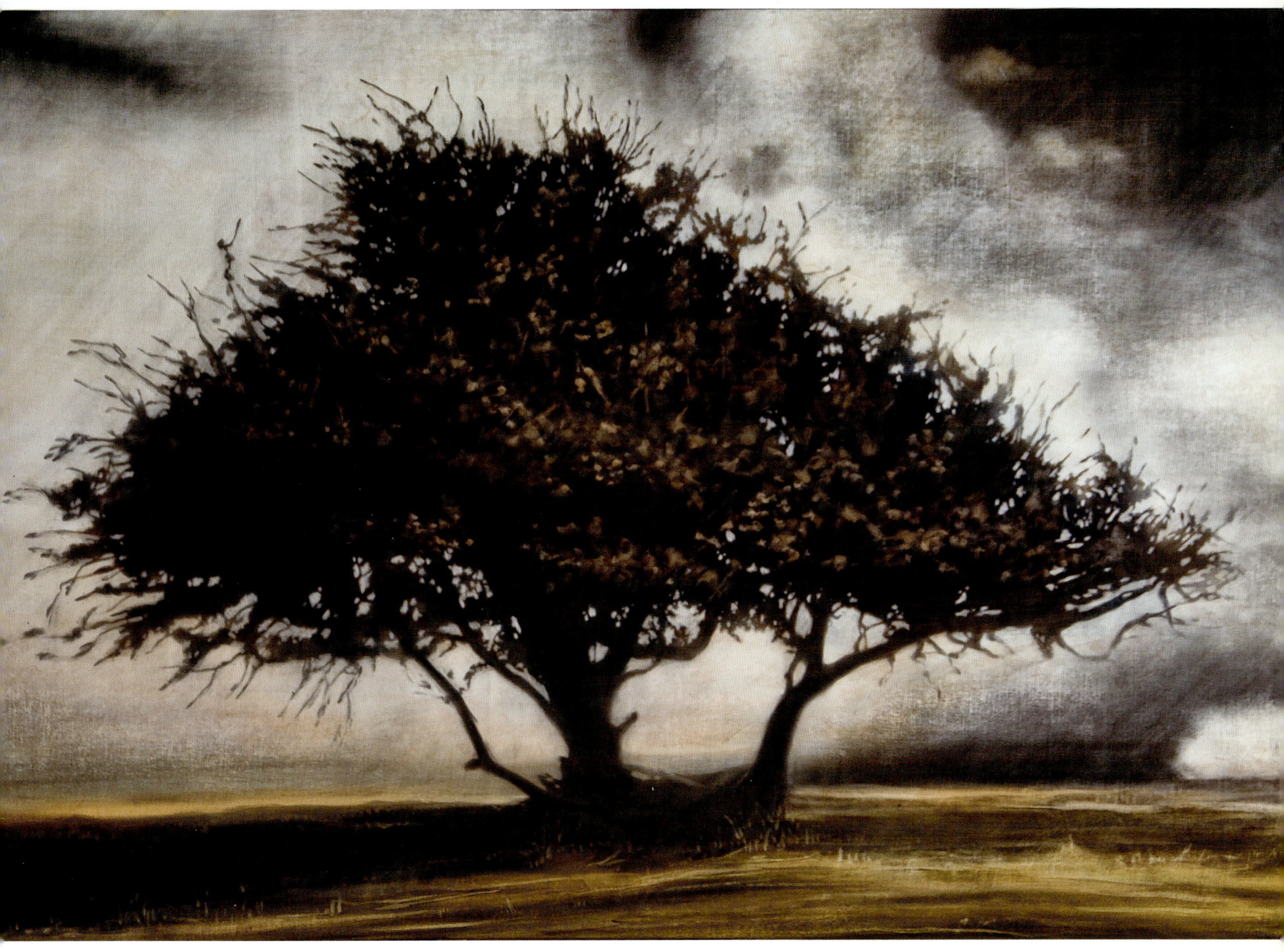

Tree and sky, 2007, oil and charcoal on canvas, 48" x 72"

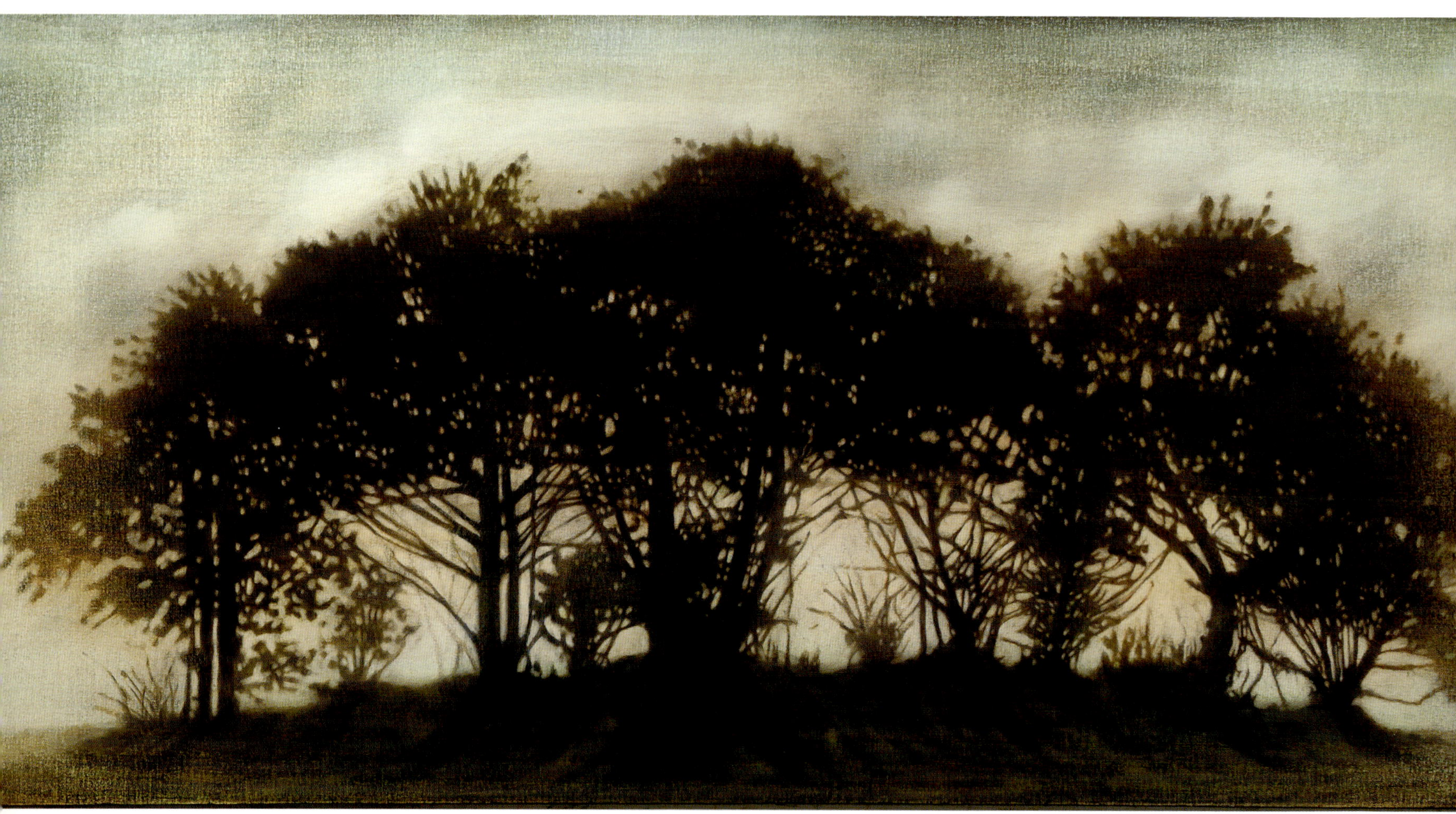

Line up of trees on a small hill, 2010, oil and charcoal on canvas, 30" x 60"

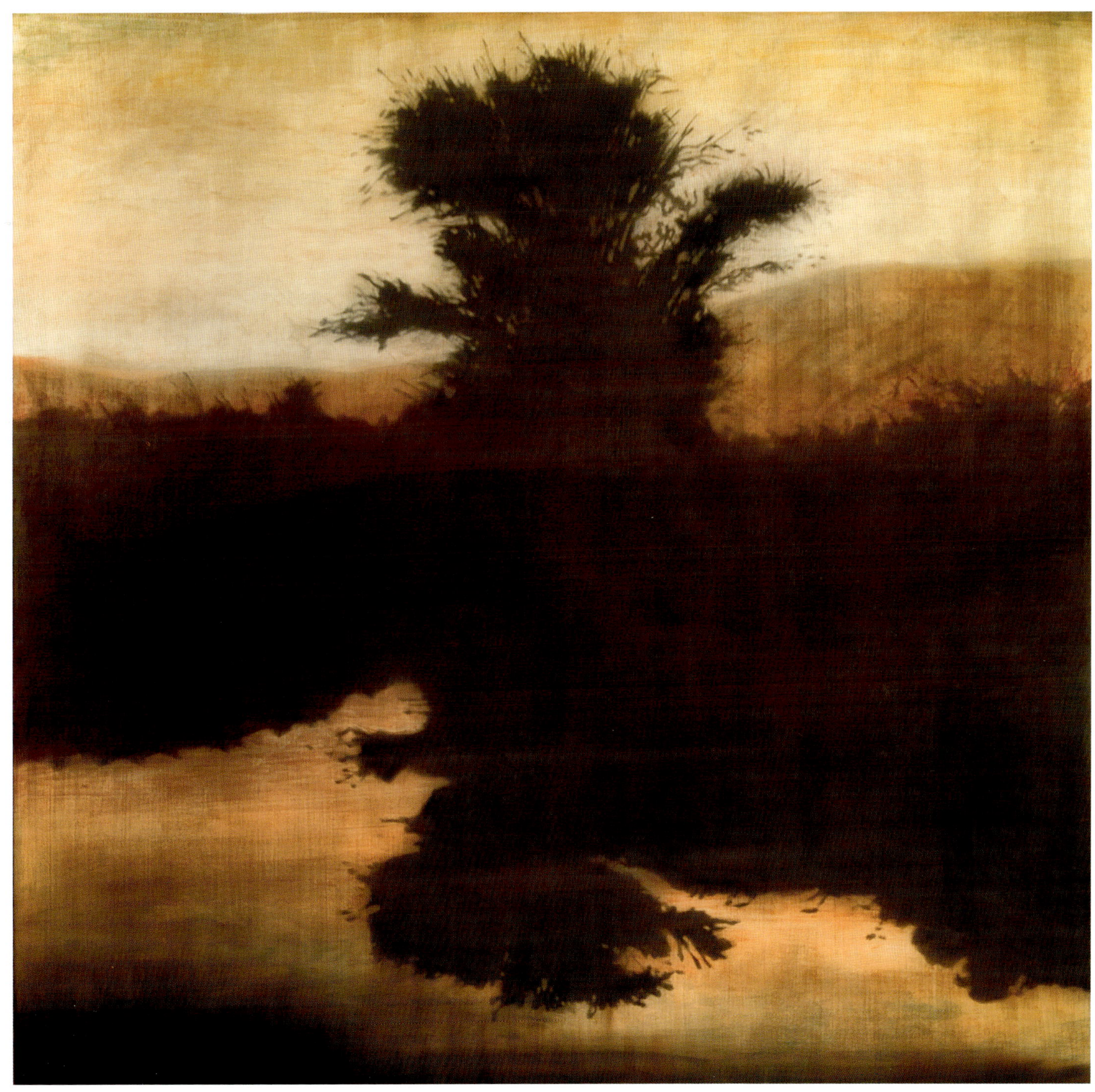

Dark bush with reflection, 2006, oil and charcoal on canvas, 36" x 36"

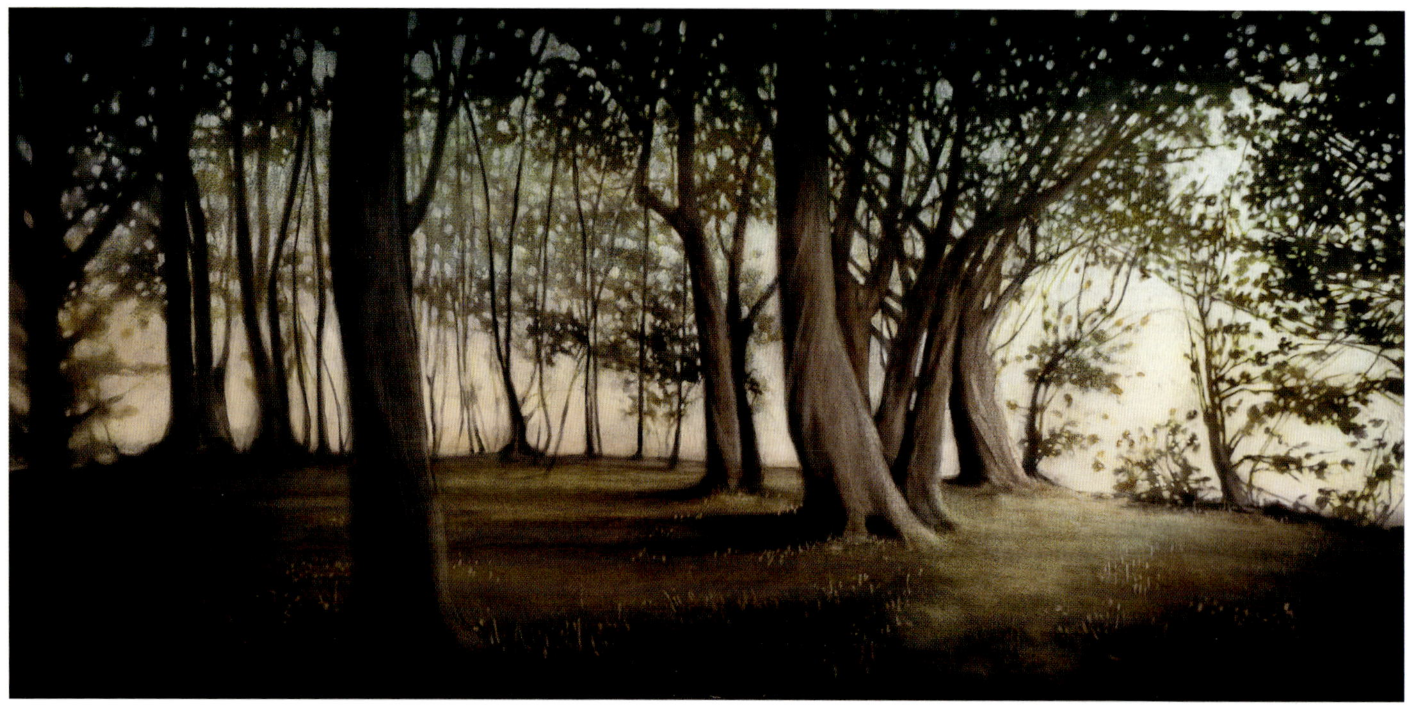

In the park, 2011, oil and charcoal on canvas, 36" x 72"

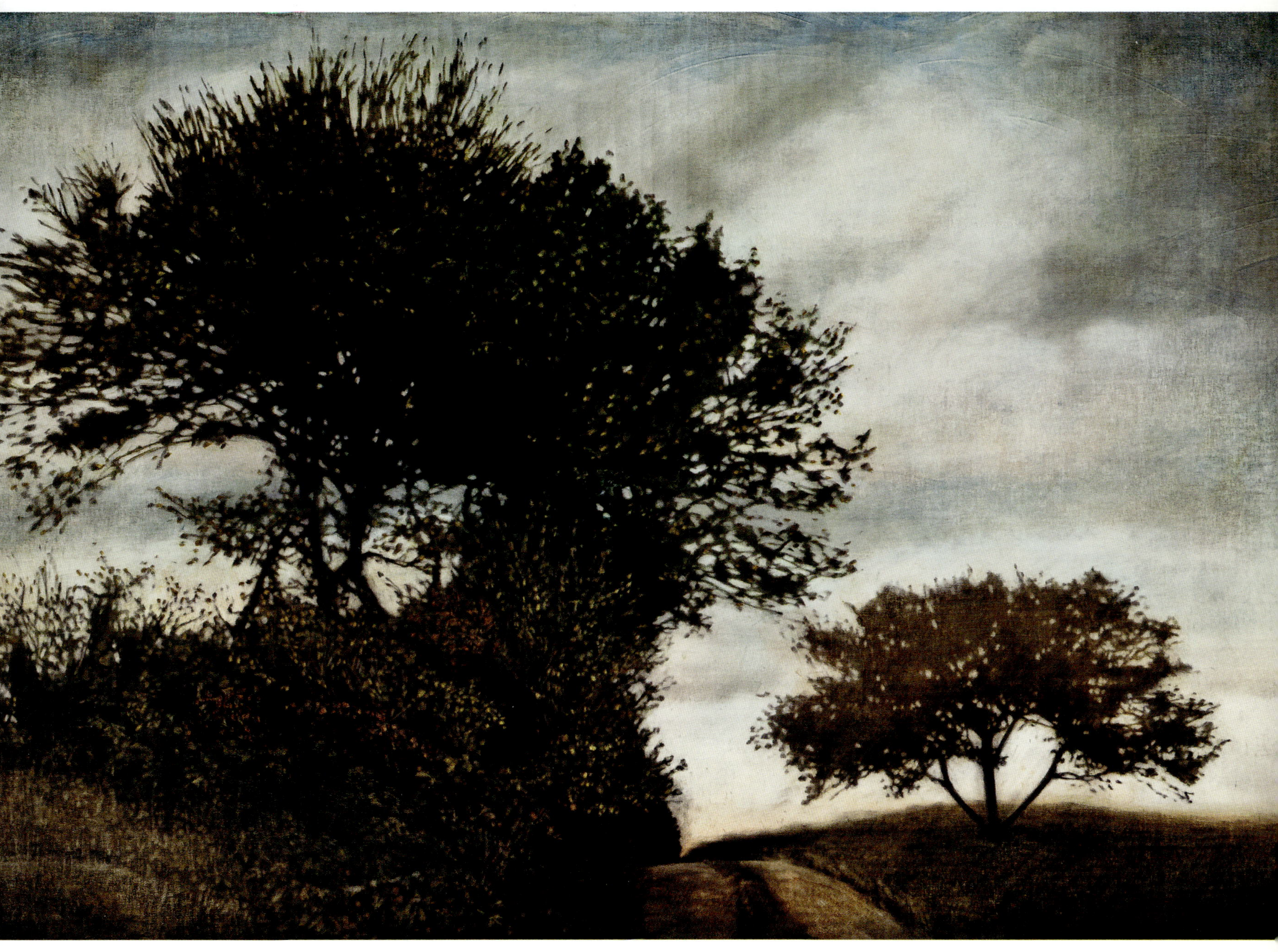

Road with trees, 2009, oil and charcoal on canvas, 48" x 72 "

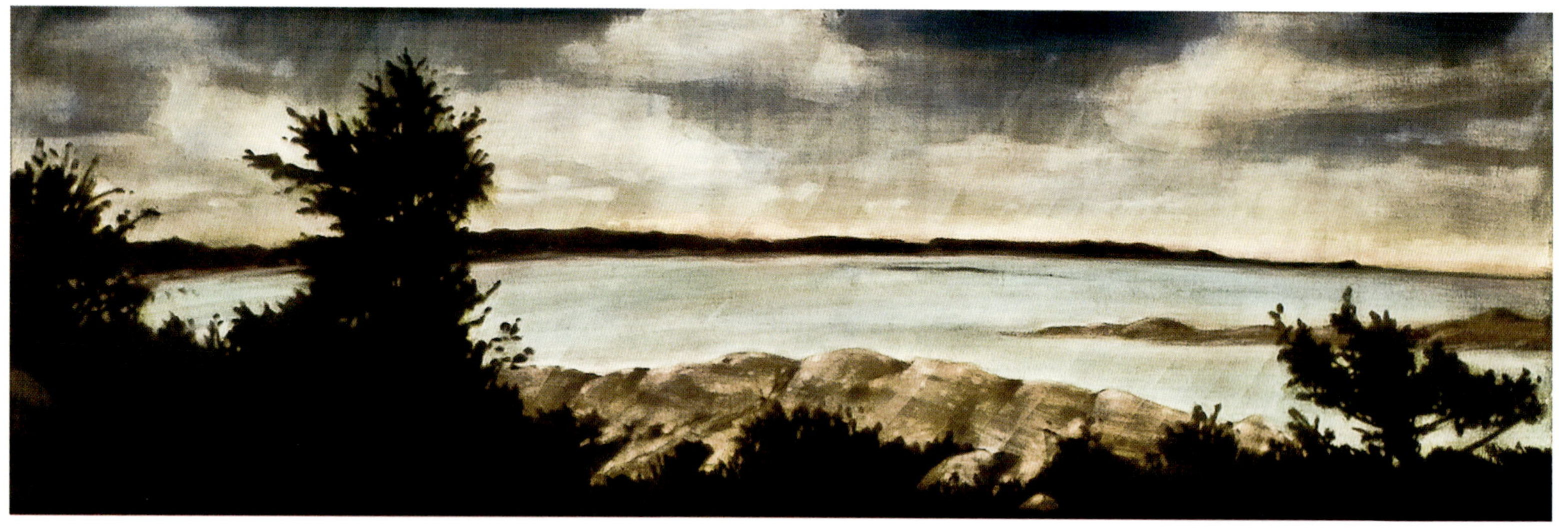

The bay, 2008, oil and charcoal on canvas, 18" x72"

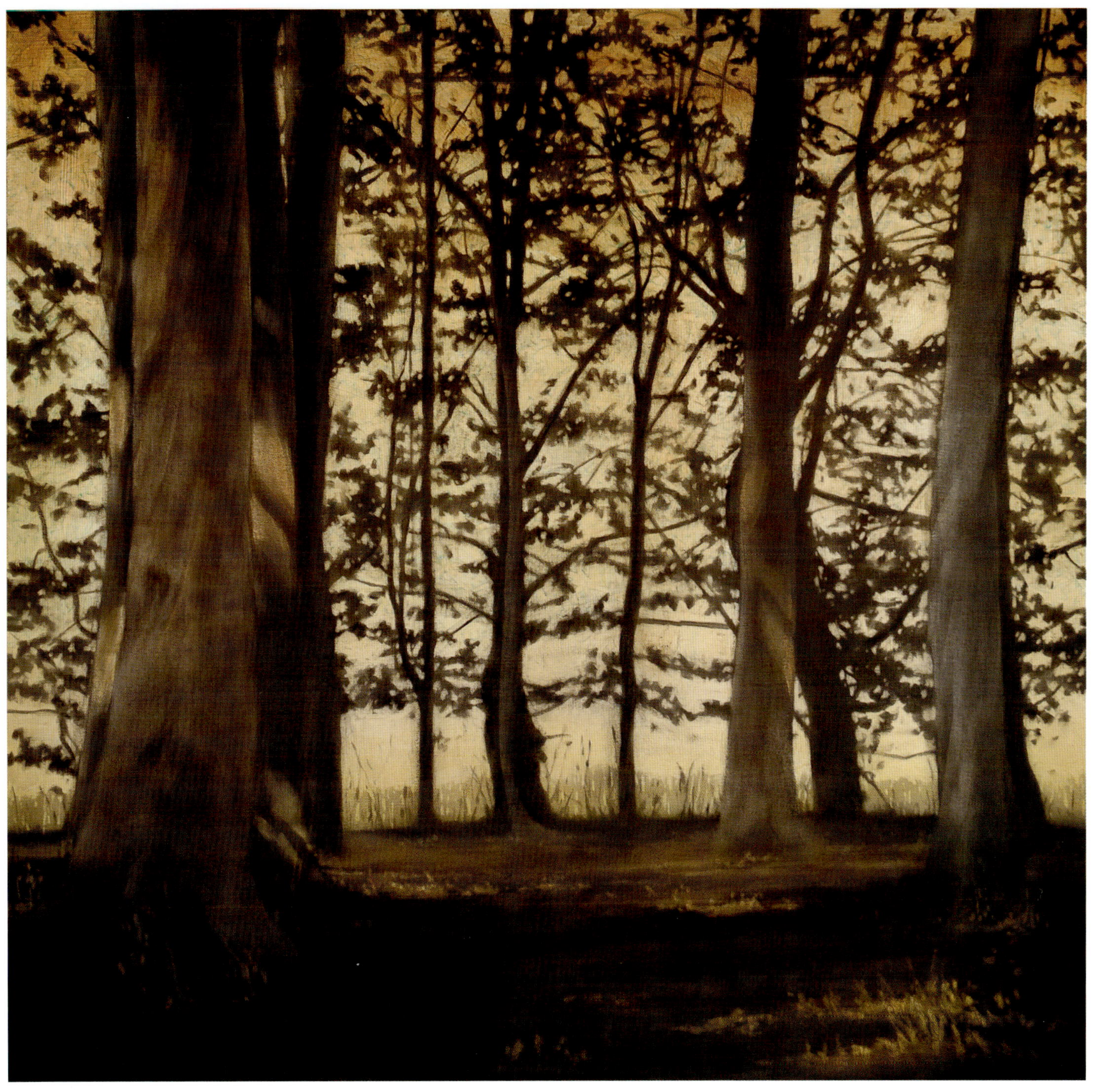

Grove (close-up 1) 2011, oil and charcoal on canvas, 48" x 48"

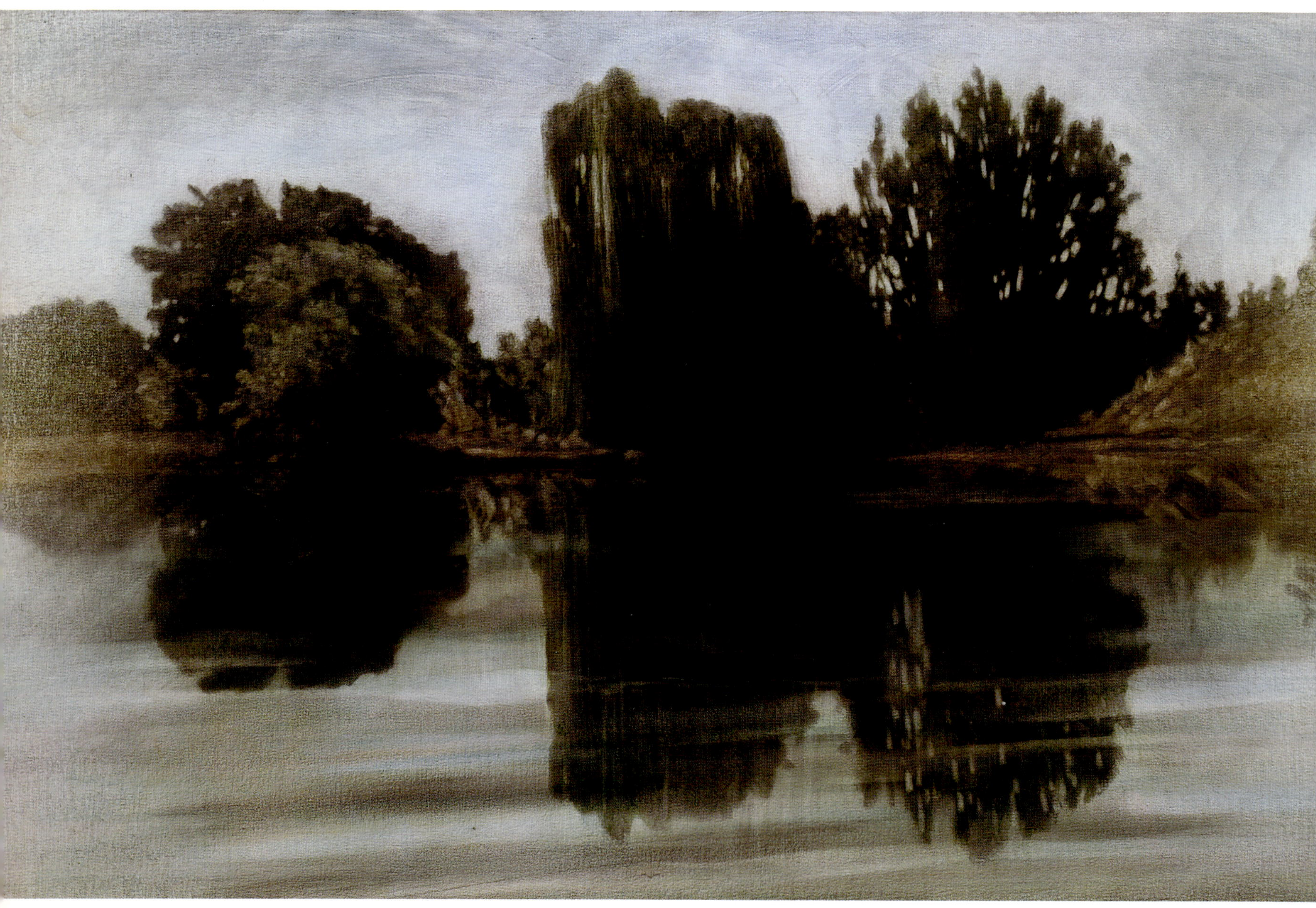

Reflections in the Arboretum 2011, oil and charcoal on canvas, 30" x 48"

Contributors

Stephen Hutchings lives in Ottawa, Ontario. He frequently works on large-scale projects such as billboard-sized drawings, outdoor sculptures, and both site-specific and gallery installations. His work has been extensively exhibited in public and commercial venues across Canada and is in many important corporate, public and private collections throughout Canada, the United States and Europe. His art practice includes painting, printmaking, photography, and video work.

www.stephenhutchings.com

Colleen Sharpe, Curator of Art at the Glenbow Museum, worked with Stephen Hutchings on the *Landscapes for the End of Time* exhibition.

Petra Halkes is an independent art writer, curator, teacher and artist who lives in Ottawa. Her book, *Aspiring to the Landscape: On Painting and the Subject of Nature,* was published by the University of Toronto Press in 2006.

Mary Reid is Curator of Contemporary Art and Photography at the Winnipeg Art Gallery. She is the author of numerous articles, catalogues and books, including a book about Wanda Koop, *On the Edge of Experience,* published in 2010 by the National Gallery of Canada and the Winnipeg Art Gallery.

Vincent Varga is Executive Director and CEO of the Mendel Art Gallery in Saskatoon. Varga has played leading roles in art institutions and museums across Canada and in the United States, including the Art Gallery of Windsor, SITE Santa Fe, McMichael Canadian Art Collection, The Edmonton Art Gallery, and The Banff Centre.

Published by the Glenbow Museum

Library and Archives Canada Cataloguing in Publication

Halkes, Petra
Stephen Hutchings : landscapes for the end of time.

Essays by Petra Halkes, Mary Reid and Vincent Varga.
Catalogue of an exhibition held at the Glenbow Museum, Calgary, Alta.,
Dec. 11, 2010-Mar. 13, 2011 and then travelling to other venues.
ISBN 978-1-895379-61-7

1. Hutchings, Stephen, 1948- --Exhibitions. I. Reid, Mary, 1972-
II. Varga, Vincent III. Hutchings, Stephen, 1948- IV. Glenbow
Museum
V. Title. VI. Title: Landscapes for the end of time.

ND249.H883A4 2011   759.11   C2011-902768-2

Copy editing by Andrea Murphy
Printed and bound in China

Roads Collection of the Winnipeg Art Gallery; Gift of the artist, 2010-86.
Abyss Collection of the Alberta Foundation for the Arts
Towards Shadowland Collection of The Glenbow Museum
Bush, June 1991 Collection of Museum London

More information on Stephen Hutchings and his work can be found on his web site:
www.stephenhutchings.com

Glenbow Museum

The Glenbow Museum
130–9th Avenue S.E.
Calgary, Alberta
Canada T2G 0P3
www.glenbow.org

Acknowledgements

There are many, many people who have been important for this project: Jeffrey Spalding for his initial support and zeal, and for his love of painting; Scott Thornley for his inspiration, both personally and professionally, and for his incredible generosity; Roman Borys of the Gryphon Trio for his enthusiasm, and for his amazing abilities as a collaborator, organiser and muscian; Vincent Varga for his unwavering and life-giving friendship; Mary Reid for always being there for me for so many years; Petra Halkes whose love of art seems to know no bounds; Andrea Murphy for her stellar editing skills, her prodigious memory, and her persuasive arguments — all of which have been instrumental in shaping this book; Pascal Nadon and Kim Lippert for their excellent and timely help in the studio; Jennifer Kostuik, of the Jennifer Kostuik Gallery in Vancouver, who is such a huge part of my professional life, for the commitment and vision that she brings to both my work and to her gallery; Gisella Giacalone, of the Mira Godard Gallery in Toronto, for her support and dedication to me and to my art over so many years.

Most importantly, I would like to acknowledge my family who has made this project possible; without their love, I would have nothing to say. This includes the support of my parents and my sisters; my amazingly talented daughter, Julia, who is uniquely creative and one of the most adept people I have ever met; my son, Sebastian, who is a pure artist in the deepest and most sincere meaning of that term, whose ideas and discussions have added immensely to the development of the End of Time concept, who introduced me to Messiaen's Quartet in the first place and who has been such a terrific studio assistant over the years. Finally, I want to acknowledge Jennifer Stead, my love, my wife, who is such a strong person, an inspired artist, and an incredible inspiration for those she teaches, and who is, above all else, a truly great partner in life, for now and for the end of time.

— *Stephen Hutchings*